D0794124

3 1232 00149 1754

Organic Agriculture

ORGANIC AGRICULTURE

Economic and Ecological Comparisons With Conventional Methods

BY

Robert C. Oelhaf

ALLANHELD, OSMUN & CO.
MONTCLAIR

A HALSTED PRESS BOOK
JOHN WILEY & SONS   *NEW YORK CHICHESTER BRISBANE TORONTO*

ALLANHELD, OSMUN AND CO. PUBLISHERS, INC.
19 Brunswick Road, Montclair, N.J. 07042

Published in the United States of America in 1978
by Allanheld, Osmun & Co.
Distribution: Halsted Press,
a division of John Wiley & Sons, Publishers
605 Third Avenue, New York, New York 10016

Library of Congress Cataloging in Publication Data

Main entry under title:

Organic agriculture.

  Bibliography: p.
  Includes index.
  1. Organic farming. 2. Agriculture. 3. Organic
farming—Economic aspects. 4. Agriculture—Economic
aspects. 5. Food, natural. I. Title
s605.5.066   338.1'6   78-7347
ISBN 0470-26427-6

Printed in the United States of America

Dedicated to the modern organic farmers, often struggling in isolation, seeking to bring a new way to modern agriculture, based on a sense of working with nature, rather than overpowering her

Preface

While some economic topics may usefully be analysed in isolation, the economics of food production cannot. Economic judgments are closely involved with the underlying technical issues. And ethical questions cannot be avoided if the discussion is to be relevant to real human welfare.

It is precisely this broad background necessary to understand the economics of organic agriculture that fire my interest in the subject. My training in theology, science and engineering determined an awareness of more than purely economic issues. I have also had a more personal interest in food and nutrition arising out of a concern for the health of my own family. In 1971 we began experimenting with raising organic food on our farm in Shenandoah Valley of Virginia.

As an economist, the question of profitability is of course a major concern. Profitability ought not be maximized in isolation from other policy goals. But if organic food is so good, why don't people raise it and eat it? I brought these concerns into my course on the economics and technology of the major American industries. I was fortunate in receiving encouragement and support from the University of Maryland Economics Department, at which the major work on this book was done. A National Science Foundation Traineeship and a National Defense Education Fellowship provided financial assistance during the preliminary phases of the work. These are also acknowledged with gratitude. I am also thankful for continuing research support from the U.S. Environmental Protection Agency.

Many good people have helped me along the way. I am particularly indebted to John Cumberland, for initially suggesting this general area for research. The careful comments of Professor Cumberland on earlier drafts and also those of Professor John Wysong, were extremely helpful in tightening the argument. Professor Clopper Almon helped with the models, and Professor Neri Clark with the issues related to crop production technology. Hy Cohen, the editor, was most helpful in pinpointing areas needing clarification.

This book could not have been possible without the cooperation of dozens of organic farmers, wholesalers, and retailers, who were generous with their limited time in explaining their operations to me and in providing necessary data. I am grateful to them for their help.

Finally, I wish to offer thanks to God, who brings things together into being.

Whatever failings remain after all this assistance are, of course, the responsibility of the author.

R. C. Oelhaf
Kimberton Farms School

Contents

LIST OF TABLES AND FIGURES

TABLES

FIGURES

Organic Agriculture

1 Introduction

Modern Agriculture: Productivity and Problems

Our modern system of agricultural production brought high levels of productivity to American farms. We not only produce more food, but we do it on less land and with less labor. Table 1-1 shows the increase in yield per acre between the 1930s and the 1970s for some of our major crops. Some yields rose remarkably, particularly for the key animal and human food crops: corn, wheat and potatoes. One of the main factors responsible for the increases is agricultural research, which has led to new plant varieties, more responsive to fertilizer, capable of closer spacing, and compatible with machine harvest. Good weather and irrigation played a role as well.

Yet these gains were made at a heavy cost. The side effects of the modern agricultural chemicals and machines raise serious questions about the overall benefits of the new technology. Chemical fertilizers and pesticides pollute our air and water. Agricultural chemicals, including hormones and antibiotics, leave residues in food that may cause cancer or genetic damage. Other aspects of food quality have also changed for the worse. Further, soil and energy resources are being depleted. Instead of recycling our wastes back onto the land as fertilizer, we allow them to pollute our water. We use non-renewable energy resources to produce artificial fertilizer. In the future we may be forced to make radical adjustments in such agricultural practices.

The new technology has also increased the advantages of large–scale production (economies of scale), with adverse social effects in both rural and urban areas. And the old diversified farm is becoming a thing of the past, as farmers tend more and more to concentrate crop and livestock production in particular regions. Large regions are cultivated to a single crop or strain. For example, two states, Kansas and Oklahoma, produce

Table 1-1.   Yield Comparison for Major United States Crops, 1930s and 1970s

Crop	Yield Per Acre		Percent Change
	1937-1939	1971-1973	
Grains			
Corn (bu)	28.3	92.1	240
Wheat (bu)	13.7	32.8	139
Rice (bu)	49.4	102	107
Cotton (lb)	248	489	96
Beans			
Soybeans (bu)	19.7	27.7	41
Edible Dry Beans (bu)	15.2	20.5	35
Hay (tons)	1.35	2.14	51
Vegetables			
Potatoes (bu)	123	387	214
Tomatoes (bu)	113	227	101
Lettuce (crates)	136	317	133
Snap beans (bu)	84	120	43
Carrots (bu)	363	522	44
Fruit			
Apples (bu)	400-600	2600-3000	333-650
Strawberries (crates)	69.4	306	342

Sources :   USDA 1940; 1975. Apples, Childers 1975.

over one-third of the nation's wheat. This increased regional concentration has led to concern about the system's vulnerability to pest outbreaks.

Alternative Agriculture

Agriculture's catalogue of sins may be impressive, but what are the alternatives? One alternative is commonly known as "organic agriculture," or "organic farming." Organic farming requires the total elimination of the most damaging chemicals. Such restrictions would presumably satisfy most concern about pollution and human health.

But what about yield? Would a national changeover to organic agriculture doom a large percentage of our population to hunger or worse? Even if we could feed ourselves, what of the rest of the world, for whom the United States has become a breadbasket? Former Secretary of Agriculture Earl Butz warned, "Before we go back to an organic agriculture in this country, somebody must decide which 50 million Americans we are going to let starve or go hungry" (Butz 1971). On the other hand, organic farmers assert that they often obtain yields which are equal to those of their conventional counterparts (*e.g.*, Koepf 1976).

Who is right? Both sides at times exaggerate or gloss over embarrassing facts. To resolve the issues, we must look at the alternative technologies, and measure their achievements in the field. Numerous studies have considered adjustments in the conventional system. But the severity of the problems may call for more drastic action. If major changes in agricultural practice are needed, incremental analysis may not be satisfactory. Modern agriculture is a system of interrelated parts. Modifying one component— by a pesticide ban, for example—may cause large-scale crop loss. Yet this result is no indication of what would happen if a *different* production system were used. It is the purpose of this study to come at the problem from the other side. Rather than look at changes in the conventional system, we will look at production potential under *alternative* agricultural regimes. Estimates will be presented for the production potential of major food crops in the United States under a national system of organic agriculture. These estimates should be useful in recommending agricultural policy not only for the United States, but also for other nations considering the adoption of conventional technology.

Market Failure

We live in a society traditionally characterized by decentralized decision-making. People are free to choose those products that bring them most satisfaction, and businessmen are free to choose that set of inputs which is most productive. One of the great virtues of an effectively competitive economic system is that, ideally, those methods of production that maximize net benefits to society will rise to dominance. Consumers will be as well off as they could possibly be, given the limitations of resources and human capabilities. Competition should guarantee minimum cost production, and that each element of the production system will be used to its best advantage.

Unfortunately, in the real world, free markets don't always achieve the ideal. And such "market failure" is particularly widespread in agriculture.

Competitive markets fail us primarily because costs or benefits arising from a particular decision are not borne by the decisionmaker. For example, a farmer who sprays his fields with a pesticide may benefit a conventional neighbor, when the neighbor's pests are killed by spray drift. On the other hand, an organic farmer may suffer when spray drift kills predators he was relying on to eat *his* pests. Sometimes markets fail to provide enough of a particular good or service, because once provided it is consumed by many people with practically undiminished intensity. Such goods are called "public goods" and will be undersupplied without public agency support. A good example is research on biological control of plant pests.

Markets also can fail to achieve an optimum for society because the decisionmakers lack the information needed to make a correct decision. Much of a farmer's information on pesticides comes from salesmen, who have an obvious tendency to be somewhat biased.

Comparing Whole Systems

The side-effects of agricultural technology are large, and their impact is felt throughout the whole economy. Any attempt to place a dollar figure on the full costs and benefits of adopting the modern agricultural system, or any alternative system, would be futile. It is scarcely possible to construct realistic models of large, complex systems with interrelated and far-reaching effects, especially when most of the parameters are unknown (Mishan 1971). Nevertheless, if we wish to compare conventional agriculture with its alternatives, comparisons must be made, and they must be made between whole systems. What then is to be done?

Actually we are making choices between complex systems every day, without the aid of analytical analysis. Take the decision of choosing a career with the goal of personal happiness. How is this to be achieved? Any kind of simple application of calculus to various qualities would be superficial in the extreme, might produce a preference by a quirk of the mathematics.

In the case of agriculture, we are comparing a total system of conventional farming with a total system of organic farming. A fair appraisal requires understanding that comes from a deep immersion in both systems. Decisions must be a matter of intuition, not deduction. All factors must be weighed within the mind of the human decisionmaker. To facilitate this understanding, we begin with a review of the main character features and interrelations and implications of both systems. The key structural features are highlighted in such a way as to give a fair picture of the whole systems. These pictures must then be juxtaposed against the value system or goals of the decisionmaker. For example, if the goal is to maximize private initiative in application of new technology, then the present system appears most congenial to that end. If more humanistic values are introduced, such as human health and the welfare of future generations, then the organic system may be favored.

In a pluralistic society, a variety of systems satisfies the diverse goals of consumers and producers. Public policy plays the role of providing goods of a public nature and seeking to maintain a climate of fair play in which one system or firm does not dominate by virtue of artificial (non-technical) advantages or by imposing burdens on others. Unfortunately, federal agricultural policy has often betrayed its neutral role by artificially favoring conventional agriculture and neglecting areas which could assist organic farmers. Any fair appraisal of the two systems must take account of this bias.

Agricultural Research

Before turning to the comparison of conventional and organic agriculture, we must pause for a look at the context in which these differences have arisen. Research has been the driving force behind the revolutions that have swept American agriculture. This work has been carried out by federal and state government agencies, by supplier industries (who often fund university laboratory research), and by foundations. Thus research priorities are not set solely by the agricultural sector; to a large extent they are the result of conscious public policy. It is of some interest therefore to examine the quality and direction of this research.

Publicly supported agricultural research is carried out by the U.S. Department of Agriculture and by the federal- and state-supported land-grant college complex. The new technologies are taught in college class-rooms, and state extension workers bring the new knowledge directly to farmers.

There are four main lines of criticism of agricultural research and the system of food production which it has fostered: research has often been of poor quality; it has benefited the large-scale operator at the expense of the small farmer and farm worker; research and extension have neglected external (social) costs; and food quantity has in some ways received higher priority than food quality. We will deal first with the quality of research.

Over half of agricultural research is now carried out by supplier industries. These industries more and more also supply supportive information services as well, replacing the traditional state extension agents (Ball and Heady 1972). Under these circumstances, the quality and direction of government-financed research becomes more important. Government programs may have to balance any excesses in the private sector.

A recent study of agricultural research by a committee of the National Academy of Sciences (NAS 1975) faults the United States Department of Agriculture (USDA) for neglecting basic scientific research. In particular, the report presses for greater effort in increasing productivity through study of photosynthesis, crop nitrogen fixation (from the air), and direct manipulation of crop genetic material. Also, alternatives to chemical pesticides and less energy-intensive methods should receive high priority (Wade 1975). These conclusions are similar to those expressed in an earlier report by another advisory committee under NAS auspices (CRA 1973). The latter report described the whole working atmosphere of the USDA agricultural research system as antithetical to significant progress in basic research. It cited poor leadership attitudes, wrong funding priorities, organizational stumbling blocks, and low-quality and duplicative research work. USDA administrators have criticized the reports for being self-serving. After all, the scientists on the committees would like to be receiving more research money! One of the main problems in recent years is the fact that research funds have not been expanding, so that as priorities begin to change, new people cannot be hired. The current staff is ill-prepared to embark on new work (Wade 1975). A bureaucratic superstructure and organization by commodity have also hampered research. Prompted by criticism, a major reorganization of the Agricultural Research Service (ARS) was undertaken in the early 1970s (Wade 1973a; 1973b). Research on the neglected areas is now being supported (Kendrick 1976). But it takes many years before such work pays off at the farm level.

Of particular interest in the NAS study are the references to nitrogen fixation and alternatives to chemical pesticides as crucial neglected areas of research. It is precisely lags in these areas which make organic farming difficult. Modern organic farming may be viewed as an attempt to replace chemical technology by biological technology. Whether the close ties of chemical supplier industries to agricultural research establishments are responsible for this void may be debated. At any rate, the agricultural research laboratories have given organic farmers less help than they have the conventional system. This theme will be taken up in some detail in Part I and also in chapter 10.

A Tale of Three Eggs

As an example of the revolutions in food production, let us look at eggs. Until the last few decades, eggs had been produced in the same manner for generations. A few dozen or perhaps a couple of hundred chickens were kept in a henhouse on a farm, which also raised a variety of other foodstuffs. The chickens scratched in the dirt, ate bugs and worms, were fertilized by the roosters, and ate feed raised by the farmer. In the fields, weeds were controlled by cultivation; insect and other pests by crop rotation, planting time and other traditional measures. There was some for the bugs and some for the farmers. The eggs were collected, candled, and packed by hand. Many genetic improvements have been made in the chickens and in the feed and in biological control of pests since our grandparents' time. These improvements make such traditional production considerably more efficient. Eggs are still raised in this way by a few farmers. These eggs are now called "organic" eggs and the farmers who produce them, "organic" farmers. In some places you will not be able to tell if you have received such a product, however, since state marketing orders may not allow any statement as to how an egg was raised to appear on the box.

Overwhelmingly, however, modern eggs are produced in large "egg factories" housing thousands or even millions of birds (Wilson 1966; Singer 1975). The system is totally mechanized, with conveyer belts providing food in carefully controlled quantities. Mixed with the feed are antibiotics to speed growth and prevent disease. The individual cages, averaging about one-third of a square foot per hen, provide little room for exercise. Twice during their one-year lives, hens are debeaked—a painful operation into the quick of the beak—to prevent the cannibalism that would result from overcrowding.

Since hens will lay eggs without being fertilized, roosters are dispensed with, saving feed. The feed is raised many states away, on a farm covering thousands of acres, fertilized with materials which require much energy to manufacture and which may pollute streams and wells. In the fields, weeds, insects and other pests are controlled with chemicals, some of which end up in wildlife, some in the feed.

Back in the egg factory, the eggs drop through the floor and are automatically conveyed to the sorting and candling area where they are mechanically packaged, untouched by human hands. The other product, chicken manure, is potentially a valuable fertilizer, but it often becomes a water pollutant unless a local farmer is interested in hauling it away. The eggs are washed to remove the natural protective coating which may have been dirtied, and replaced with a chemical coating which keeps the eggs from drying out during storage. The whole system has been carefully engineered to maximize egg output and minimize cost, including feed, number of chickens, labor and equipment. However, little is known of possible effects of the new system on human health (Hall 1974). Many pesticides are readily stored in fat; eggs contain a lot of fat.

The third stage in egg technology began in the 1970s. Recently many people have been concerned about animal fat intake because of a possible association with heart disease. The food system has responded with a new "egg" substitute in which the egg yolk has been completely replaced. The name of one, "Egg-Beaters," implies going nature one better. According to standard nutritional analysis, this artificial product is just as nutritious as a wholly animal-produced egg; in fact, the lack of cholesterol is deemed by many consumers to mean a *better* product (FPD 1975). Unlike their cousins, non-dairy creamer and margarine, the egg substitutes are still largely made from the substance they are designed to replace. (Egg whites constitute over 80 percent of the ingredients.) And also, unlike the other common substitutes, the new "egg" prices are higher than their natural competitors.* In many cases, however, technology has improved on the price as well as the chemistry. Since taste can be controlled by chemistry

*Prices were found to be 32 to 65 percent higher in a survey made by the author in Washington, D.C., July 1976.

and taste preferences manipulated by advertising, a cost advantage can result in the gradual displacement of the earlier technology, as the non-dairy creamers displaced cream and Pream, the Powdered Cream.

Convenience and changing lifestyles have also played a role in the demise of the egg and other natural foods, as consumers switched to fast-food type meals. Per capita egg consumption declined 31 percent between 1945 and 1975, despite a 40 percent decline in price relative to other food. (Most of this fall in consumption took place prior to the cholesterol scare.) The egg producers are fighting back at the substitutes. Federal legislation has recently established a tax on egg producers to be used for a private institute to promote eggs. The $5 to $7 million that will be raised is still small compared to some $100 million that will be spent on advertising by cereal manufacturers, considered a main competitor in the breakfast food business (Samuelson 1976).

PART ONE

Conventional Agriculture: Main Features and Critique

2 Farm Labor and Economies of Large-Scale Production

Two strong trends of modern agriculture have been the substitution of capital for labor and the increasing size of farm units. Since organic farming appears to be more compatible with diversified, small-scale, labor-intensive farming, a bias within public policy toward large-scale and capital-intensive operations is an important consideration in evaluating the viability of organic farming.

Substitution of Capital for Labor

Capital inputs, particularly machinery, and the associated chemicals, have been replacing labor on farms. The price of labor has been rising faster than prices of other inputs. And technological change has favored this substitution. Publicly financed research helped establish the technical possibilities for substituting other inputs for labor. Technological change can be classified as labor-intensive, neutral, or capital-intensive. Government sponsored agricultural research has not been intentionally capital-intensive: the emphasis has been on simply increasing output (Quance and Tweeten 1972). Nevertheless, much of the effect *has* been to cause a substitution of capital for labor. If labor is made more productive, there will be an incentive to expand scale, and this is often accompanied by increased mechanization. There was no effort to balance industry bias toward capital-intensive developments.

An example of an innovation that is labor-intensive would be development of new varieties which have some highly desirable nutritional or taste quality, but require special handling, such as various specialty vegetables

13

marketed to home gardeners. The innovations that have had the largest impact on agriculture have been capital-intensive. An example is a new tobacco-harvesting machine with a minimum efficient scale of 40 acres; it will replace the traditional hand-harvesting if and when tobacco allotments are ended. The tobacco harvester illustrates the connection between capital-labor substitution and economies of large-scale production. The substitution can be made by lowering the labor input and/or increasing the size and mechanization of the operation.

Economies of Large-Scale Production

Many cost advantages of size, or economies of scale, are inherent in modern technology and social organization; others are peculiar to agriculture. Improved management techniques, radio and closed-circuit TV allow centralization of supervision of many workers and operations. Large-scale firms can hire specialized managers and take advantage of the comparatively high fixed costs of information handling. The increased homogeneity of conditions made possible by planting a single crop, called monocropping, makes for easier supervision and decisionmaking. Pest control and government supports remove a good deal of the risk to the individual farmer from growing single crops on large-scale, highly mortgaged, highly capitalized farms with a high proportion of purchased inputs. There are, of course, always the pecuniary economies of scale: volume discounts related to size or purchasing power, and higher prices for the products. Supply discounts of 10 percent and a 5 percent bonus on selling price are not uncommon (Krause and Kyle 1970).

Federal programs, on balance, have had a bias toward helping large-scale firms. Past price support programs helped the large farms more because the payments were tied to acreage. Because of indivisibilities in equipment purchases, output control programs that are simply proportional to acreage are more likely to benefit large farms than small. The latter tend to be relatively overcapitalized compared to the amount of land and labor used (Kyle *et al.* 1972). While extension and education programs have been scale-neutral or even beneficial to the smaller farmer by providing management he could otherwise not afford, the *kind* of information received has been more helpful to expanding or larger growers.

The net effect of all these influences has been toward increasing the average size of farms and decreasing their numbers. The larger family farms are still virtually as efficient as large-scale industrial farms (Madden 1967). Nevertheless, it is the farms with largest sales which have been increasing in numbers most rapidly. Between 1959 and 1964, farms with sales over $1 million grew 178 percent, the fastest rate of all size categories. The smaller the sales class, the less rapidly the numbers increased (Wirth and Rogers 1970). The advantages of the very large farms are, however, mainly pecuniary—rather than real-cost savings—in the areas of tax, purchase, credit access, and sales price (Ball and Heady 1972). In sum, the economies of scale of the large family farm are primarily technical, involving real productivity gains; those associated with the very large-scale, industrial-type farms are mostly pecuniary, involving no real benefit to society.

Input trends in agriculture are illustrated in Table 2-1. The amount of labor used dropped markedly, and land rose modestly. But use of other inputs rose greatly from the mid-1930s to the early 1970s. During this period labor productivity measured by output per manhour also increased greatly, to about four times what it was in the 1930s. This increase was largely due to the large relative increase in the use of the other inputs. Increased productivity is generally assumed to imply improvement. But productivity measures are slippery. The farm worker is supported by other workers in input industries and also in transportation, processing, storage, and wholesaling industries. And productivity increases may be at the expense of other policy goals. There may be serious external costs, borne by others, arising from either the new technology or out of the *process* of changing. Furthermore, it is not at all clear *a priori* that output maximization will result in maximum satisfaction for the average farmer. These will now be examined in turn.

Side-Effects of Substituting Capital for Labor

Social effects. Scale changes and decreased labor use have had a broad impact on society. The whole fabric of rural life has been radically altered. A downward regional multiplier effect has resulted in a depopulation of rural areas as businesses and other support industries closed down due to

Table 2-1   Changes in Farm Inputs, 1930s to 1972

Input	Percent Change, 1930-34 to 1972
Labor	− 72
Real estate	+ 22
Mechanical power and machinery	+ 235
Fertilizer and lime	+ 1508
Feed, seed and livestock purchases	+ 543
Total inputs	+ 21

Source: ERS 1969;   1973.

the outmigration of farmers and farm workers. The investment loss and the human suffering are not included in the lower food prices; neither are lost cultural values. "Food is a cultural, not [merely] a technological, product," says Wendell Berry (1974, 1977). "A culture is . . . a practical necessity, and its destruction invokes calamity. A healthy culture is a communal order of memory, insight, value, and aspiration."

The farmer has also suffered financially from the lower food prices resulting from increased productivity. As prices fall, people do not buy proportionately more food; the demand for food is comparatively inelastic. In recent decades, only during the worldwide crop failures of the early 1970s did American farmers receive incomes comparable to urban workers.

Also excluded from food prices are the costs of adapting rural poor to urban life, the increased welfare and health costs in the cities. The study of social effects has been neglected in federally funded agricultural research (Wade 1973; Hightower 1973). A study of the benefits from development of a mechanical tomato harvester concluded that it would have been to society's advantage to develop the machine even if all workers were compensated for lost wages at $1.65 an hour (Schmitz and Seckler 1970). But what about compensation for moving to, and living in, a city slum? Or what if they had been paid a fairer wage? The balance would no longer clearly favor the machine.

The disappearance of small farms and farming communities has also had effects on urban dwellers' amenities and options (cf., Krutilla 1967). Those who like to drive by picturesque family farms have been losers. Owners of second homes, however, have benefited from cheap caretaker and maintenance service.

Environmental effects. Regional specialization has its own adverse side effects, mainly on the environment. The top four cattle-feeding states had 45 percent of the nation's cattle and calves on feed in January 1975. Broiler production is even more concentrated. During 1974, four states accounted for 53 percent of sales; eight for 78 percent (USDA 1975). Concentration of economic activity leads to cost advantages in handling inputs (feed and feeder animals) and outputs. But environmental costs are neglected. One of these costs is the pollution from feedlot runoff. Until recently, clear water had little or no private cost attached to it. Manure wastes from animal feeding operations and also food processing wastes were discharged into waterways, causing health hazards (to be discussed in the next section). Paradoxically, large-scale feedlot operators argue both that they are more efficient than small-scale firms, and that they will be driven out of business if strict pollution control measures are enforced (Breimyer 1975). Both may well be true. Economic "efficiency" depends on the groundrules laid down by society. As long as pollution is allowed, organic farmers operate at an artificial disadvantage. It would appear that small farmers would be favored by strict pollution controls. Nevertheless, there are significant economies of scale in processing wastes that would favor the large operator (Darrow 1972).

Large farms use more pesticides per acre than small farms (Fox *et al.* 1968). In 1964, farms with sales greater than $40,000 were roughly twice as likely to use pesticides as farms with sales of less than $10,000. Whether this is inherent to large-scale operations remains to be seen, however. Large farmers have better access to capital, obtain volume discounts, and have a different crop mix. Large-scale growers also spray more because they are more likely to be subject to industry marketing orders or processor specifications, which often require culling out produce with even minor insect damage. Small growers will, on the average, cater more to a local market, so that preservation may not be as important (DeBach 1974). On the other hand, a large grower pools his risks over many fields, so that he may avoid treatment if the expected loss is less than the cost of treatment. This appears to be the case with corn rootworm damage in the Midwest; the damage is hard to predict and only sporadic in occurrence (cf., EPA 1974). Weeds are more effectively controlled by cultivation by small-scale farmers, who are better able to supply labor on an as-needed basis (Berry 1971).

Modern mechanized harvesting lowers some risks of crop loss at the expense of increased risk to the consumer. The shift to field-shelling ("combining") of corn has saved labor and transportation costs. And the probability of crop loss has been lowered compared to the old field-drying method (Gavett undated). But grain must be slightly wet when harvested. Crops must be dried promptly, generally with liquid propane or natural gas. Any delay can allow growth of molds, some of which produce carcinogenic toxins. Others are implicated in abortions and heart failure (Brett 1975). Machine harvest often requires auxiliary chemicals (Chapter 12).

There is one last side-effect of regional concentration which is of particular interest to organic farmers. The regional markets for the small diversified producer have dried up. Diversification becomes very costly. The situation has been worsened by the expansion of suppliers and food processors into farming. Whether through farm ownership or forward contracts, such "vertical integration" has virtually eliminated free markets in some product lines and regions, as in the case of broilers and some fresh vegetables (Kyle *et al.* 1972).

Increased Risk of System Failure. Regional specialization increases the risk of system failure. Farmers now plant a single variety over vast regions. Farmers cannot save seed from the new hybrids, so they are dependent on seed companies for each new crop. Resistant mutant strains of diseases can spread rapidly once they appear and destroy a large portion of a major crop. The corn blight of 1970 resulted in a production decrease of 10 percent from the previous year, even though acres harvested were up 5 percent (USDA 1975). But some states suffered a 50 percent loss. Similar outbreaks have occurred in oats and wheat. The Irish potato famine of the 1840s is a well-known example of the dangers of genetic uniformity (NRC 1972). Fortunately, there is evidence that genetic uniformity is going out of favor with farmers. Each new variety seems to have its own disease resistance and susceptibility. By mixing varieties, a diversified soil ecology is established which is less favorable to attack by any one pathogen. This has already been done commercially with lima beans and oats (Baker and Cook 1974).

A more intensive selection process may make it possible to avoid the ratrace of attempting to stay one step ahead of the pests. Standard breeding seeks control for a pest through a resistant gene, but new pest varieties arise, often within a few years. The new approach seeks to select a set of resistant genes which together would provide resistance to a wide pest varietal range. The price is some susceptibility to a low degree of infestation. The benefit is the reduced probability of epidemic outbreak (McNew 1966).

Genetic Loss. Another side-effect of the homogeneity of crop plantings over wide areas is the loss of genetic material for use in developing new strains of plants. Old open-pollenated varieties are being replaced by new high-yield varieties all over the world. This is of course in the best interests of the farmers involved, but the plant breeder is in need of the old gene pool maintained by local and regional varieties. For example, two types of pea and nine strains of peanut make up 95 percent of the United States production. As the gene pool shrinks, pests gain resistance to pesticides. As larger areas are planted to the same crop, the capacity to maintain a fair margin of safety in producing new crop varieties becomes rapidly more difficult. Recognizing the danger, the Agricultural Research Advisory Committee of the USDA and National Academy of Sciences has pressed for strong action, particularly a large increase in the $100,000 a year appropriated for the National Seed Storage Laboratory (NRC 1972; Miller 1973).

Appropriate Technology

While technological change will generally involve the use or improvement of some tool, there is nothing inherent within technology which demands that things be done on a grand scale. Technology can also be designed on what has been called a human, appropriate or intermediate scale (Schumacher 1973). For example, an innovation in cucumber harvesting for the fresh market is a bicycle-tired cart on which the picker reclines and pedals with his feet. Machine harvesting requires that all produce ripen at the same time. Researchers were unable to develop such a cucumber plant for the fresh market. The cart allows many passes over the field without damaging the plants. The efficiency was estimated as great enough that workers could be profitably paid $6 to $7 per hour.

Appropriate or intermediate technology is defined as a technology which is on a human scale. It is not primitive, but neither is it so overly mechanized that the human being may feel more an extension of the machine than vice versa. More positively, appropriate technology is an Aristotelian Golden Mean of maximizing human satisfaction, creativity and fulfillment in *work*, not simply in consumption, as is the view of conventional economic analysis. Maximizing production, the accepted goal of agricultural research, does not necessarily maximize job satisfaction.

Before proceeding, a caveat is appropriate for those who would return to the horse-and-buggy era. Many farmers love the power and prestige of chemicals and big tractors. What appears appropriate to social planners seeking to engineer ideal human beings may be different from what makes farmers happy. Nevertheless, past agricultural research has focused on large farms, and the result has been an unmitigated disaster for small farmers who were unable or unwilling to adapt. A small versatile tractor may be more "appropriate" than either horses or giant specialized equipment.

If we are concerned with farmers' welfare, allocation of research funds must reflect farmers' desires. The size distribution of farms in 1973 is given in Table 2-2. Because of the larger number of farms in the small size categories, equity would argue for focusing research (and extension services) there, for example, attempting to increase efficiency (lower average costs) for these farms. It *is* possible that the potential for reducing costs is greater at larger scales of operation. If that is the case, the large numbers in the small size category would not weigh as heavily in allocation of funding. On the other hand, there are many Americans who would like to become small farmers, if only it were economically feasible. These potential farmers would also benefit from small farm research.

If a hypothesis of decreasing marginal utility of income or other source of satisfaction is introduced, the case for research efforts aimed at increasing efficiency of small-scale farming becomes stronger. For the incomes of small farmers (from farming) are significantly lower than those of large-scale farmers.

Naturally, when considering research allocation, the farmer's welfare is not the only consideration. The rest of us (and farmers, too) benefit from overall productivity gains. Nevertheless, value added in agriculture (farmers' sales less farmers' purchases) is now less than 1 percent of our Gross National Product (GNP). National economic policy hardly needs to place much emphasis on reducing the farm share of food cost any more (cf. Raup 1972).

Table 2-2   Size Distribution of Farms in 1974

Sales Class	Number of Farms	Percent
>$100,000	109,000	4
$40 to 100,000	337,000	12
$20 to 40,000	563,000	20
$10 to 20,000	332,000	11
< 10,000	1,503,000	52
Total	2,844,000	100

Source: ERS 1974.

Past agricultural research concentrated almost entirely on increasing efficiency of large-scale farms (CRA 1973). Only recently has labor-intensive agricultural technology been taken seriously (*e.g.*, Heady 1975). Research on intermediate technology has long been neglected. A small beginning has now been made by two federal agencies. The Agency for International Development (AID) has set aside $20 million, but their program is still in the planning stage. The Community Services Administration is spending $3 million on a small facility in Montana, which is also making grants in the $5,000 to $50,000 range (P&E 1976: MacKenzie 1975). The fact that most research has been on a small scale and privately funded—while more "appropriate" to appropriate technology—has meant in practice a general bias toward large-scale technologies.

Rural development projects can have the effect of increasing the rewards to small-scale farmers. The small farmer is not fully utilizing his abilities (human capital). Off-farm employment can fill this gap (Mayer 1970). Direct marketing is another option being fostered by many states as an aid to small farmers and a move toward regional self-sufficiency.

Whether or not a dispersed form of agricultural ownership and control could be fostered through technological change, it could be established by public policy for purely social reasons, namely, the fostering of social and economic democracy and freedom. A potential side-effect might be improved environmental and food quality. Federal irrigation projects have included limitations on the acreage of beneficiaries. North Dakota has prohibited corporate ownership of farmland for many years. Limits on vertical and horizontal growth of corporations could be set nationally (Breimyer 1973; Breimyer and Barr 1972), or incentives could be introduced through government assistance or financing (Ball and Heady 1972). The status quo has not been ordained by forces beyond our control. Decisions made now will shape the agriculture of the future.

Animal Production

Maximizing profit in animal production has meant larger and more mechanized units. Animals spend much or all of their lives in giant meat, egg, or milk factories. Efficiency is increased by the use of growth regulators: hormones and antibiotics. Antibiotics also help to control disease, which is a serious problem. Lack of fresh air, soil, sunshine and exercise lowers resistance. Close confinement encourages the spread of contageous diseases. Feed rations are geared to optimal growth, not necessarily optimal health, making the situation more conducive to sickness.

While animal welfare groups may be dismayed at the animals' living conditions (*e.g.*, Bellerby 1970), it is hard to resist the economic incentives. The use of hormones cuts feed requirements about 10 percent, and the rate of gain is increased between 9 and 18 percent, depending on whether the cattle are being pasture-fed or finished in a feed lot (Cunha 1972). The net saving was about 3.5 cents per pound to the consumer in 1970 beef prices, or probably twice that in 1976 with feed prices roughly doubled. (Feed prices fell in 1977.) Since less feed is needed, less manure is produced, and thus waste disposal from concentrated feeding production operations is less costly (Kiesner 1971).

It should be evident that the elements of this system work very effectively together. Hormones and antibiotics are an important factor in the profitability of large feedlots. Over three-quarters of the meat and eggs produced in the United States come from animals that have been treated with these chemicals (Cunha 1972). The antibiotics used are a by-product of concentrating them for human use. In 1970, 1,300 tons were used in animal feed (Kiesner 1972).

The use of these substances, however, has serious implications for human health. One of the widely used hormones, DES (diethylstilbesterol), a female hormone, has been shown to cause cancer in test animals. It has also been implicated in some cases of human cancer where the DES was used experimentally to prevent miscarriages (Weiss 1973). Residues are periodically found in beef liver. The use of DES has been gradually restricted in the United States in recent years. Earlier use as a neck implant for growth stimulation has been banned. But it is still in limited use, and other hormones which may not have been tested for effects on humans are also available.

Some people have allergies to antibiotics, so that they may have ill effects from ingesting residues (FDA undated). But the more important problem stems from the fact that humans are susceptible to some of the same diseases that affect animals. Widespread use of antibiotics such as penicillin, tetracycline, and streptomycin in animals results in a selection among bacteria populations which favors resistant strains. Thus, these important tools of modern medicine may become less effective in treating human disease (Hall 1974). In other western countries, antibiotic use in animals has been banned for some time in cases where the drug is also used to treat humans. Other dangers may be in store. Scientists have recently discovered that some types of bacteria can pass disease resistance to other bacteria and even to other species, a phenomenon known as "transferable drug resistance" (Crossland 1975).

3 Soil Fertility and Food Quality

The two major differences between conventional and organic agriculture lie in their approaches to soil fertility and pest control. Accordingly, we will now turn our attention to methods of increasing fertility. In order to understand the critique of conventional agriculture, it is necessary to review briefly the relevant aspects of soil science. Only those facts needed to understand the issues will be covered.

Organic farming is a biological technology attempting to supercede a technology based primarily on the science of chemistry. Thus, to understand the economics of organic farming, we must begin with an understanding of soil biology and of its potential impact on crop production. An analysis of technological alternatives must involve a comparison of technologies. In this case, the technological differences relate in a large way to the soil. This chapter will also serve as a brief feasibility study of organic fertilization.

Soil fertility is the area of major ideological conflict between conventional and organic agriculture. To what extent and in what manner does the method of fertilization influence food quality? The generally accepted position is succinctly stated by an Iowa State University textbook on soils: "Organic and mineral fertilizers are equally good for plants and for animals or people eating the plants for food" (Thompson and Troeh 1973). Until the mid-1960s, the Food and Drug Administration (FDA) went somewhat further, holding that, "Composition [of plants] is controlled by hereditary factors or genes," (not the kind and extent of fertilizer used) (Nelson 1959). It is now generally admitted by all sides that soil conditions affect nutrient levels. Still, "Today's general food supply can provide adequate amounts of all nutrients necessary to good health" (FDA 1973). Two key words are "can" (not "does") and "nutrients." The word "nutrients"

23

implies that the importance of food lies in nutrient levels only, a contention denied by advocates of organic farming.

The organic farming groups assert not only that imbalances in the soil may lead to imbalances in plant nutrients, but also that "Vitamin and mineral content of the food are related to the humus content of the soil" (DeHart and DeHart 1962). Further, some go beyond a simple appeal to nutrients. "Some things chemically the same may be very different as conductors of living energy" (Balfour 1975). This last assertion should be recognized as something of a different order from considerations of relative amounts of nutrients. Minerals are chemicals and, if missing, can simply be added. Modern man tends to view himself and his fellow creatures and plants as special arrangements of chemicals, no more, no less. As a famous Harvard nutritionist put it, ". . . all foods are chemicals. You and I, too, are chemicals—so much water, protein, fat, carbohydrates, vitamins and minerals" (Stare 1961). Living beings carry on certain characteristic functions which differentiate them from the nonliving. But any suggestion of a non-physical life-energy, vital force, or soul which inheres in living beings has been rejected by conventional academic thinking because of the present lack of empirical evidence. Nevertheless, the belief that there may be such a difference between the living and the dead persists in some circles, turns up among advocates of organic farming, and leads to a particular concern for living relations in the soil. It is worth noting that the same rejection of non-physical aspects of living beings also characterizes the American medical establishment. Cures which operate through energy paths, like chiropractic, osteopathy, and acupuncture, are similarly rejected. We will return to this parallel in coming chapters.

Soil Components and Their Properties

The major differences in practice and opinion between farming methods relate to the treatment of the soil. People and animals depend on plants and animals for food; plants depend on the soil. Plants do need air for oxygen, carbon dioxide and, through soil bacteria, nitrogen. But availability requires penetration of air into the soil, so we are brought back to the soil. Aside from air and water, there are three main soil constitutents: minerals, living organisms, and the remains of formerly living organisms.

Minerals. The mineral components, derived from the rocks of the earth, come in all sizes, from stones through sand and silt to clay. Soils vary widely in their relative amounts of sand, silt, and clay, but a good proportion is around 20 percent clay and 40 percent each of the others. Such mixtures are known as loams. The larger particles gradually weather and release mineral nutrients for use by plants. The clay particles, the smallest particles of rock, have electrically charged locations which can attract, hold, and make available to plants, charged atoms of elements known as ions. They can also adsorb (hold on the surface) organic molecules and microbes. (Organic in this context means "from life," that is, containing chains of carbon atoms.) Some of the ions dissolve readily in water, and the character of their reaction with water determines whether soil provides an acid, neutral, or alkaline environment for the plant roots and soil life. For example, calcium carbonate has an alkaline reaction in solution; calcium sulfate an acidic. Most crops grow best when acid and alkaline components are balanced, that is, when the soil reaction is close to neutral.

Organic Matter. The second major category of soil material is the organic matter: decayed or decaying remains of formerly living plants or animals. This material is of two types: crude organic matter, in which the structure of the parent plant or animal is still discernable; and humus, composed of a wide variety of high molecular weight (heavy) organic molecules. The humus content of soils can range from virtually zero to practically 100 percent in reclaimed peat bogs. Average cropland ranges from about 2 to 5 percent humus. When sod is plowed up for agricultural use, the humus content declines and, over a period of years, approaches an equilibrium value depending on the crop and fertilizer program. Once the equilibrium level is reached, the soil stabilizes, even under heavy chemical fertilizer use. Despite common organic propaganda to the contrary, humus *is* replaced with plant residues under conventional chemical as well as organic fertilizer programs. Plots cropped continuously for over a hundred years using chemical fertilizer are still fertile and productive (Russell 1961). The humus content of sandy eastern United States soils has probably been increased since cultivation began (Allaway 1975). Nevertheless, compared to conventional farmers organic farmers can, and generally do, achieve higher humus levels in their soils. And chemically treated soils are able to maintain their organic matter content only because their soil life is so weak that it cannot break down the organic materials.

Humus serves a number of vital roles in the soil. Like clay particles, it has an ability to hold nutrients needed by plants. Ions are of two kinds. The first, positively charged, called cations (because they are attracted to the cathode or negative terminal of a cathode ray tube), includes most of the metals, such as calcium (Ca^{++}), magnesium (Mg^{++}), sodium (Na^+, from Latin *Natrium*), potassium (K^+, *Kalium)* and iron (Fe^{++}, or Fe^{+++} *Ferrium*), and also ammonium (NH_4^+). The others are negatively charged, called anions, and are usually nonmetals, such as phosphate (phosphorus combined with oxygen, PO_4^{---}), sulfate (SO_4^{--}), nitrate (NO_3^-), nitrite (NO_2^-), and chloride (Cl^-). The capacity of clays and humus in a soil to hold and make available these ions is an important measure of fertility. The ability to exchange the metal ions (in a neutral solution) is called the "cation exchange capacity." A soluble chemical fertilizer can wash away in the next rain unless there is a high cation exchange capacity to hold the nutrients until the plants need them. Thus humus is complementary to chemical fertilizers. Humus also ties up certain ions which otherwise tend to make phosphates insoluble.

A second way humus holds and offers minerals to plants is in "chelated" form (giant claw-structured molecules). Trace minerals can also be added in synthetic chelates. The humus also serves as an effective buffer, regulating the balance between acid and base in the soil solution. The more humus, the more effective the buffer (Allison 1973).

Humus adsorbs large quantities of water in comparison to its weight. This is clearly most important in dry seasons or years or regions. Both this and the capacity to hold nutrients is important for sandy soils. With the increasing reliance on irrigation, this quality has been less important. Energy and water shortages could lead to a reevaluation, however.

Humus also helps avoid damage from too much water. Clay soils are kept open and air is allowed to penetrate and water to drain out—both necessary conditions for satisfactory plant growth. Humus improves soil "tilth," making the soil easier to plow. It is also of particular value in regulating soil heat. The dark color absorbs heat, helping soil to warm up in the spring. And the high specific heat (capacity to hold heat) helps to stabilize the soil temperature.

Decaying organic matter provides plants with nutrients and other benefits which are not avilable in its absence, though bacteria can synthesize vitamins. Auxins (plant hormones or growth regulators) are released. These and other large molecules can be absorbed by the roots of plants. While some plants can *only* live off organic material, *all* plants can absorb organic compounds from the soil (and also carbon dioxide). In fact, any water-soluble substance can be absorbed through plant roots, not just mineral ions. Thus, plant nutrition is really different from animal nutrition in *degree*, not kind (Krasil'nikov 1958; Bear 1953). Soil organic matter includes many biologically active substances such as enzymes, vitamins, auxins, and amino acids. Soil fungi, living on organic matter in the soil, produce antibiotics. A high humus content helps control some plant pathogenic fungi.

Soil life. The third important component of soils is the living portion, the soil life, which comes in all sizes, from microscopic to small animals. Most important for plants are the microorganisms, mainly bacteria and fungi. These microbes live on organic material in the soil, converting it into humus and also other metabolic products influencing plants. They also obtain energy by converting the ammonium form of nitrogen found in plant residues and some fertilizers into the nitrate form. There are more than four tons of microbes in the plow layer of one acre of fertile soil (Krasil'nikov 1958).

Compared to soil chemistry, soil biology is many orders of magnitude more complex. Besides the difficulties of dealing with living organisms instead of simply chemicals, there are probably thousands of different types of microorganisms inhabiting soils. They interact with each other, with the soil minerals, and with plants. They may only live a few hours. Life cycles are poorly understood, and it is still not even possible to obtain an accurate survey of soil fungi populations.

Microorganisms can be either beneficial or harmful to plants. Fungi predominate in acid soils; bacteria in neutral to alkaline. Most plants exhibit some degree of close mutual association (symbiosis) with soil microorganisms. For example, plants exude substances from their roots which encourage some microbes and discourage others. These substances (and also decay products) may affect the growth of other higher plants, one of the reasons for success or failure with crop rotation and companion planting (mixing species for mutual benefit in a field). With monocultures (planting the same crop over wide areas) and continuous cropping (planting the same crop year after year), toxins exuded by microbes and plants (dead and alive) build up and the natural fertility of the soil for that crop may decline, though toxins can often be leached out by water. Toxicity also depends on the season, being lowest in the spring. Soil microbes are affected as much or more than the higher plants. Plant excretions may also be toxic to other plants, as grass excretions to apple trees (Krasil'nikov 1958).

Symbiosis, including actual "infection" with fungi, is common. The mycorrhizal (little root) fungi are particularly interesting. When a fungus infects a plant root, it sends its filiaments into and between the plant cells, trading nutrients for carbohydrates made by the plant. The plant may even absorb portions of the fungus itself. Outside, the fungus provides the plant with root-hair-like projections which funnel nutrients back to the plant. The fungi also produce plant hormones (auxins). This arrangement is most common in forest soils, which tend to be acidic, but is also present in many croplands. In the latter, if plants are not growing well, fungal infection (in legumes, for example) can lead to early root death and less growth (Russell 1961).

Bacteria also invade plants beneficially, the most well-known being the root-nodule bacteria which fix (convert into usable form) atmospheric nitrogen within the roots of legumes. Some non-legumes also exhibit a similar symbiosis. Plant growth is weak when the corresponding microbe infection is absent. The same type of symbiosis occurs in plant leaves. The spores pass from plant to plant through seeds (Krasil'nikov 1958).

Plants absorb such organic nutrients as vitamins and antibiotics when a vigorous soil life surrounds the roots. The microbes also transport nutrients to plant roots and often transform inorganic nutrients to organic forms prior to plant absorption. For example, they may make inorganic phosphate avilable (Krasil'nikov 1958).

Bacteria of the same species (azobacter, for example, which fixes nitrogen in legumes) exhibit adaptive variability; that is, they undergo great changes in shape and activity depending on plant root influence and other factors. For bacteria to be effective in promoting crop growth, they must be of the specific type required (Krasil'nikov 1958).

Plants provide, in the region of their roots, the "rhizosphere," an environment which encourages microbe growth. Plants exude a wide variety of substances from their roots, including various proteins and amino acids, vitamins, auxins and toxins. Some of these substances are used by the microbes for food; dead plants provide food also. All these relations are specific to particular plants and microbes. How different these relations are from the simple relations between plants and chemicals! A few chemicals promote the growth of almost all plants.

Plants also improve the soil structure in the neighborhood of roots, making the rhizosphere more hospitable to microbe growth. The poorer the soil in organic substances, the less vigorous the life in the rhizosphere. The microlife benefits humans and animals by destroying pathogenic organisms in manure. Bacteria are also able to destroy some herbicides and other chemicals. The products of microbial metabolism can exert marked effects on plant life, influencing seed germination, early plant growth, and biochemical processes within the plant.

Increasing Soil Fertility

Except for some virgin, highly fertile soils, soils in their natural state do not normally provide satisfactory yields without some assistance from man. Since any effort has its cost, maximum yields will not be sought, unless a farmer attaches some value to high yields for their own sake. Growers seeking to publicize a particular fertilizer program may seek maximum yield, but the strongest argument is, of course, increased profit. Assuming profit maximization, methods of enhancing soil fertility will be carried out as long as the marginal value of yield increment exceeds the marginal cost of the improvement. The soil fertility can be radically altered by such investments as drainage and irrigation systems, but we will discuss only fertilization techniques, since these are what distinguish organic from standard agriculture and raise the significant public policy issues for this study.

There are three major nutrients which generally have the most marked effects on crop yields: nitrogen, phosphorus, and potassium. A host of minor elements are also needed, and humus and soil life also make their contributions. Fertilizers are labeled according to their content of the three major nutrients, according to a traditional scheme. The percentage of nitrogen (N) by weight is listed first. Then the percent of phosphate, PO_4 (actually calculated as P_2O_5), is listed, but only that which is readily available to plants (soluble in citrate solution). Last, the percent of potassium oxide, K_2O, is listed; that is, it is assumed that the element potassium (K) is present in this special form, even though it generally is not. Potassium oxide is commonly known as potash (since it was originally obtained from pot ashes), so that this is called "percent potash." Thus a "10-10-10 NPK" fertilizer is 10 percent nitrogen, 10 percent phosphate (actually 4.4 percent phosphorus), and 10 percent potash (actually 8.3 percent potassium).*

There are four types of fertilizers which may be added to soils: nitrogen and three corresponding to the three soil components—organic matter, minerals and soil microlife.

Organic matter and nitrogen. Organic matter is an end product of any life process: animal and human manures, food processing wastes, garbage, crop or other vegetable residues, dead bodies. When a legume crop is turned under to provide nitrogen fertilizer, this is known by analogy as "green manure." Some such materials are necessary if humus is to be formed. Humus-like materials can also be supplied by processing some soft coal (lignite) deposits and some shales. If properly chosen, a complete plant fertilizer can be obtained from organic materials. More often, organic farmers add mineral fertilizers to supply major nutrients which may be lacking, usually phosphate and potash. Minor nutrients are generally adaquately supplied by organic fertilizers.

The materials may be applied directly to fields and disked or plowed under or, in some cases, sprayed on the fields or crops. If incorporated directly into the soil in undigested form, and if the nitrogen content of the residue is low, initial decomposition of the organic material by soil bacteria may draw down the nitrogen reserves of the soil so much that a nitrogen *deficiency* is produced for a period of time, perhaps a few months. This is only one of many examples of the delicate nature of organic fertilizers.

Decomposition can be hastened by composting. Crop residues in the field can be "sheet composted" by spraying with bacteria and disking into the top soil, or simply by disking in and letting nature take its course. Adding a nitrogen fertilizer speeds decomposition. More commonly, especially among organic farmers, plant and animal wastes are piled up and allowed to form humus, or compost, a process which takes up to a few months under favorable circumstances of moderate moisture and good air circulation. Composting has some real positive features. The heat generated kills harmful bacteria and weed seeds. The nitrogen percentage is raised, as some of the bulk is lost to the atmosphere as carbon dioxide. (Nitrogen can also be lost unless care is taken, though it may be added through bacterial action.) Compost can be reformulated to provide more

*Potassium oxide, K_2O, is 83% potassium and 17% oxygen by weight. Thus if a fertilizer is 10% K_2O it must be $0.83 \times 10\% = 8.3\%$ K; that is, 8.3% potassium.

of one nutrient, such as nitrogen, by chemical treatment (Fryer and Simmons 1976), but whether the fertilizer produced is "organic" by the standards of organic farmers is questionable. Since composted materials have been decomposed and turned into humus, they are more readily available to plants than in the raw form. On the other hand, there is less bulk.

When legumes are grown in soil that is comparatively lacking in nitrogen, bacteria in their roots will transform atmospheric nitrogen into nitrate plant food. If the crop is then plowed under, the succeeding crop will be blessed with an organic nitrogen fertilizer. Commonly a legume like alfalfa is grown "in rotation" with corn to obtain this nitrogen fertilizer benefit for the corn. Typically, alfalfa adds 50 to 150 pounds of nitrogen in a season. Unfortunately, if the legume crop is fully harvested (for hay), the soil will be *depleted* of nitrogen, not enriched. However, especially in warm climates, legumes can be planted between corn rows in late August, to provide a winter cover as well as nitrogen. Vetch planted in this manner can add 133 pounds of nitrogen per acre (NRC 1975).

Soils receive nitrogen from many sources. Nitrogen is added to the soil in rainwater, mostly as ammonia and organic matter which had been earlier lost. From one to 20 pounds may be added per acre per year in this manner. (Evidently little is fixed by the atmospheric electrical discharges during thunderstorms.) There is possibly some direct absorption by plants of nitrogen compounds from the air, and some nitrogen is fixed by non-symbiotic bacteria and blue-green algae. The latter contribution is uncertain, perhaps around 12 pounds per acre, perhaps as high as 50 to 100 pounds in sods. When manure is used as fertilizer, it promotes soil life to the extent that an amount of nitrogen is fixed from the atmosphere approximately equal to the amount in the manure (Dhar 1961). Under most American field conditions, only a small amount of nitrogen is produced from these natural sources (Allison 1973).

We may conclude that the total nitrogen which may be derived from natural sources, including crop rotation, is in the range of typical amounts of chemical fertilizer used on heavy feeders such as corn, between 100 to 200 pounds per acre per year. (See Table 3-1 below.) Sufficient organic matter must be present to nourish the nitrogen-fixing microorganisms, however. Generally, under recently prevailing economic conditions in this country, it is easier to use chemical sources of nitrogen.

It is often implied by apologists for conventional agriculture that the only value of organic fertilizers is in adding mineral nutrients. Some value in improving soil structure is also usually acknowledged. But not only can these fertilizers contribute to nitrogen fixation from the atmosphere, humic substances derived from organic matter have positive effects on plant growth in their own right, even in sterile solution. The plants grown with added humus are "bigger, more intensely colored and their root systems better developed" than controls. Different effects are obtained depending on the material used for compost (Krasil'nikov 1958). Higher yields and vitamin content have been obtained in test plots when pure humus was added to the soils (Senn and Kingman 1973).

Manufactured nitrogen fertilizers. Nitrogen is in many ways the critical plant nutrient. It is difficult to obtain, not being found in geological formations. Its use often produces dramatic yield increases (although other major nutrients generally must be increased proportionately). It is at the same time the major cause of pollution from agricultural lands. Any organic waste containing protein has some nitrogen, and, with sufficient organic matter and care, sufficient quantities of nitrogen can be obtained from natural sources to produce top yields. But the simplest way to supply nitrogen is with manufactured chemicals. "Inorganic" nitrogen fertilizer production begins with the synthesis of ammonia (NH_3) from a mixture of gaseous nitrogen and hydrogen (H). The energy and the hydrogen for this process generally is supplied by natural gas (mostly methane, CH_4), which helps to explain the strong position of petroleum companies in fertilizer production, and the energy-dependence of modern agriculture. Ammonia can be liquified ("anhydrous ammonia") and squirted directly into the soil where it dissolves in soil moisture and is adsorbed onto the soil particles as ammonium ions. Soil bacteria then gradually convert the ammonium to nitrate over a period of weeks. Plants absorb both forms. Fertilizer is easier to handle and formulations may be easily varied if the ammonia is made into a solid salt such as ammonium sulfate or ammonium nitrate before spreading on fields. Or synthetic urea (an "organic" chemical!) can be made by a simple reaction with carbon dioxide.

Phosphorus and Potassium. Phosphate and potash fertilizers are obtained from natural deposits, which may be mined, crushed and applied as is to fields. "Rock phosphate" is mostly apatite, $Ca_5(PO_4)_3$ F. Potassium chloride (KCl), "muriate of potash" or simply, "potash," is the common naturally occurring form of potassium.

While some purification of the potash is possible, the major choice in application concerns the phosphate. Rock phosphate is fairly insoluble and thus makes little phosphate immediately available to plants. Conflicting claims over its usefulness probably arise because its solubility depends on where the rock was mined (how tight the crystals are) and on the soil conditions. A slightly acid soil is needed to leach the phosphate from the crushed rock, so that natural phosphate works well with manure, which tends to acidify the soil (Thompson and Troeh 1973). Organic farmers also find rock phosphate more helpful than conventional farmers because humus ties up metals that tend to make phosphate unavailable, and bacteria can also assist in making the phosphate available.

Rock phosphate may be reformulated to make the nutrients more concentrated and more soluble. Sulfuric acid treatment produces a mixture of calcium phosphate and calcium sulfate which is known as "superphosphate." Treatment with phosphoric acid is more expensive, but yields the more concentrated pure substance, calcium phosphate, "triple superphosphate."

Organic farmers often refer to phosphate rock as "organic" fertilizer, to contrast with chemically processed phosphate. Since rocks are in fact minerals, this terminology can cause some confusion. Because of the high solubility of mined potash, organic farmers generally favor other sources of potash, such as organic wastes or wood ashes.

Bacterial fertilizers. Bacteria are widely used as fertilizers in the Soviet Union, but less so in this country. Yield increases of 10 percent to 25 percent or higher are reported (Krasil'nikov 1958). Interest in bacterial soil inoculants has picked up in the last few years in America (See, *e.g.*, Fogg *et al.* 1973). One small firm is marketing a mixture of "blue-green algae" and other bacteria in the spore stage, which is fortified with chelated trace minerals. Trials by farmers and at least one university indicate that semi-annual inoculation ($12 per acre cost) provides yields equal to or greater than typical commercial nitrogen fertilizer applications (of, say, 150 lb. per acre). Better soil structure and crop quality also may appear (Hay 1977; Kinsey 1976). Bacteria are also used to inoculate composts, enhancing the speed and quality of the compost process. The results vary with crop, compost type, and bacteria used (Krasil'nikov 1958).

Use of chemical fertilizer on major crops. Four crops are the recipients of 55 percent of the total chemical fertilizer used in the United States: corn, cotton, soybeans, and wheat. These crops also account for 61 percent of the land so fertilized. Table 3-1 shows the average percent of harvested acres receiving fertilizer for these crops, and the average rate per acre receiving fertilizer in 1975. Corn is clearly the heaviest user of chemical fertilizer: 94 percent of harvested acres receive nitrogen at the rate of 105 pounds per acre. Almost all farmers today use hybrid corn, which has been bred for excellent response to nitrogen fertilizer.

Chemical vs. Organic Fertilization

Manufactured or chemical fertilizers have some clear advantages over organic. Chemical fertilizers are easier and cheaper to handle. Only those nutrients actually missing need be added. Manure is messy and its nutrients can be lost quickly to air or water unless handled carefully. Organic fertilizer is expensive, bulky, and comparatively slow-acting (unless composted or high-grade, such as seed meals or slaughterhouse wastes). Maximum yield requires a spurt of nutrient-intensive growth

Table 3-1   Fertilizer Used on Harvested Acres of Major Crops in the United States in 1975

| Crop | Acres Receiving Fertilizer (percent of total crop) | | | | Rate Per Acre (lb) | | | Total U.S. Harvested Acreage (1000 acres) |
	Any Fertilizer	N	P_2O_5	K_2O	N	P_2O_5	K_2O	
Corn	94	94	86	82	105	58	67	66,573
Cotton	65	65	43	33	78	50	55	9,307
Soybeans	28	18	25	26	15	40	53	53,533
Wheat	63	63	43	21	46	35	35	68,861

Source: ERS 1976.

early in the season. Organic farming advocates often point out that plants put on the bulk of their growth during the warm summer months, when soil organisms are most active releasing nutrients from organic fertilizers. But plants, organically raised or not, are then concentrating on bulk, using carbon from the air, and average percent mineral content declines (Thompson and Troeh 1973). A green manure crop *can* provide this burst of available nutrients if turned under prior to planting (Allison 1973).

Despite their advantages, however, chemical fertilizers have serious drawbacks, as already indicated. The main side-effects are on soil life and water quality. Fertilizer manufacture also generates pollution, and more pollution is generated indirectly by the neglect of organic wastes. There may also be more subtle effects on human health through changes in food quality, which will be explored in the following section.

Soil conditions. Chemical fertilizer may have an adverse effect on soil life, particularly if the soil is highly acid. Short-term effects can be balanced by adding lime at the same time. On a heavy clay soil, a program of continuous cropping with a heavy feeder like corn and exclusive reliance on chemical fertilizers can lead to poor drainage, a more impenetrable soil below the surface layer, and lower fertility. High short-run yields are traded for long-term decline in production. Subsoiling equipment is now available to open up such soil at modest expense. It should be recalled that shortsightedness was not invented by chemical fertilizer companies and agribusiness. The history of agriculture is a history of soil erosion and exploitation of natural resources. Over-grazing, over-irrigation, replacing forest cover with farmland—these can create permanent infertility, even change climate.

Water pollution. If used carefully and in moderation, adverse effects of chemical fertilitzer use on water quality may be avoided. Unfortunately, this has often not been the case. Chemical fertilizers do not supply humus, so the nutrient and water-holding capacity of the soil may be less than with organic fertilizers. (Some humus is always supplied by decaying plant residues.) This lower capacity leads to faster leaching of nutrients from the soil. The nutrient loss is aggravated by the higher solubility of chemical fertilizers, particularly nitrogen fertilizers. The runoff from nitrogen and phosphate fertilizers into streams and rivers and eventually lakes feeds algae which multiply rapidly. The situation is substantially worsened by human and animal sewage and food processing wastes, which also contribute these nutrients (more than farms, actually), as well as organic material. Note that organic fertilizers also cause pollution if highly concentrated, but this generally occurs when the goal is waste disposal rather than fertilization. The growth and decay of these microorganisms and the digestion of the organic material leads to depletion of the oxygen in the water. Fish and other higher life forms are inhibited or eliminated. Recreational values may be severely lowered. This pollution can hasten the natural process of aging and dying of a lake, as has happened with Lake Erie. In the streams, pathogenic organisms, which would otherwise remain dormant in the soil, are activated by the anaerobic conditions (without oxygen or air), and outbreaks of previously rare diseases may occur (Commoner 1971).

Nitrates do not just pollute streams. They are so soluble that they leach down through the soil into the ground water that feeds springs and wells. High nitrate concentrations in drinking water can cause death in infants and are also harmful to adults. Dangerous concentrations of nitrate have been observed in some midwest wells (Commoner 1971).

While up to 70 percent of phosphate fertilizer may be lost in runoff, this is due mainly to erosion, since phosphates are relatively insoluble, even in superphosphate form. It is thus argued that phosphate pollution is more a function of poor farming practice than of fertilizer choice. Once in the streams, superphosphate *is* more soluble, thus presumably more available, but in longrun equilibrium, phosphate from rock phosphate will also become available.

It should be recognized that water pollution is not so much a matter of the *use* of chemical fertilizers, as of the *misuse*. An application of chemical fertilizer which does not exceed the soil's capacity for holding nutrients (cation exchange capacity) will cause little pollution. The safe level varies greatly with soil conditions, but 100 pounds of nitrogen per acre is generally considered safe. In some cases, perhaps even 300 pounds would not result in significant leaching (Martin *et al.* 1970). Heavy manuring causes the same nitrate problems as heavy chemical application. Furthermore, chemical urea can be formulated (for example, combined with formaldehyde) to be insoluble and release its nitrogen only slowly over a period of weeks (Teuscher and Adler 1960).

Depletion of the ozone layer. Nitrogen fertilizers have been implicated in depletion of the upper atmosphere ozone layer, which protects us from cancer-causing ultraviolet rays. Some of the nitrogen in fertilizer is converted into the gas nitrous oxide, which escapes to the atmosphere. This gas speeds the decompostion of the ozone (Shapley 1977).

External costs in production. Some ill effects of fertilizer *are* strictly a matter of use, however. These are the side-effects of fertilizer manufacture. Some pollution results directly from nitrogen fertilizer manufacture, but the main side-effects stem from the use of energy. Nitrogen fertilizer requires much energy to produce, especially natural gas. This consumption has many implications, which will be discussed in Chapter 6.

Phosphate fertilizer is strip-mined, mostly in Florida. Not only is much land despoiled in the process (although much can be reclaimed), but a great deal of water is required for purifying the gravel deposits. The rinse water contains such fine particles of clay that it must be held in settling ponds, perhaps for over a decade. Radioactive substances have been raised to the surface, and radioactive radon gas is emitted by the ponds. Irreversible changes in the resource base are occurring. Salt water is encroaching on Florida's fresh water reserves, subsistence of surface areas has occurred, and our own national phosphate reserves which are extractable at current prices may be exhausted by the year 2000. In fact, *world* reserves may be used up within a few more decades. The United States currently has 30 percent of world reserves (Love 1976).

Organic wastes. It may be suggested that, since farms contribute less than other sources to water pollution, focusing on agricultural pollution is misplaced and somewhat unfair. This point of view neglects the fact that the reason we have non-farm pollution is to a large extent the same as the reason we have agricultural runoff. As a society we are not recycling our wastes from the industrial and household sectors back to the agricultural sector. In a free market, the costs of this system are not borne by the participants: farmer, businessman, consumer. Economists call such costs "external" costs. The full social cost of using soluble nitrogen fertilizer includes not just the pollution caused by the fertilizer runoff, but also the pollution caused by the waste products which are *not* recycled. This becomes clear if we consider that if a zero-release of pollutants were imposed upon sewage treatment and food processing plants and feed lots, the supply price of the raw waste material might well be negative. They would have to pay people to haul it away. The price would be the subsidy necessary to induce farmers to use all the materials which must be disposed of in a non-polluting fertilizer program, assuming no cheaper alternative was available. In the long run, new technology would be developed, to make it possible to sell processed waste as a profitable by-product. This has already happened in some places under the pressure of current restrictions.

Another organic material which could be partly used for fertilizer is garbage. Much urban refuse has in recent years been placed in "sanitary landfills": valleys of garbage interleaved with soil. The anaerobic decomposition of this organic material over a period of years eventually begins to release significant quantities of methane, making the area dangerous for residences. An explosion has already occurred in Richmond, Virginia (McAllister 1976). Landfills can also release poisonous organic chemicals into groundwater if not separated from the water table (Robertson *et al.* 1974). Ocean dumping of garbage and sewage sludge threatens recreation at nearby beaches. In the summer of 1976, New York City garbage began washing up on some Long Island beaches, forcing them to be closed. Other beaches may also be threatened by giant sludge pools, as well as garbage (Frank 1976).

Institutional barriers hindering use of organic fertilizers. Government regulations and policies have hindered the use of organic fertilizer, both actively and passively. Chemical fertilizer has been subsidized, even given away, by government agencies. The use of manure and sewage sludge, on the other hand, has been subject to sanitary and aesthetic restrictions, particularly in regions where farming overlapped with residential land use. There has been conservatism among sanitary engineers and a fear of germs, despite successful use of sewage sludge in some areas of the world for generations. Spray irrigation with sewage effluent and fertilization with compost has been successfully carried out in the last decade by many United States municipalities, including some in Michigan, Illinois, Ohio, and Pennsylvania (see, for example, Manson and Merritt 1975).

Strict labeling is usually beneficial to consumers. Under the guise of consumer protection and in response to chemical fertilizer interests, some states are restricting the marketing of natural products. Strict labeling and reporting standards for organic soil-amendment fertilitzers, like the humate products, have been set (Hinnen 1975). Some states now require a minimum NPK content in order for a product to be marketed as a fertilizer. Organic fertilizers usually do not qualify for federal fertilizer subsidies. Special restrictions, not applying to chemical fertilizer, have been imposed on use of manure products when pollution might occur. As a result of this pressure, organic fertilizers and soil amendments have been forced out of some state markets.

The organic fertilizer industry is a small one composed of small firms. Because they are small, the firms cannot afford to pay for tests in all the states which may require them (Taylor 1976). There are special problems associated with testing and marketing natural products, which will be explained in following chapters. Brand loyalty is important to these firms because they are marketing naturally occurring materials. Maintainance of consumer loyalty after market development is a serious problem. Products are differentiated by certain additives and combinations. Listing ingredients on the label would undermine brand loyalty and hinder market development. Nevertheless, inactive ingredients are admittedly a serious problem in the soil amendment industry. Many "organic" soil amendments are now on the market which are mainly crushed rock, selling at prices as high as 200 times the price of the ingredients. Since extension agents generally do not give advice on these organic fertilizers, the farmer is on his own, and may neglect a useful product or waste his money on an overpriced one (Taylor 1975).

Human Nutrition

Human well-being is the ultimate goal of food production, as it is of any economic activity. Health is a function of many things, including the amount of food, its quality, and the level of pollution. Defenders of conventional agriculture argue, in effect, that this function is separable; that is, that increases in output and consumption would lead to increased welfare independent of any measure of quality or associated pollution. This is clearly not true in the case of pollution, as explained above. But what of quality? Organic farmers are often reluctant to talk quantity, for they believe that this is a misleading measure. Many believe that as quantity increases, quality decreases. If fertilizer choice makes a significant difference in human nutrition, output comparisons (to be developed in Part III) must be made on the complex basis of human health indices rather than the simple intermediate variable, crop yield.

What is the effect of chemical fertilizer on animal and human nutrition? There are two subsidiary questions. First, is there a positive or negative effect on the measureable nutrient content of the crop due to the fertilizer program? And, second, is there any demonstrable effect on animal and human health? These two questions can be investigated independently and the answers may not necessarily be the same. While the former is easier to test, the latter is the real concern. Nutrition is a very complex affair, and new essential nutrients or vitamins are still being discovered, not to mention possible interactions between nutrients, intestinal bacteria populations, and the genetic makeup of the individual consumer.

The issues can be broken down in a different manner, producing at least one simple answer. If soil nutrients are out of balance due to natural deficiency or overly zealous and improper fertilization, then animals eating the food will suffer (Albrecht 1975). An obvious example is iodine deficiency resulting in goiter. Some soils have naturally toxic levels of certain trace minerals, for example, selenium. Plants grown in such circumstances will in general also be less resistant to pest attack, requiring increased pesticidal efforts. We will first look at evidence regarding particular nutrients; then more complex studies of consumer health will be reviewed.

Soil imbalance. Chemical fertilizers may interfere with the uptake of other nutrients. When ammonia or ammonium is added to a soil, the ammonium ions displace other positive (metallic) ions from their sites in the soil particles and force them into solution, where they may be leached out by rain or irrigation. The same thing happens when potash (K^+) is added. However, calcium, which is the main element endangered, can be easily brought up to higher levels by liming (adding calcium carbonate). Often the soil cation exchange capacity becomes unbalanced with these few ions, and deficiencies of other nutrients can thus occur, since plants tend to absorb more of those nutrients which are more concentrated. If potassium is in excess supply, plants build up high levels at the expense of calcium and magnesium (Bear 1953). If there is a plentiful supply of a particular nutrient in the top few inches of an acre of soil, the soil is not technically "deficient." Nevertheless, the *plant* may be deficient if there is an excess of a nutrient which competes for the plant's attention (is a close chemical substitute), or if the nutrient is not in available form. This is important for both animal and human nutrition and also for susceptibility to pest attack.

Excessive nitrogen fertilizer has been linked to various adverse quality changes in produce: "Resistance to mechanical damage at harvest and during transport, in potatoes; a reduction in favorable proportions of graded fruit and vegetables; losses of flavor and above all a decline in keeping during winter storage" and an increase in disease (Schuphan 1970). A decrease in the essential (limiting) amino acid methionine, and thus in the usable protein, can also be observed (Schuphan 1972). In potatoes, yield increases with nitrogen applications of up to 180 pounds per acre, but protein quality and other quality features such as taste peak out at 45 pounds per acre. Though crude protein produced per acre continues to increase, usable protein per pound of produce decreases. Similar percentage decreases in vitamins and minerals can be observed (Schuphan 1972).

Organic fertilization programs can also lead to soil imbalance. There is a tendency to oversupply potassium and undersupply phosphate. Imbalances in long-time organic gardens have been observed that are sufficient to decrease plant resistance to pest attack and probably to significantly lower the nutritional quality. "This is a common occurrence in organic gardens where heavy applications of manure or wood ashes have been made . . . The food raised there would probably kill any cattle eating it" (Harnish 1976).

The minor plant nutrients, essential though needed in trace amounts only, are known as the micronutrients or trace elements. They may be easily neglected in using chemical fertilizers, which are formulated from more or less pure chemicals. Micronutrient deficiencies are hard to detect. Yield may be down and deficiencies present, yet no evident symptoms show in the plants. Even if supplied, micronutrient availability is better and lasts longer with manure than with chemical fertilizer. If added in chemical (pure salt) form, some of these nutrients are readily tied up by precipitation and locked up in insoluble form in the soil. For this reason, application of micronutrients as a "foliar" (on the leaves) spray on the growing plant works best, especially for iron. Trace minerals can also be added to the soil in chelated form, that is, tied to large molecules, but available to plants (Thompson and Troeh 1973). A common organic micronutrient fertilizer is seaweed.

Even though excessive use of chemical fertilizer may cause nutrient imbalance in particular crops, this doesn't necessarily mean that humans will suffer. Most people eat a wide variety of food obtained from various geographic regions, and so can obtain all the minerals they need from a balanced diet, providing they eat unrefined foods. It would take a widespread soil deficiency to have any significant impact on any large number of people. There may be such a deficiency, however. The most likely candidates are zinc, magnesium and sulfur. Zinc deficiency symptoms, for example, include "loss of appetite, loss of sense of taste [!], delayed healing of burns, accidental wounds, or surgical incisions," and serious reproductive problems (Allaway 1975). Magnesium deficiency can cause nervous disorders. Much as such symptoms may sound common, they can of course have many causes. The use of zinc as a fertilizer is increasing in response to the possibility of a deficiency. But it is often more efficient to supply a deficient nutrient in feed supplements than through feeding the soil.

Vitamins. Fertilizer may affect vitamin content. But usually genetic makeup is more important than soil conditions (Allaway 1975). What about differences between organic and chemical fertilizer? Many investigators find no significant difference between nutrient levels of plants fertilized with equal amounts of organic and inorganic fertilizers (Beeson 1972). Few reported comparisons show an attempt to control for nutrient value of the fertilizer. Even when equal levels of NPK are used for the organic and chemical plots, a one-year trial may not be fair to the organic, because nutrients are released gradually. This may account for the fact that some researchers *have* measured differences, even depending on the type of compost used. Differences are small, however, and do not always favor organic fertilizer, though they usually do (Koepf *et al.* 1974; Krasil'nikov 1958; Allaway 1975).

Schuphan (1974) observed a striking increase in vitamin content in test plots when fertilization was achieved with compost rather than with chemical fertilizer. He studied nutritional value and yields of vegetables over a 12 year period. Results for four vegetables, representing the major classes, were reported: spinach, savoy (a type of cabbage), potatoes, and carrots. Four types of annual fertilization were used on each crop: (1) NPK at the rate of 88 (to 284)–99–178; (2) stable manure, of, unfortunately, comparatively poor condition, at 13.5 tons per acre; (3) both chemical fertilizer and stable manure; and (4) biodynamic (see Chapter 7) compost at 39 tons (!) per acre. (The compost was made with manure and other organic matter.) Except for potatoes, yields with the compost and the manure were considerably lower than those with chemical fertilizer, declining 4 to 80 percent, depending on soil type and crop. However, the lower yields were to a large extent compensated for by increased nutrient content, particularly higher potassium, vitamin C, phosphorous, iron, and usable protein—in many cases more than 50 percent higher. Sodium and nitrate levels were comparatively low in the organic produce, considered a positive nutritional factor (see below). Organically grown produce also has a relatively higher percent of roughage.

Results of the first three years of a six-year Swedish study begun in 1971 provide evidence of higher quality of organic potatoes and grains. Conventional and organic (bio-dynamic) plots were set up by both the Agricultural College of Sweden and by a nearby biodynamic research group. Macro-nutrient fertilization levels were comparable. Many quality variables were tested, including nutrient content, storage life, and flavor. With only a few exceptions, the conventional products were of lower quality (Dlouhý 1977; Pettersson 1976).

Nitrates. Nitrate in water supplies and in food is becoming a recognized danger. When nitrate is in excess in the soil, it is not fully converted to protein, and may accumulate in plants in quantities of up to 5 percent of their dry weight. A high likelihood of excess occurs during periods of drought or cloud cover, when plant growth is not rapid enough to make full use of nitrogen fertilizer. The nitrogen can come from organic sources as well as chemical fertilizer; in fact, a nitrate problem can appear in any fertile soil. But over-fertilization with feed lot wastes is a main contributor. (Viets and Hageman 1971). The food plants most readily affected are annual grasses, cereals cut at the hay stage, and some leafy vegetables, such as kale, turnips, spinach and beets.

Schuphan (1973) investigated nitrate uptake in spinach in shade and in full sun. With full sun, nitrate content increased only modestly with nitrogen applications of less than 100 pounds per acre. (Nitrate nitrogen was less than 15 milligrams per 100 grams dry matter.) In shady conditions, nitrate accumulation was about two and one-half times greater than with the plants in full sun. Nitrate concentrations increased rapidly for fertilizer applications above 100 pounds nitrogen per acre, reaching levels of over 70 milligrams per 100 grams for 200 pounds per acre applications.

The average spinach yield in the United States of about 140 cwt (hundredweight) per acre (in 1974) corresponds to a fertilization rate of about 70 pounds, apparently within safe bounds. It should be noted that commercial application rates may go much higher (rates as high as 288 pounds per acre have been recorded in Germany).

Why are we concerned with nitrate content of plants? Because in some cases nitrate is converted to the toxic nitrite that reacts with hemoglobin in the blood to inhibit oxygen transport. Nitrates also react with other nitrogen compounds to form nitrosamines, some of which are carcinogens (Allaway 1975).

Fortunately, single-stomached animals like man are less likely to be affected by nitrate uptake than multi-stomached cattle and sheep in whose rumen bacteria readily reduce nitrate to the toxic nitrite. Infants under four months of age are susceptible, however, due to lower stomach acidity than adults (Wolff and Wassermann 1972); baby foods have been found to reach excessive levels of nitrite when improperly stored.

The reaction between nitrates and other compounds to form carcinogens occurs in water polluted by organic wastes and nitrates, so these poisons enter our drinking water. This may be a factor in the high cancer incidence in certain cities (Shapley 1976). Fortunately, it does appear possible to breed plants for low nitrate uptake (Kehr 1974).

Genetic changes. Protein content has a clear relationship to nitrogen fertilizer levels, since nitrogen is incorporated into plant material mainly as protein. However, the percentage of other nutrients declines, due to dilution. This is partially a result of the new hybrid varieties, which have been bred for rapid growth and good response to nitrogen fertilization.

Studies of the feed value of heavily fertilized corn confirm that most of the nitrogen absorbed goes into making protein. But the added protein is of a lower quality and more difficult to digest. (Sauberlich *et al.* 1953; Mitchel *et al.* 1952). And nitrogen not fully converted to protein is in the corn as toxic nitrates and free amino acids. Many studies claiming high protein in chemically raised grain measure only nitrogen content and assume it is all in protein—an obvious bias. Some hybrids have a lower protein content than the old open-pollinated corn, and the average protein content of feed grain in the United States has declined (Perelman 1978). Since both cattle and humans in this country consume plenty of other protein sources besides grain, this decline has not caused a nutritional hardship. Hybrid corn can be selected for high protein content (Kavanagh 1957; Zillinsky 1975).

Often nutritional changes in new varieties have been fortuitous, whether for good or ill. Such changes, which may relate to pest control needs as well as human health, are being investigated by the Food and Drug Administration. Vitamin content may be enhanced. For example, the vitamin A content of sweet potatoes and carrots has risen because breeders have selected for yellow color, which happens to be caused by the vitamin precursor carotene. On the other hand, natural toxins may increase at the same time. Irradiating potato seed tubers to increase yield causes an increase in a toxic alkaloid of 60 percent (Miller 1974). Alkaloids have caused human and animal death from over-consumption of potatoes. Potatoes can be bred for lower alkaloid content. However, the alkaloids apparently serve the function in the potato of protection from insects and fungi. Thus, breeding for human consumption can have unintended side-effects on pest control needs. With cucumbers, breeders confront a trade-off between pest resistance and human health. The bitterness factors in cucumbers are also attractants for spotted cucumber beetles. So breeding bitterness out lessens pest attack. But the bitterness factors are carcino-static in humans (Kehr 1974). The decisions involved in plant breeding for human health are not necessarily simple.

Interactions among nutrients. The nineteenth-century approach to nutrition and health was to isolate and measure particular nutrients. This approach was understandable as a first step in a fledgling science. In the same manner, biological and physical sciences began with classification of living creatures and rocks. Many sciences have progressed beyond classification into analysis of relations between substances, creatures, and environments. The science of nutrition has not so progressed (Hall 1974). Nutrient recommendations are formulated for isolated substances and are standardized for the population as a whole. Yet the value of a food may very well depend on the combination or interaction of its nutrients, and also on the person eating it. Many people cannot digest milk sugar (lactose), including a large percent of the black population (Patton 1969). The consumers' physiology may even change in response to the food ingested (Dubos 1965).

The same considerations apply to negative nutrition, or toxicology, the analysis of food poisons (Hall 1974). The accepted approach, in academia and regulatory agencies, remains that of the early stage of science: isolated element analysis rather than multiple element or element-environment analysis. Poisons are allowed in foods if, when given alone to healthy test animals, no acute poisoning results. No consideration is given to combinations of chemicals, interactions of chemicals with disease (such as a weakened liver, which normally processes poisons), nor to possible long-term effects. In the latter category, cancer is of primary concern, since there can be a latency period of 20 to 30 years between initial exposure and the appearance of the disease. A good example of chemicals acting in concert, but not alone, is nitrates and amines, explained above.

Another example of the interaction of elements in a system arises from the use of ethylenes to fight disease and rot in fruit and vegetables.

Apparently ethylene is harmless in itself, but a byproduct of its manufacture and heating is a proven carcinogen in animals (Mintz 1976).

The idea that analysis of single entities in isolation is sufficient to understand their effect makes as much sense as an economist analyzing labor in isolation from capital or capital in isolation from labor. Isolated from each other, we might conclude that neither makes any significant contribution to the industrial process, and that there is no evidence that either has any value. Of course, working together, far more is accomplished than by either in isolation. This is known as "synergism," a more than proportional effect from the operation of two elements of a system working together. Put another way, the whole is greater than the sum of its parts. This elementary idea is neglected in the science and application of nutrition and toxicology (Hall 1974).

Whole system studies. Since human health is so complex, nutritional science has tended to focus on nutrient levels rather than on the more difficult question of health. But in fact there is no guarantee that more of a particular nutrient in a food means it is better, unless it is to treat a particular known nutritional deficiency. An increase in one nutrient may result in a decrease in another, perhaps as yet undiscovered, factor. Not only malnutrition, but also overnutrition, particularly overweight, are associated with various degenerative diseases. Excessive or unbalanced nutrient intake can have adverse nutritional consequences. The nutritive value of a food is not a matter of certain nutrient composition, but the total effect on the health and well-being of the consumer, including levels of known and unknown nutrients, their associations, and perhaps other unknown factors (Beeson 1972).

There may be still another dimension to nutrition, however. Some philosophers and consumers believe that there is more to the quality of life and food than physical nutrients. Orthodox Jews must have their animals raised and killed in a certain way. It was the belief of ancient peoples that the quality of life of the food influenced the consumer. Some recent experiments cast an interesting light on this. If certain worms are trained to avoid a given stimulus, and then these worms are ground up and fed to other worms, the consumer worms continue to behave in the same manner as the trained worms for a period of time. Does the living quality of the food or of the fertilizer have any effect on the consumer? We know that plants absorb not only simple chemicals, but complex organic molecules.

If there *is* more to food than chemical nutrients, perhaps this can be picked up in experiments. Pfeiffer (1938) carried out a series of experiments in which animals were fed organically raised and conventionally raised feed. In one test, organically fed hens laid sooner, laid more eggs, had more eggs hatch, and experienced less egg spoilage. In another study, mice, calves and cows were offered a choice of food. The preference was strong for the organically raised, which comprised almost 100 percent of the food eaten. Another study, of the mortality rate in mice and turkeys, found about a 30 percent lower mortality rate for organically raised animals. (For a review of these studies, see Linder 1973.) No statistical analysis accompanies these reports, so it is impossible to tell how likely it is that the observed differences were merely chance occurrences—a failing, unfortunately, that is common in organic investigations. The fertility of mice, rabbits and bulls fed organic feed has been investigated in Europe. Animals fed on chemically fertilized fodder had significantly lower fertility—the more fertilizer, the lower the fertility. Chemically fed animals suffered from atrophied uteruses and testicles, less live births, lower semen mobility and higher biochemical stress. Conventional chemical analysis could find no significant differences between the two feeding programs (Aehnelt and Hahn 1978).

A long-term feeding experiment was carried out on an English dairy farm over a period of 30 years (Balfour 1975). The farm, Haughley, was divided in half and each treated as a self-contained unit. The cows were from the same stock and as evenly matched as possible. Each part raised all its own feed, and the only export of significance was milk. (Both also exported some eggs and vegetables and culled cows.) The two sections were treated differently in one way: method of fertilization. One section, the conventional or "mixed" section, used mineral (inorganic) fertilizers in recommended amounts, in addition to the manure available from the farm animals; the other, organic, section used only manure.

Both sections exported milk and imported only a feed supplement to correct for any possible mineral deficiencies. The conventional used a mineral lick, the organic, seaweed. Both recycled the manure back to the soil. The conventional section supplemented the manure with regular applications of chemical fertilizer. The organic section obtained needed plant nutrients from the air (nitrogen fixed by soil bacteria) and from the subsoil via deep-rooting herbs planted in rotation with the feed crops.

Many detailed records were kept of the Haughley experiment, but the most striking results were these: Though the mixed section produced more feed and the cows ate more feed, the cows on the organic section produced, on the average, more milk! Fortunately, enough data are given in the report to determine the significance of the differences.

The following differences between the two sections were tested to see if they were statistically significant, that is, to see how likely it would be that the differences were mere chance occurrences: (1) milk per acre, (2) milk per feed unit, and (3) milk per cow. The first, milk per acre, was not significantly different between the two sections. ($t_8 = 0.275$. Only five years' data were available.) This occurred despite the fact that chemical fertilizer was imported into the mixed section. The mixed section produced more feed per acre, so that the organically fed cows produced more milk per pound of feed, 44 percent more over the five years. And this difference *is* significantly different from zero at the 0.01 level; that is, the probability that both sections produced the same amount of milk per pound of feed is less than one chance in a hundred. ($t_8 = 5.93 > t_{0.005,\,8} = 3.36$. A two-tailed test was used.) The third comparison also favored the organic section and was also statistically significant at the 0.01 level ($t_8 = 4.6 > t_{0.005,\,8} = 3.36$): The organically fed cows produced 10 percent more milk per cow on the average than the conventionally fed, even on the reduced feed input! This is quite a productivity edge. These differences are impressive, and are at variance with conclusions and assumptions of standard agricultural research.

Differences in health between the two herds were small, particularly at first. After the second generation of cows began to take over, observers had an impression of higher stamina on the organic section. A less vague comparison was made between numbers of cows culled for failure to breed: 17 percent of the organic herd versus 35 percent of the conventional. The organic cows had a longer working life, but twice as many stillbirths.

It is possible that the differences observed in some of these experiments were artifacts, results of some other influence, such as a flaw in the chemical fertilizer program. But if the chemical program were not deficient in any manner, what then? Would the total nutrition experiments come out differently if an ideal chemical program were used rather than simply the one currently in use or recommended by inexpert or even biased extension agents or fertilizer salesmen? The differences in feeding experiments may also depend on feed freshness, availability of water, even the experimenter's feelings toward the animals! Certainly changes to more artificial, and thus possibly less complete, methods may introduce some risk into the food system. For example, the effect of refined flour on the British populace was not noticed until the national emergency of the Boer War in 1899, when recruits were in significantly poorer health compared to those in earlier wars (Hall 1974).

Advocates of alternative agriculture predict declines in vitality and fertility, particularly after two or three generations (Steiner 1924). In fact, fertility in America *has* declined during the 1970s. Will listlessness follow? Some critics of the younger generation would say that sloth is already upon us! The reflection that there is a high correlation between nationalist groups and concern for food quality should give pause for reflection. We are proud that our harvests are generally far better than the Russian. But perhaps they know something we don't know. We may not know who is right for some time.

Conclusion. In the final analysis, the important issue in the debate between organic and conventional fertilization is the effect on human health. Although the evidence is still not conclusive, nutrient levels appear to be higher for organically raised vegetables, and perhaps in better balance. Total nutrient output per acre is probably higher for chemical fertilization. Contrary to the assertions of some chemical fertilizer spokesmen, plants can and do absorb whatever substances are present in the soil, and pure humus can have a positive effect on plant growth.

Tests of the effect of production methods on consumer health, vitality, and fertility are rare. The most impressive are the studies of bull and rabbit fertility. The declines in fertility were large and statistically significant. And the Haughley experiment showed that organically raised food can have more real food value. Whether and in what manner a similar feed efficiency might apply to humans remains to be seen.

Enough questions have been raised about possible superiority of organically raised food to avoid dismissing such contentions out of hand. A risk to national well-being exists. The paucity of data forestalls the application of a simple numerical adjustment in gross yield per acre. Our comparisons between organic and conventional food production will be made on the basis of the intermediate variable, yield. However, we must recognize that a lower yield under organic husbandry will probably be compensated for to some extent by higher nutritional quality.

4 Plant Pests and Their Control

The preceding chapter explained how organic and conventional agricultures differ in their approaches to soil fertility. In this chapter, we turn to the other major difference between the two methods: how they handle plant diseases and insect pests. As in their approach to soil fertility, conventional farmers tend to rely upon chemicals to control pests. Their organic counterparts, however, again turn primarily to biology.

Crops are subject to a variety of pest attacks. These include bacteria, viruses, and fungi (NRC 1968a); soil-dwelling roundworms or nematodes (NRC 1968b); insects (NRC 1969); and the larger animals. Also they suffer from competition from other plants, that is, weeds (NRC 1968c). Under natural conditions a balance is achieved between plants and their pests, through natural competition, selection, and predator-prey relationships. Such control is going on all the time in all ecological systems. The natural balance is generally not optimal for human food production, however. With human intervention in the form of agriculture, new circumstances may create favorable conditions for the multiplication of disease or insect pests, and lead to the need for pest control measures.

In the first section of this chapter, the technical characteristics of the main pest control alternatives will be described. We will see why chemical pesticides have such an appeal to the farmer, even though they pose serious dangers for human health and the environment. With this background, the economics of pest control development and adoption will be analyzed. First some estimates of crop loss in the absence of pesticides will be examined. These estimates are subject to qualifications, but give us some idea of the magnitude of the problem. Then we examine costs and benefits of developing new pesticides. It turns out that the ratio of the benefits to the costs of developing new biological controls is far larger than that for new chemical pesticides. The following section explains how this arises from the failure of pesticide supply markets to reach a social or economic optimum. The final section summarizes the argument of the chapter. It explains how the present domination of chemical pesticides in the pest control market arises from the technical characteristics of the control options; our societal institutions, particularly patents; and the interactions of the farm firms and the supplier industries. The present conditions favor chemical use and make organic farming comparatively difficult. This situation is neither optimal nor inevitable, but it is rather the result of strong incentives within the agricultural sector and its supplier industries, and the failure of government policy to remedy the defects of the private markets.

Methods of dealing with pest attacks can be classified in three ways: preventive or curative; biological, chemical or integrated; and eradicative or management-oriented. The organic farmer must perforce emphasize preventive non-chemical methods and pest management. The common approach among conventional growers is chemical and eradicative. However, a strong movement among entomologists and environmentalists has developed to foster a more receptive attitude toward integrated control and pest management (DeBach 1974; Luckmann and Metcalf 1975). Like the last chapter, this one will describe the main options and note the advantages and disadvantages to grower and society, that is, the internal and external costs and benefits. There are many methods of pest control available, both old and new. The most useful appear to be cultural and classical biological controls, resistant varieties and chemical pesticides.

Cultural Control and Resistant Varieties

Traditional and organic pest management emphasizes prevention of pest damage by choice of resistant varieties and manipulation of the plant's growth and environment. The latter is known as cultural control, a type of control through (non-human) biological agents, or using biological and ecological knowledge, which we shall call biological control.

Cultural control. Proper fertilization enhances the plant's capacity to resist insect attack. A high humus content inhibits soil-born pathogens (diseases). Predacious fungi, which attack nematodes, are encouraged. Antibiotics are produced by microbes that are well-fed (Allison 1973). Among the most important contributions of organic fertilizers, especially manure, is the limitation of the germination of pathogenic spores and their rapid digestion by the active soil life that it stimulates. Other spores germinate and are quickly digested by the microlife (Baker and Cook 1974).

On the other hand, excessive use of nitrogen fertilizer, though increasing yield, may lead to decreased plant resistance to pests, including rust, mildew, lice, and mites (Schuphan 1972). Thus, there is a linkage between heavy use of fertilizer and pesticides. Yet weak growth, due to under-fertilization, is also conducive to pest damage. Seaweed, as both a fertilizer and foliar spray, has recently been shown to increase resistance to pests. (See Chapter 12.) Foliar sprays also remove dust which is more harmful to pest enemies than to pest insects (Debach 1974).

Planting and harvesting can be done at times that minimize pest damage. For example, fall Hessian fly damage to winter wheat can be eliminated by late planting, after the brood has hatched and starved. Harvesting imme-diately upon maturity can reduce insect damage to potatoes, peas, and cabbage (DeBach 1974). The conscientious handling of crop residues, cultivation, and water management can also be helpful.

An appropriate crop sequence, or rotation, provides fertilizer for heavy feeders. It also can help in pest management. Since many pests are specific to particular plants, planting different crops in different years causes large reductions in pest populations. On the other hand, planting the same crop year after year, "continuous" cropping, often encourages pest buildups and requires more emphasis on curative measures, such as chemical pesticides. For example, grass, corn, or small grains following legumes generally greatly reduce legume damage from white grubs, which do not reproduce well on grains (DeBach 1974). Some pests, however, may be handled more easily with continuous cropping (Perry 1972). Green manures are effective in changing soil conditions and thus enhancing control of soilborne pests; for example, soybean green manure controls scab in potatoes (Baker and Cook 1974). Crop rotation does require more planning and the availability of more harvesting equipment.

An appropriate temporal mixture of crops and non-crops can also assist in pest control. Some plant combinations produce beneficial results in one plant or the other. However, sometimes the presence of a particular plant is harmful. These effects may arise from chemicals exuded by the plants, or from harboring pests or predators. Plant diversity makes for a more stable local ecology, helping in pest control (Luckmann and Metcalf 1975). On the other hand, a simplified ecosystem can simplify applied biological control (DeBach 1974).

Resistant varieties. A highly effective method of preventing pest damage is through breeding resistant varieties. Types of corn have been developed that are not very susceptible to damage from European corn borer, and varieties of wheat that are immune to wheat rust disease. Benefits are substantial, to farmer, environment and consumer. Pests are eliminated without any increased effort on the farmer's part, and probably with decreased input cost. Nevertheless, substitution of resistant varieties for pesticides has not been widespread: The major success stories, as in the case of wheat rust, involve instances where chemical treatment failed, giving the impression that genetic manipulation has been viewed as a backup to chemicals, rather than vice versa (DeBach 1974). This is understandable in economic terms. Genetic selection does have its limitations. The smaller the number of characteristics being selected for, the more likely the success. New varieties have been primarily advertised on the basis of yield (Smith 1966). Yields are associated in the purchaser's (farmer's) mind with seed, but pests are associated with growing plants. The temporal separation of cause and effect makes the results of preventive treatment less visible. Thus, it is not surprising that plant breeders tend to focus on the more marketable aspects of their product. There is a further long-run difficulty. Varieties may not be permanently resistant, for pests can change, too. A finite or even shrinking gene pool faces pests which continue to adapt through mutation (increased by pesticides) and natural selection. It is possible that this loss of genetic material can be counterbalanced by direct intervention into the crop's genetic material, a goal of current research.

The fact that in many cases selection has been primarily for yield rather than pest resistance has contributed to increased pest damage to crops despite higher levels of pesticide use (see below). If commonly available seeds are used in comparisons of organic and conventional farming, results will be biased in favor of the latter. Thus, we see the fallacy of attempting to compare systems by making a substitution *within* one of the systems. Vigorous growth of the hybrids does help to control weeds. New hybrid rice varieties were *more* susceptible to weed competition, however, because they grew closer to the ground.

The international institutes that do much of the pioneering work on rice and corn (maize) have begun to breed consciously for compatibility with low pesticide use. An increasing percentage of the new rice varieties developed at the International Rice Research Institute (IRRI) in the Philippines is resistant to more than one pest, some to six of the major pests. To limit herbicide use, IRRI is developing varieties with better leaf coverage and faster early growth. This work has been stimulated by the recent shortages and high prices of agricultural chemicals and fuel in underdeveloped countries (IRRI 1975).

Two important conclusions may be derived from the above discussion. First, presently available varieties are not ideally suited to organic farming. And, second, there is considerable room for improving organic farming technology through research.

Animal breeding. Chicken breeding has also neglected disease resistance and climatic adaptation in favor of efficiency of feed use and egg production. Susceptibility to disease is handled by chemicals, particularly antibiotics and vaccination. Disease mortality dropped from 20 percent in 1940 to 15 percent in 1966, but leukosis (blood cancer) is still widespread (Wilson 1966).

Chemical Pesticides

A chemical pesticide is a chemical that kills pests. Chemicals can also be used to control pest populations via behavioral effects. The latter approach is entirely different in its ecological implications, and will be considered separately under biological controls. When distinctions are made between chemical and biological control, the former refers to chemical pesticides.

Chemicals have been used for many years to kill pests in agriculture. Arsenic compounds were quite commonly used before World War II, and a public debate continued for years regarding safety (Whorton 1974). Since World War II, however, much more effective chemicals have been developed, and a large industry has arisen to manufacture, promote, distribute, and develop new chemicals. Currently about 1500 substances are registered for pesticide use in the United States (NRC 1975). In 1973, 1.36 billion pounds of pesticides were manufactured in this country, about 600 million pounds were exported and about 32 million imported. In 1975, domestic use was between 800 million and one billion pounds (USDA 1975; NRC 1975). Almost all of this was manufactured. Importation and use of natural pest-control materials, pyrethrum flowers and extract, and rotenone-bearing roots, totaled only a little over three million pounds.

Domestic sales of pesticides increased from $1.04 billion to $2.47 billion between 1971 and 1975 (NACA 1976). Deflated by a price index of agricultural chemical prices (which does not include fertilizers) (CRB 1975), this is an increase of 46.5 percent in real terms (constant value dollars), or about 10 percent a year. Despite increased prices and federal restrictions, demand has been increasing, spurred by increased food prices and increased land area under cultivation (and also by increased pest resistance). Total out-of-pocket costs for our society must include public expenditures, but these only add about $60 million or 2 percent to the private cost of pesticide use. Government agencies spend about $30 million for pesticide research, $22 million for registration and regulation of use, and $5 million for monitoring and regulation of residues (NRC 1975).

New chemical pesticides are still being invented, and the old ones are modified to achieve greater toxicity to the pest, and/or less toxicity to the plant being protected. Since these substances are made up of large manufactured molecules, there is considerable flexibility in how they can be reshaped. There are many synthetic pesticides that are more toxic to the pests and less toxic to the user than the old inorganic pesticides of the pre-World War II era (McNew 1966). New pesticide development is highly selective. Many chemicals are tried as possible pesticides; few are chosen. In 1974, 70,597 compounds were screened; in 1975, 84,787. Yet new chemicals registered in those years numbered only 8 and 10, respectively! In 1975, the average wait between invention and final regulatory approval was eight years (NACA 1976).

Despite the widespread use and environmental impact, "It is 'normal' for us to have only the vaguest idea of how much each compound was used and where, and then only after half a decade's lag" (NAS 1976). Total pesticide usage by crop is shown in Table 4-1 for 1966. Cotton and corn together accounted for almost 50 percent of use. Apples, tobacco, soybeans, and citrus followed. The type of pesticide that is important for major crops can be seen in Table 4-2. Potatoes, citrus, and other fruits (mainly apples) account for two-thirds of fungicide use. Corn accounts for over 40 percent of herbicide use. And cotton and corn receive 60 percent of the insecticides, with cotton alone receiving 47 percent. In sum, the major recipients of pesticides are corn, tobacco, cotton, soybeans, apples and citrus.

It may be noted that the largest user of pesticides is a non-food crop. Much of the cotton insecticide treatment is counterproductive (DeBach 1974). These considerations alone indicate that over 25 percent of insecticide use could be eliminated with little effect on food supply. Because of lack of information on the alternatives, farmers use more pesticides than they really need. The potential of biological control on fruit and vegetables is very good; in many cases, half of the insecticide use could be ended with no loss in yield (DeBach 1974). Peanuts can be grown in dry climates where fungi are not a problem (Ford 1975). The only major crop with a serious loss potential appears to be corn, with its heavy dependence on both herbicides and insecticides.

The widespread use of pesticides testifies to their apparent benefit in crop production. Pesticides are compatible with modern technology. Herbicides work less well with crop rotation than with continuous cultivation, since residues may damage a different crop. Insecticides are more efficient with low humus and low moisture, low soil temperature, and low cultivation. These factors encourage pesticide loss through volitilization (Lichtenstein 1966).

Side-Effects of Chemical Pesticides

Cooperating with other technological innovations, pesticides have contributed to the high yields and stable output of modern agricultural production. As experience and use increased, however, many side-effects became apparent, mostly detrimental. Side-effects of fungicides are apparently small compared to herbicides and insecticides (Marsh 1972), so the following discussion will focus on the latter two.

Effects on crop. Pesticides frequently have effects on the plant treated as well as on the target pest, even when used at normal application rates (NRC 1968c). Sometimes these effects are simply related to yield, and so should be rather easily associated with the pesticide used. But many times the effects are less obvious. A number of pesticides increase nitrogen levels in

Table 4-1 Farm Use of Pesticides on Crops in the United States in 1966

Crop	Pesticide Use (million pounds of active ingredients)	Percent of Total Use
Cotton	86.0	26
Corn	70.2	21
Other field crops	43.8	13
Vegetables	25.3	8
Other fruit	22.5	7
Apples	18.5	6
Tobacco	17.2	5
Hay, pasture and range	15.5	5
Soybeans	13.6	4
Citrus	8.5	3
Peanuts	4.0	1
Rice	2.8	1
Total	328.2	102

Source: Eichers et al. 1970.

Table 4-2 Pesticide Use on Major Crops by Type of Pesticide, 1966

Crop	Pesticide Use (percent of type by weight)		
	Fungicides	Herbicides	Insecticides
Corn		41	17
Wheat		6	1
Soybeans		9	2
Peanuts	3	3	4
Irish potatoes	12	2	2
Alfalfa		1	3
Pasture and rangeland		9	
Apples	28	3	6
Other fruit and nuts	14		
Citrus	13	3	2
Cotton	1	6	47
Tobacco[a]			3
Other	29	14	13
Total	100	100	100

[a]Tobacco accounts for one-third of "miscellaneous pesticide use," mostly soil fumigants.

Source: Eichers et al. 1970.

treated plants, and a few cause decreases in some plants. The higher nitrogen levels lead to increased mite and aphid infestation, particularly on apple trees. The lower mechanical strength of cell walls also may lead to successful pest attack (Schuphan 1974). Thus, an apparent need is generated for further pesticide treatment. The total benefit of using pesticides may be considerably less than the sum of the benefits associated with each individual pesticide use. The user generally does not have the information to make this distinction, however. On the other hand, sometimes there are positive effects on other pests, lessening the need for other treatment.

Changes in mineral composition in treated plants have frequently been documented. Sometimes a pesticide-supplied trace element enhances yield, as zinc on potatoes. Increases in vitamin content occur occasionally, but they are small compared with those associated with varietal differences (Salomon 1974). Soil type makes a big difference. So does pesticide purity. Petroleum oil sprays on fruit trees retard fruiting and photosynthesis. Frequently used on citrus, these sprays markedly lower the vitamin, acid, and mineral levels in fruit.

Pesticide absorption by plants depends on crop, variety, and soil condition. Soil residues are deposited in fruit as well as root (Lichtenstein 1966; 1973). Pesticide residues in the plant may affect flavor. Lindane residues are mostly concentrated in the fibrous roots of potatoes and carrots, rather than in the tubers and taproot. But off-flavor may nevertheless occur. When BHC, a pesticide that commonly affects flavor, was added directly to food, no off-flavor resulted. Apparently the effect is not simply from the residue, but from some physiological change in the plant or some metabolic product of the pesticide. Processing may bring out the off-flavor.

Changes induced in the plant by pesticides can affect more than flavor. Take the widely used herbicide, atrazine. When it is fed to yeast, no mutations result, but recent research discovered that the corn *raised* on atrazine-treated fields *does* cause mutations when fed to yeast. This means that there is a good chance that people and animals eating corn raised on herbicide-treated fields may have an increased probability of getting cancer (Galston 1976).

Some herbicides have been found to have positive side-effects that are perhaps more important than their direct effects. MH is used extensively as a spray prior to harvest to prevent crop growth during storage, particularly of potatoes and cabbage. Several herbicides such as 2,4,5-T speed maturation; 2,4-D is effective in preventing early fruit drop.

Since a good crop is fairly well assured with the use of pesticides, risk is removed, and the farmers can afford to invest in other inputs. Their marginal product is increased, and risk of loss from higher fixed costs is decreased.

"Preventive" chemical treatment. Pesticide companies have commonly recommended, and farmers have often followed, spraying on a regular "preventive" schedule, independent of evidence of pest infestation. But even if pests are visible, they may not be a potential economic problem. This type of overkill not only results in more pesticide use (and sales), but also in making pest control more difficult when it is needed. Frequent exposure to pesticides leads to selection in favor of resistant varieties of the pest. Often predators are damaged more than the pest, resulting in a resurgence more damaging than the original infestation. And decimation of the predators may cause new, previously innocuous, pests to emerge as serious economic threats. Finally, pesticides may cause adverse effects on plant physiology, allowing pests to reproduce more strongly. In practice, DeBach estimates that such negative results occur almost as frequently as actual effective control. All these effects have been observed and carefully documented, particularly for the use of DDT, for example, on cotton and citrus crops (DeBach 1974).

Insecticides. Only about 4 percent of the insecticides used on crops today are of the old inorganic type, primarily arsenic and lead compounds (see Table 4-3). Their use has declined because of "unfavorable mammalian toxicity, persistent residues, the problem of insect resistance, and low efficacy in comparison with synthetic organic insecticides" (NRC 1969). Most current concern focuses on the newer synthetic organic insecticides.

Natural organic insecticides, mostly pyrethrum, derived from an East African relative of the chrysanthemum, make up less than 1 percent of

---

Table 4-3   Insecticides Used on Crops in the United States, 1966

Insecticide Class	Use on Crops (percent of total)
Inorganic	4
Natural organic	a
Synthetic Organic	
Organochlorine	56
Organophosphorus	25
Carbamate	8
Other	a
Petroleum	7
Total	100

aLess than 1 percent

Source: Eichers, et al. 1970.

insecticide use, and less than 0.05 percent of insecticides used on crops. Their toxicity to mammals is low, to insects high, especially when accompanied by chemical synergists. The high relative price continues to limit sales.

Petroleum oils make up about 7 percent of insecticide use. Although large doses of petroleum distillates are poisonous to humans, FDA has ruled that small residues are of such slight danger that no limit has been set. The main reason for the small use of petroleum oils is their toxicity to plants. Growers, including organic ones, commonly apply an oil spray to fruit trees during their dormant period, when effect on the tree is presumably negligible.

The synthetic organic (meaning "containing carbon" in this context) insecticides made up 89 percent of sales in 1966. They rapidly established dominance following their introduction after World War II. They are of most interest because of their wide use and potential harm. The three types are: organochlorine, organophosphorus, and carbamate.

Chlorinated hydrocarbons, or organochlorines, include DDT and its relatives, chlorobenzilate, difocol and methoxychlor; benzene hexachloride; lindane; and the cyclodienes, aldrin, dieldrin, chlordane, heptachlor, endrin and toxaphene. They are highly toxic to insects in most stages of development. Absorbed by surface contact or ingestion, they kill through effects on the central nervous system. They are less effective on piercing and sucking insects. In recent years they have been gradually replaced by the other synthetic organics.

Pest resistance has been an increasing problem for chlorinated hydrocarbons, especially for DDT, the first and most widely used member over the years. Under public pressure, DDT was finally banned from routine crop use by the Environmental Protection Agency (EPA) in 1973, and its use in the United States dropped to 1.1 million pounds, down from 23.5 million the previous year (ASCS 1974). The use of aldrin and dieldrin has also been severely restricted. It is evident from the number of family members that a variety of substitutes is available, even within the family, though at somewhat higher price. There are similar problems with other compounds in the group, however, so that it appears that public pressure and visibility (and perhaps obsolescence) had as much to do with the ban as environmental and health considerations (Graham 1970). Whether EPA has the backbone to push for further restrictions in the face of mounting industry counterattacks is a serious question, raised by the protest resignation of the three EPA lawyers who led the battle against aldrin and dieldrin (Carter 1976).

Many family members are highly persistent (long-lasting) in the soil and in plants and animals. In soils, for example, DDT gradually degrades (changes) to DDE, a related pesticide, which is even more stable. Thus, just because no pesticide residue is detected does not mean that there is no residual effect from some derived chemical form. Still, the organochlorines are less persistent than the inorganic pesticides they replaced. Former orchards may continue to show spotty growth at the tree sites for many years after conversion to other crops, due to arsenic residues in the soil (Allaway 1975).

When used on crops, the organochlorines are carried off from farms by wind and water run-off (primarily erosion), evaporation, and as residues in food. Because of their chemical stability, they or their metabolites accumulate in body fat, and the concentration increases as they move up food chains. One result has been the inability of predatory birds to reproduce due to weakened eggshells. The consequent disappearance of the robins was recounted in *Silent Spring* (Carson 1962; see also Rudd 1964). Sublethal effects apparently act via lesions on the thyroid (Jefferies 1975). The sudden release of the residues from body fat during stress can result in serious poisoning, even death, and has been implicated in a number of bird and fish kills. Fish eggs are highly susceptible. In the ocean, residues also accumulate in the food chains, and may be contributing to a decrease in ocean life. Behavior modification, such as loss of coordination, has also been observed (Hunt 1966). Levels of DDT above safe tolerances have been detected in human milk. This contamination coincides with a return to breast-feeding, stemming from recognition of the benefits to mother and infant, including cancer-prevention in the former. California sought to limit DDT use on feedgrains in the 1960s to solve this problem, only to have its bees decimated by substitute chemicals (Swift 1969). A connection between these residues and the difficulty encountered by humans trying to lose weight—that is, metabolize their own body fat—appears possible but has not been documented. These environmental and human health hazards are balanced against the general lack of toxicity to the applicator.

The second group of synthetic organic insecticides, the organophosphorus or phosphate insecticides, is numerically the largest. More than 200,000 have been synthesized. They are systemic insecticides; that is, they are absorbed by and distributed throughout the plant, and are useful against a wide variety of insect pests, on animals as well as plants, including the sucking insects which thwarted the organochlorines. Many phosphates have low toxicity toward plants and animals. Unlike the organochlorines, they are readily transformed in the environment or in plants and animals into other substances. Parathion is toxic to birds on contact, but most are not, and they all degrade so rapidly that widespread environmental impact is avoided. The third class, carbamates, is similar to the phosphate insecticides in its properties. One of them, carbaryl, is toxic to the honeybee.

The toxicity, as measured by the dose needed to kill 50 percent of rats (Lethal Dose for 50 percent, or LD50), varies widely within each group.

Most of the phosphate and carbamate insecticides are more toxic in large doses to warm-blooded creatures than are the chlorinated. The popular phosphate parathion has a contact LD50 of 2.5 mg/kg body weight, compared to 15 for the most toxic chlorinated, endrin, and 2500 for DDT. There have been only one-fourth the deaths from organochlorines than from the phosphate group, even though three times as much of the former has been used (NRC 1969). The less persistent pesticides tend to be more hazardous to the farmers. Thus, on the average, there is a trade-off between danger to users of the insecticides and danger to non-users.

The manufacture of insecticides can also be dangerous. Allied Chemical Corporation achieved notoriety by poisoning employees, soil, and neighbors at a Virginia plant which manufactured kepone, a relative of DDT which is carcinogenic in animals. (The plant was actually owned by a firm under contract with Allied.) Presumably employee poisoning, whether in manufacture or in use, is reflected in user costs. Production wastes also generate pollution, however. Kepone killed the bacteria in the local sewage treatment plant and continues to contaminate the James River (Smith 1976).

When pesticide accidents cause crop loss, the federal government compensates the affected farmers. Bee keepers were being compensated an average of $1.5 million a year in the early 1970s (NRC 1975). Thus are pesticide manufacturers and users blessed by Congress in the same manner as nuclear power plant builders and operators. When the public picks up the tab for negligence, there is little incentive to be careful.

Weed control with herbicides. Weeds compete with crops for moisture and nutrients and can cause significant output loss. There are two main systems for handling these problems (Allison 1973). The traditional and organic method of weed control is through tillage: plowing under before seeding, and cultivating from time to time during the growing season. For the organic grower, this method has the added advantage of causing nutrient release from the soil's organic matter following each cultivation. For the chemically oriented farmer, this is a disadvantage. Since he is not adding organic matter directly, he needs to conserve it. Compaction of the soil, causing loss of structure and fertility, is a danger that increases with the increased use of heavy equipment and the decrease in organic matter. Modern large machinery makes contour plowing difficult, and thus increases the likelihood of erosion loss (Carriere 1976).

Advocates of organic farming often remind us of these disadvantages of herbicides. However, certain problems facing the conventional farmer can be avoided by the use of "minimum tillage" or "no-till" techniques. In dry-land farming, special equipment is available to cut weeds off below the surface and form a "trash mulch." In more humid regions, herbicides are used to control weed growth before planting and during the season. These methods provide the additional benefits of decreasing erosion and in-creasing infiltration of rainwater into the soil, both less of a problem in the presence of high organic matter content.

No-till has other advantages. Proper tillage is dependent on proper weather conditions; substituting chemicals avoids this dependency. For example, heavy rains can keep machinery out of the fields, while en-couraging weeds, particularly damaging in early stages of crop growth. And energy used in field operations (plowing, cultivating, etc.) is cut by two-thirds compared with conventional corn production (Wittmuss *et al.* 1975).

Minimum tillage may result in increased yield, but that depends on soil fertility, slope of the land and weather. For corn yields above about 90 bushels per acre (85 is average for the United States in the 1970s), minimum and conventional tillage net the same yields. Only with poor soil, rainy weather, or rainy weather combined with a steep slope (greater than 3 percent) does minimum tillage increase yield significantly, on the order of five to eight bushels per acre (van Doren and Ryder 1962).

Modern chemical herbicides are efficient and flexible. They are highly toxic to weeds, so they are comparatively cheap. Some kill and degrade rapidly, while others maintain control over many months. They are selective, so they can be used while crops are growing. They may be systemic, that is, act by spreading throughout the whole weed once applied to one part, so that spraying the leaves may be sufficient to kill the whole plant. Or they may be applied to the soil, deep or shallow, early or late, depending on the crop and weed characteristics. They are degraded by soil organisms over differing time periods, depending on the chemical, from a few days to over a year (Day 1966). These characteristics help explain the rapid growth in herbicide use. Between 1965 and 1969, herbicide sales grew at an annual rate of 22 percent a year, compared to only 8 percent for insecticides.

Herbicides may cause some decrease in yield if crops are grown in rotation. Residues of broad-leaf herbicides used with corn may inhibit soybean growth, and grass-type herbicides used with soybeans inhibit corn (Hall 1972). But these drawbacks can be avoided by additional fertiliza-tion, or avoiding rotation, or using the correct pesticide in moderation. Compared with cultural control (tillage) of weeds, herbicides offer consid-erable advantages to the farmer.

The benefits to society from being able to obtain cheaper crops with less erosion must be weighed against the dangers to human health from the residues. A popular group of herbicides is the phenoxy, including 2,4-D and 2,4,5-T, which made up 16 percent of herbicide sales in 1969, and about half that in the early 1970s (ASCS 1974). A confidential report to the United States Department of Agriculture in 1968 showed that 2,4,5-T was teratogenic (caused birth defects) (Epstein 1970; Bevenue and Kawano

1971). No action was taken by government agencies until 1970 after the facts had been leaked to the press. Most uses of 2,4,5-T were suspended, except for use in rice production. By 1972 it was discovered that the birth defects were caused by an impurity, dioxin, and new production cut the dioxin level by a factor of over 200. Nevertheless, an appeal of the suspension by Dow Chemical was unsuccessful (Davis 1974). This would appear to be a case of "closing the barn door after the horse has gone."

Long-run effects on human health. Adverse environmental effects of pesticides have been widely discussed. The battle has been largely fought over the issue of "birds or people." However, early reports probably confused DDT with PCBs, polychlorinated biphenyls, industrial chemicals that are chemically similar to DDT. Annual production of the two has been comparable (Zweig 1973). The ill effects of pesticides are not limited to birds, but have important consequences for human health as well.

Testing of pesticides (and other additives and contaminants in human food) is carried out primarily on the basis of acute toxicity, that is, effects from short-term, comparatively high doses. Studies normally span three generations in rats and mice and two years in dogs. Tolerance levels are usually set 100 or more times lower than the "no-effect" level in test animals. If a substance shows up as a carcinogen in test animals, no detectable level is allowed in human food. (The lowest detectable level changes from time to time with improvements in analysis.) It is fine to test for acute toxicity, but what if there are undetected effects on humans, effects that may not show up for many years or generations? Our limited testing is unlikely to find out (HEW 1969). Cancer may take 20 to 30 years to appear. And animal experience is especially unreliable in tests for cancer, mutations, and allergies which are less transferable between species than acute toxicity (Fournier 1971).

Some 80 to 90 percent of human cancer may be caused by chemical contamination of the environment and food (Marx 1976). Since widespread use of chemicals began after World War II, it is not surprising that appearance of the disease on an epidemic scale has not yet occurred. The cancer death rate did turn up sharply in 1975, however, recording a 5 percent increase in the first seven months compared with a 1 percent yearly increase previously (NS 1976).

There is evidence that some of the pesticides do cause cancer (aldrin [EPA 1975], and DDT [HEW 1969]), and possibly also birth defects and genetic mutations. Associated contaminants may also be harmful as was dioxin in the herbicide 2,4,5-T. And the treated plant may be carcinogenic, even though the pesticide itself is not. In the past, pesticides have not been checked regularly for mutagenicity, although many are suspect and the laboratory procedures are known (Epstein and Legator 1971).

Recently the pesticide industry has adopted such testing as a screening device to avoid the possibility of later regulatory problems (Kolata 1976).

The Food and Drug Administration sets maximum residue levels for foods, but some scientists question whether any minimum safe dose can be specified for potential carcinogens or mutagens, since one molecule may be sufficient to do the damage to one cell, which could begin the fatal chain reaction (Carper 1970). The probability of adverse effect would be proportional to the number of molecules. Then even a small probability spread over 200 million people could result in great misery. A small probability of damage would not show up in tests unless astronomical numbers of animals were used. The National Institute of Health is planning some such experiments, using millions of mice. This cannot be done for more than a few of the thousands of chemicals that have been introduced into the human environment—much less for the possible interactions between them.

The same argument applies to the continued use of DES. Residues of DES are not detectable in meat (except some liver samples). Current methods can find residues which are present at levels of a few parts per billion or greater. But there are over 10^{20} molecules in an ounce, the number depending on the size of the molecules. Thus, there could still be some 10^{11} (one hundred million billion) molecules of a chemical contaminant in an ounce of food, and the danger would go undetected.

Even the limited testing currently performed is apparently not being adequately carried out. The Environmental Protection Agency checked 25 reports on 23 pesticides; only one was satisfactory. The others lacked sufficient data and/or analysis. The EPA instituted reforms, and required reregistration of all pesticides by October 1977.

In a way, it is a little late in the game to be trying to find out whether pesticides cause cancer or other long-term damage. Exposure is already widespread. Even if it were conclusively proven that DDT causes cancer, what could be done? If all world production and use were terminated, it would still take decades before there would be significant reduction in amounts carried in human tissues (Zweig 1973).

If genetic mutations are occurring in the human population, it could take many generations for them to show up (Lederberg 1971). The testing procedure also neglects a number of other factors: possible interaction between residues and other food additives; hazard of metabolic products; increased susceptibility of the young and the sick (because tests are run on healthy animals); and the possible adverse nutritional effects of induced metabolic changes in the food (Hall 1974). All these considerations indicate some degree of increased risk to consumers and society from continued use of chemical pesticides. The cost of obtaining the information for an informed consumer choice appears to be prohibitively high. So decisions must be made on the basis of a person's desire to avoid risk. This desire will vary from person to person and forms part of the basis of organic food demand.

There is an indirect effect of the combination of nitrogen fertilizers and pesticides on cancer incidence. Both technologies lead to a decrease in crude fiber in the diet. Heavy use of nitrogen fertilizer leads to a smaller percent fiber and also to increased pesticide use. Pesticide residues tend to concentrate in the outer and oily portions of foods, which are the richest in fiber, as well as in the major nutrients (vitamins, minerals, unsaturated fats) (Schuphan 1972). Refining and peeling protect against residues, but lower nutrient intake. Recently an association has been established between low crude fiber intake and certain degenerative diseases, particularly heart attacks and cancer of the lower gastro-intestinal tract (Reuben 1975). Thus, avoiding one form of cancer may lead to another.

Inadequate data and the necessity of subjective evaluation of damage to wildlife and threat of risk subvert detailed, quantifiable cost-benefit analyses of overall liabilities and benefits from pesticide use. An attempt to quantify the costs of pesticide side-effects in a Florida county (Edwards 1969) illustrates the problem. A sophisticated decision model was developed, but the estimates of external costs were mostly guesses.

Biological Control

"The value of organochlorine insecticides in the production of cotton . . . is beyond question" (Davis *et al.* 1970). USDA researchers have extolled the necessity of chemical controls. The value of chemical treatment on cotton is now better understood. In many cases, it is essentially zero, or even negative. In California, the yield of cotton grown without chemical treatment is identical to that with chemical treatment. Spraying simply encourages the bollworm by destroying its predators (Adkisson 1971). Control of the bollworm by natural predators is one example among many of successful biological control of plant pests along "classical" lines, involving the introduction and/or encouragement of biological agents which act to control plant pests.

Classical biological control (DeBach 1974). There are three kinds of agents used in classical biological control: insect predators, which feed on insect pests as adults; parasites, which lay eggs in pests or pest larvae, and whose offspring then devour the pest; and pathogens, or pest diseases. The last, pathogens, have been least successful. The insect must eat the bacteria, fungus, virus, etc.; the pathogen does not seek out its prey as an insect does. Also inhibiting progress has been a cautious attitude on the part of federal regulators. They have been slow to approve the use of insect viruses, despite the fact that there has been no evidence that these pathogens affect humans. The first registration of an insect virus occurred in January 1976 (Carter 1976a). Only a few bacteria are registered. Because danger to humans is unlikely, it would make sense to have less rigorous testing requirements for biological controls than for chemical (Djerassi *et al.* 1974).

A good biological control species needs good searching ability so it can find the prey; high reproductive rate with respect to the prey; specificity in its attacks, so it does not harm non-target species or waste its effort; and the ability to tolerate the required climatic conditions.

Biological controls may be introduced in three ways. They may be conserved by environmental manipulation, that is, cultural control (discussed above at the beginning of the chapter). They may be imported from foreign countries, often to control a pest that itself has been inadvertently introduced. For example, milky spore disease was introduced from Japan to control Japanese beetles. And control species may be mass-produced and released in the fields at appropriate times during the season. This procedure, known as augmentation, is necessary when climatic or other conditions preclude natural establishment of the control organism in effectively large numbers.

One of the most successful augmentation programs involves the use of parasitic wasps, such as trichogramma, against the cotton bollworm and many other pests. The wasps are raised by the governments of Mexico and Russia, but are little used in this country, even though yields increase as insecticide use falls. In Russia, various species of wasps are used on wheat, corn, sugar beets, cabbage and apples. Wasps have been introduced in Maryland by university researchers for the control of aphids on soybeans and weevils on alfalfa. As a result, spraying of chemical pesticides on soybeans has virtually ended in the southern region of that state (Schwecker 1975). Green lacewings are produced commercially in California for use on a number of crops.

Soil microbes are more difficult to handle than insects. There are probably antagonists for all soil microbes. But there are serious production problems. Microbes produce antibiotics only in the presence of antagonistic species, and microbes may lose their ability to produce an antagonistic substance, that is, the ability may not be fixed by heredity (Krasil'nikov 1958).

Biological controls often need to be introduced over wide areas to be effective. The wasps, for example, have a range of over a mile. Thus biological controls may have large external benefits to other farmers at no cost to the user (characteristic of a public good).

What is the potential for classical biological control? Evidently it has been exploited hardly at all. Potential predator insects number over one million species. Most pests have a number of enemies, some over a hundred. The most effective predators so far have been the hymenoptera (wasps), but only about 10 percent of these species have even been identified and described. There exists no biological information on some 97 percent of the estimated number of wasps. And characteristics of subspecies are important, too, for they may be more effective or specific for a particular pest. Only a small fraction of these insects have been tried.

Insects. Interest in importing control species or diseases arose about one hundred years ago when it became apparent that plants were often attacked by a pest that had been imported from another part of the world *sans* predator. Since that time, only a few hundred have been tried, against both insects and weeds, with many notable successes. Of about 5,000 known pests worldwide, attempts have been made to control 233 species. By 1970, some degree of control had been achieved for over half of these, 130 species. Complete control, or reduction to economic insignificance, was achieved in 42 cases; substantial control in 58, and partial in 30. This is a respectable showing compared to the number of insect species that frequently cause serious damage in the United States: about 150 to 200. An additional 400 to 500 species may cause serious damage from time to time (NRC 1969), but many infestations occur in response to misused chemical pesticides.

Some successful examples of biological control of insects include the total elimination from pest status of red scale (a leaf-sucking insect) on citrus in California, and the sugar cane leafhopper and beetle borer in Hawaii. The scale was brought under control by a beetle and a fly; the sugar cane pests by a fungus and a number of insects. One notable failure appears to be the case of the gypsy moth. However, a number of potential predators remain to be tried, and new ones have been introduced in the last couple of years. It may take a number of years for a predator to become established.

Weeds. About a hundred weeds have been studied, and 50 attempts at biological control have been made. Of 27 reported studies, 75 percent achieved some level of successful control. Some of these have been rather dramatic. About 1900, the prickly pear escaped from homes in Australia and rapidly established itself in over 60 million acres by 1925, ruining them for any possible agricultural use. The following year, a parasitic, cactus-feeding insect was introduced, and total destruction of the plague was achieved seven years later, with a return of this wasteland to productive agricultural use.

Other biological methods. A number of other possible methods of pest control have been and are being developed, but none appears to have the potential of classical biological control described above (DeBach 1974; Pimentel *et al.* 1965). These other biological controls are compatible with other control methods; in some cases considerable success has been achieved.

Release of large numbers of sterile males has achieved complete control of screwworm fly, formerly a devastating pest of animals in the South. While an annual release is required, permanent control is achieved. But only certain types of pests are susceptible, ones with a relatively constant density.

Pheromones (sex attractants) can be used to control specific pests. As with other biological methods, this one must be applied over a wide area to be effective. The European fruit fly was eradicated in Florida through the use of attractants in 1956–1957. Pheromones and insect hormones appear to pose negligible danger for non-target species, including humans.

Another insect species may be introduced which, because of some competitive advantage, displaces the pest species and thus eliminates it.This method has some application to flies and mosquitoes, human and animal pests. Host plants can be inoculated with a nonpathogenic strain of microorganism that displaces a virulent parasitic strain (Baker and Cook 1974). The same principle is used in biological disease control in ănimals. Bacteria cultures can replace antibiotics in dairy farming, and have also been introduced to prevent mold growth in grain storage (McCullough 1975).

Integrated Control and Insect Pest Management

Some biological control advocates believe that a realistic goal is the elimination of all chemical pesticide use (*e.g.*, DeBach 1974). But most efforts are now directed to using a combination of methods, often called "integrated control." Eradication of insect pests is not necessarily intended, but simply depression of pest populations to below the economic threshhold; that is, below a number that would inflict economically significant damage on the crop. Thus, the approach is also called "insect pest management." For in fact, a low level of pest infestation may be desired to encourage predators (Luckmann and Metcalf 1975). An emphasis on integrated control is characteristic of the pest management extension publications in China (Chiang 1976).

The failures and higher real production costs of excess use of chemical pesticides are becoming more widely recognized among farmers, as the chemicals themselves are becoming less effective and their use more restricted by government agencies. Since biological controls are often the cheapest and most effective when available, they are used first. Pest populations and weather are monitored and computer models are developed for crop systems (Giese *et al.* 1975). Chemical controls are used on a standby, as-needed basis, mainly to bring pest populations back down to the level where they are economically insignificant and may be controlled by natural predators or parasites. Full consideration is given to crop system ecology, so that predators are affected as little as possible. A number of programs have been developed in which spray applications were reduced by 50 percent, simply using the current state of knowledge. These crops include oranges, grapes and apples. In the latter, output also increased 20 percent due to the end of the insecticides' inhibiting effect on growth (DeBach 1974).

The integrated control approach has clear benefits in reducing environmental impacts of pesticides and also serves to introduce farmers to nonchemical control technologies. In this manner, chemical use can be gradually reduced. Strong forces work for continued excessive use, however, despite the progress of integrated control and management programs. These incentives are largely of an economic nature. So we turn next to the economics of pest control.

Crop Loss Due to Pest Damage

Pimentel estimated crop loss due to insects, diseases and weeds for various time periods, from 1904 to 1960 (Table 4-4). He drew upon the results of field studies of crop production with and without pesticides to estimate losses that would have occurred in the absence of pesticide use. Each loss estimate is the sum of estimated losses for a number of major crop classes. Pimentel apparently assumed that only in the control of weeds would alternative control measures be used, namely, cultivation. In the case of other pests, farmers would simply have to take their losses.

In 1951-1960, the most recent time period for which estimates are given, the annual losses come to $9.9 billion or 33.6 percent of the potential production of $29.5 billion at market prices. The total value of crop production should be about $33 billion in 1978 (ERS 1977), adjusted for an index of crop prices. Assuming a similar loss percentage and a similar crop mix as in 1960, a loss on the order of $17 billion is currently being sustained ($33b/0.664–$35b). The loss without pesticide treatment would also be proportionately larger, on the order of $20 billion.

These are impressive figures. They are, however, subject to some large qualifications. Similar estimates by USDA economists (Andrilenas 1971; Delvo *et al.* 1973; Gerlow 1973) of the increased costs of giving up the use of particular pesticides are for the most part subject to similar qualifications.

Qualifications. The total percentage loss figures are overstated, since they involve some double counting. If a crop is destroyed by both insects and disease, the loss is 100 percent, not 200 percent. The valuation is at current prices. Because of the inelastic overall demand for agricultural products, an increase in production means a decline in the social value of the production and vice versa. Because of price supports, the loss figures

Table 4-4 Annual Losses in Agriculture for Selected Periods and an Estimate of Losses if No Pesticides Were Used

Period	Insect Loss (billions of $)	Insect Loss (percent of crop)	Crop Disease Loss (billions of $)	Crop Disease Loss (percent of crop)	Weed Loss (billions of $)	Weed Loss (percent of crop)	Total Loss (billions of $)	Total Loss (percent of crop)	Potential Production (billions of dollars)
1904	0.4	9.8	NA[a]	NA	NA	NA	NA	NA	4.1
1910–1935	0.6	10.5	NA	NA	NA	NA	NA	NA	5.7
1942–1951	1.9	7.1	2.8	10.5	3.7	13.8	8.4	31.4	26.7
1951–1960	3.8	12.9	3.6	12.2	2.5	8.5	9.9	33.6	29.5
1960, no pesticides	4.8	16.3	4.2	14.2	3.0	10.2	12.0	40.7	29.5

[a]Not available

Source: Pimentel 1973.

appear more real than they are. If the losses were valued at the price crops would bring without losses, the loss figures would be substantially lower.

The trends in the losses are of interest. Percent losses due to insects and diseases have been increasing, despite the increased use of pesticides. Do pesticides cause insect damage? There has been some increase in damage directly caused by pesticide use (see the section on side-effects, above). But the main reason for increased loss is the substitution of new plants and cultural practices that trade increased production potential for decreased resistance to pest attack. It should not be surprising that a large loss would be sustained by eliminating one of the main components of modern agriculture, while keeping the other components the same, such as low-resistance strains, continuous cropping, and monoculture. This is why the production estimates of such a crippled standard system do not give reasonable estimates of production and loss under alternative agricultural regimes (see Chapter 10). And this is why we must look at real organic farms, as we will do in Chapter 12.

Crop loss and locational decisions. Certain climates will favor some crops more than their pests; other conditions may be more favorable to the pests. Thus there are natural restraints on the geographic distribution of crops. The red scale has been completely controlled near the coast of California with biologicals. But where the winter is too cold or the summer too hot, predator reproduction is hindered, and biological control is less effective (DeBach 1974). This illustrates the very difficult task of assessing the need for chemical controls, and attaching meaning to loss figures. A particular farmer might be affected adversely with a pesticide ban, yet the effect on the whole society might be much smaller, once geographic readjustments had occurred.

Since the environment has only recently become an issue, the location of farms and the development of cropping patterns and regional markets have not taken the environmental impact into account. Consequently, much land use is suboptimal from an environmental point of view. An example is the congregation of animal feeding operations with the associated manure runoff. Less obvious, but with large import, is the way in which pesticide use depends on geographical location. Insecticide use on major crops, particularly cotton, is far higher in the Southeast and delta states than in the Southwest (Eichers *et al.* 1970). If chemicals were restricted, more cotton would be grown in the Southwest. Similarly, biological controls on citrus work better near the California coast. The increased cost of crop production under a pesticide ban is not the cost of fighting the bugs in the desert, but of expanding production in more favorable climates.

Dixon *et al.* (1973) calculated that a geographical relocation of crop production that minimized private production costs would have cut insecticide use about 50 percent in 1965. About half the reduction would come from locational changes and the other half from a reduction in farmland used for crops. The authors made no effort to determine minimum pesticide use or environmental damage. They simply took a previous study of the geographical reorganization of agriculture which would minimize production costs (Heady and Brokken 1968) and looked at what changes in insecticide use would occur as a side-effect of this increase in private efficiency. Since insecticides will still have an environmental impact, even when private costs are minimized, the social optimum of insecticide use must be less than 50 percent of its use (in 1965). Presumably similar conclusions would be reached for other pesticides. If it is cheaper to grow cotton in the Southwest, why don't we? There are economic and social costs of moving, which encourage maintenance of the status quo. And government crop support programs of the 1950s and 1960s discouraged farmers from shifting land to different agricultural uses.

Other system components. The choices of variety and cultural methods are also conditioned by existing technology and regulations. McIntosh and Delicious apples are susceptible to scab disease; Baldwin are not. Continuous cropping and monoculture encourage pest buildup, so more spray is needed (McNew 1966). The farmer makes his choice of variety and system, given the fact that pesticides are cheap and easy to come by. The crop loss from not using pesticides in the current system is not a measure of loss under an alternative regime of severe restrictions on pesticide use. Thus we must look at functional organic farms rather than marginal changes in the current system.

Economic Benefits from Pest Control Research

Despite our qualifications, there are large pest losses suffered by all farmers, conventional and organic. The figures in Table 4-4 give us an impression of the order of magnitude of the losses. Losses are impressive, and indicate that considerable benefit may be realized from pest control research. This has, in fact, been the case. Historically, and still to a large extent today, research funds have been weighted in favor of chemical pesticides rather than biological controls. This imbalance has persisted even though returns on investments in biological controls have been generally higher. How this came about can be best understood through the characteristics of pest control technologies and their markets.

Research expenditures. In the 1950s, about two-thirds of the USDA's entomology research was on insecticides. Recently priorities have altered

(Hoffmann 1971). In 1977, biological control and related basic research made up almost two-thirds of the $90.4 million pest control research budget (CA 1976). And some of the chemical work is on chemicals with negligible environmental impact such as insect hormones, which we have been calling a kind of biological control. Nevertheless, private sector pesticide research still exceeds federal spending. Total expenditures by chemical firms on pesticide research came to $103 million in 1975 (NACA 1976). Assuming the recent growth rate of 20 percent per year continues, private sector pesticide research should have reached $150 million by 1977, about twice the USDA research budget for biological control.

In California, where much of the biological control research has taken place, expenditure on chemical pesticides has been far larger than that for biologically oriented work. Pest control expenditures in California in 1963 are given in Table 4-5. Biological research is mostly funded by state and federal governments, which also spend about the same amount on pesticide controls, $1,250,000. Most of the research on pesticides, or about $12 million worth, is funded by industry, however.

All state agricultural experiment stations and universities have entomology departments, but most have no biological control specialist. External funding of research is largely from chemical companies. For example, one of the largest entomology departments in the country spent $8,500 for biological control in 1969 and 1970, but $490,000 for other research, mostly on chemical pesticides (DeBach 1974).

Returns on investment in chemical pesticides. The full cost of bringing a new pesticide to market was estimated to be some $11 million in 1972 (Johnson

Table 4-5 Pest Control Expenditures in California, 1963

Type of Control	Research and Development Costs	Retail and Application Costs
Biological control (parasites, predators, and disease only)	$ 800,000	$ 300,000
Other bioenvironmental controls	325,000	2,337,000
Chemical pesticides	13,250,000	230,000,000
Total	$14,375,000	$232,637,000

Source: Pimentel et al. 1965.

and Blair 1972). This is the total cost, including failures, pilot plants, testing and marketing. Today the figure would be even higher. In 1974 and 1975, 18 new products were registered by the major pesticide companies. Total expenditures on research and commercialization of new products was $188 million for the firms, or $10.5 million per product (NACA 1976). Since this amount was invested over a ten-year period, the interest on the investment must also be added. Assuming a 10 percent return on alternative investments, we estimate that the 1976 cost of developing a new pesticide are on the order of $16 to $17 million. This would also be in line with correcting the $11 million 1972 figure for inflation. The real cost to society is actually higher, since field tests are carried out by state and federal experiment stations, partly at government expense. For example, in California government pesticide research was about 10 percent of private in 1963 (Table 4-5). Using this percent, the full cost may run about $18 million.

It is estimated that there is a net benefit in terms of crop loss avoided of about four dollars for each one dollar invested in pesticide research, marketing and application (Pimentel 1973).* Since we are looking at the total benefits and costs, not marginal quantities, it is not surprising that benefits exceed the costs. For there is in general some consumers' or

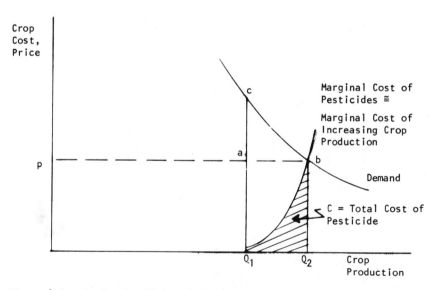

Figure 4-1. Production With and Without Pesticide Use

*Headley (1968) found a *marginal* benefit of $4 for each additional dollar spent on pesticides by farmers. But the qualifications to this estimate are so great that it is not clear what meaning to attach. See Chapter 10; also HEW 1969.

producers' surplus. If no net benefit to anyone could be measured, the project is unlikely to be undertaken. In Figure 4-1, the supply of food has been increased from Q_1 to Q_2 by the use of pesticide expenditure C (the shaded area). With value of sales = price, p, the benefits to society are $p(Q_2 - Q_1)$ plus the area of triangle abc. The *net* benefit to society (looking now only at private costs and benefits, excluding pollution, for example),

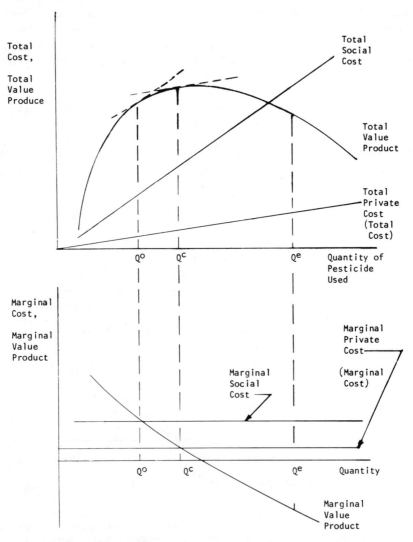

Figure 4-2.   Total and Marginal Value Product and Cost for Pesticide Use

requires that the cost of the pesticide, estimated at about $C = p(Q_2 - Q_1)/4$, be subtracted. If the innovation affects only a particular crop or region, we may take the demand as comparatively elastic, and $p(Q_2 - Q_1)$ as a good measure of gross benefits. For the economy as a whole, and for food as a whole, it is less valid, for the demand becomes more inelastic. (For a discussion of problems in evaluating benefits, see Headley and Lewis 1968.)

Also, the fact that the benefit-to-cost ratio for pesticides is four to one tells us nothing about the optimum expenditure on pesticides. Assuming that the farmer's expenditure on pesticides covers the full cost of pesticide development, we compare in Figure 4-2 the benefit or value and cost of pesticide use. The top part of the figure shows total cost and total benefits; the lower part, the respective incremental or marginal quantities. Total private costs increase with use, but social costs increase faster due to pollution and health effects. A point is reached where increments in benefits to society no longer exceed increments in costs, namely, quantity Q^c in private markets, or Q^o if producers must also consider external costs in addition to private costs. Q^c is the equilibrium quantity used in perfectly functioning private markets.* Actual use is Q^e, where the benefit-cost ratio is four. Farmers use more than Q^c because of ignorance and heavy advertising. Advertising continues until *its* marginal value product exceeds marginal additional expense. But at this higher rate of use, the farmers' marginal value product is negative. That is, pesticides are actually making a negative contribution to crop production. Clearly less ought to be used under such circumstances, not more. A number of sources (see, for example, page 69 above) estimate that the optimal usage of pesticides is about half of the current rate, Q^c on the graph, if external costs are not considered. So Figure 4-2 appears to represent the main features of the current situation.

Returns on investment in biological controls. Biological controls have admittedly been neglected over the years in favor of chemical pesticides. Could this be because of smaller potential benefits from the former? The evidence appears otherwise. Returns on investments in biological controls are often much higher.

In California over a 45-year period, returns were about $30 per $1 invested in research and application, not including benefits accrued to other states and other nations, nor programs that were only partially

---

*When farmers are using less than Q^c, incremental benefits from using more exceed incremental or marginal costs. Thus they should use more in their own self-interest. When using more that Q^c, each additional unit costs more than it is worth. Thus a rational buyer with good information will use more until marginal cost equals marginal benefit.

successful (returns are measured in terms of crop damage avoided at current prices [DeBach 1974]). Furthermore, returns from new research should be larger in regions where little effort has already been invested.

Classical biological control. For individual biological control species, total cost for introduction has typically run from a few hundred to several tens of thousands of dollars, with an average of perhaps $5,000. For example, the mealybug was controlled in California in 1928 for a cost of about $2,600 ($8,400 in 1975 dollars). The resultant saving has been on the order of $1 to $2 million a year. Average cost today runs about $100,000 to $200,000 for introduction of a new species, not including failures (Djerassi 1974).

Cultural control. If fall Hessian fly damage to winter wheat is avoided with postponed planting, yield increases by about 7 percent. Total research on this problem, between 1915 and 1935, was about $10,000 yearly, or $2 million, and current advisory costs total about $20,000 per year. If all farmers used the correct planting times, the annual saving in 1974 would have been $340 million (47,000,000 acres×27.4 bu/acre×$3.75/bu×7%) (USDA 1975). This is a current return on the original investment of almost $60 per $1 invested. (In 1974 dollars, the original $2 million investment would be worth about $5.8 million.) Chemical control is also available for Hessian fly. The original investment was small, perhaps $200,000, but annual costs would be high, so that growers opting for chemical control would receive only a $2 return for each $1 (a total of some $185 million) spent on chemicals for comparable level of control. It is unlikely that chemcials would be considered, since virtually complete control has been established with the development of resistant varieties (Pimentel *et al.* 1965).

Cotton is another crop which can utilize cultural control. Pasturing cotton fields following harvest kills over 94 percent of the pink bollworm population. This practice, however, is incompatible with heavy pesticide use (NRC 1969).

Resistant varieties. Crop savings from the development of resistant varieties can also be substantial. Development of wheat resistant to sawflies resulted in a $15 million increase in yield in Kansas alone. (Kansas, our top wheat-producing state, raises 18 percent of our wheat [USDA 1975].) Losses up to 75 percent to 85 percent of the crop had commonly occurred (Painter 1968). A Hessian-fly-resistant wheat produced a national saving of $238 million in 1964 at the average price of $1.37 per bushel (Luginbill 1969). In 1974, the price was $4.04 per bushel and 26 percent more acreage was planted, so savings would be on the order of $880 million per year.

($238 million $\times$ 1.26 $\times$ $4.04/$1.37) Corn resistant to the European corn borer saved an estimated $100 million a year. Resistant varieties are costly to develop in terms of both personnel and time. Perhaps 10 to 15 years is required for plants, longer for the larger animals.

Why the relative neglect of biological research? If returns are so high from biological control research compared to chemical research, why the disparity in research funding? This seems to be a classical case of underinvestment in a public good. New chemical controls are patentable, so that returns can be appropriated by the investor. Even if patentable, as are manufactured hormones, sex attractants, etc., biological controls are *specific* to particular species, thus severely limiting the market potential (Steward 1972, NRC 1975). For these reasons, biological research must come primarily from the public sector.

A similar situation exists in the pharmaceutical industry, where there is a lower relative expenditure on vitamins than on chemicals. Vitamins make up 8 percent of sales, yet account for only 2 percent of research and development expenditures. Anti-infectants, on the other hand, make up 15 percent of sales, yet account for 20 percent of these expenditures (PMA 1974). A similar comparison holds for relative advertising expenditures.

Market Failures in Pest Control Supply

The economic agents involved in pest control are the suppliers who decide which controls to develop and market, and the farmers who decide which to use. The extent to which the available controls are utilized depends on the functioning of the markets for purchase and sale of pest controls. Suppliers make their decisions on the basis of their estimates of the market potential of various possible pest control techniques. These suppliers are primarily large chemical companies. They may be considered well-informed about market conditions, and will invest in developing and marketing only if there is a good expectation of obtaining a fair return on such investment. In order for this to happen, profits must be appropriable by the firm making the investment. Thus the key characteristics of a potential pest control technique are patentability and size of the market, that is, potential sales. Techniques which are not patentable can be readily marketed by competitors, and thus research effort cannot be recaptured in sales. If no supplier firm is required, the farmer himself becomes the competitor and, again, no profit redounds to the innovating firm.

The market potential must be sufficient to overcome the sizable investment involved in bringing a new technique or product to market. This means that techniques that are very effective with one species are far less likely to be investigated than "broad-spectrum" controls that are effective for a wide variety of species. It is thus no accident that the private market has been very effective in innovating new chemical pesticides, which have the characteristics of high market and profit potential, but far less effective in marketing other, primarily biological, controls.

Seaweed is a good case in point (Fryer and Simmons 1976). A private company tried for a number of years, without success, to satisfy Environmental Protection Agency regulations for the marketing of seaweed as a pesticide. Finally, through the good offices of a consultant and a private philanthropist (who supplied $60,000 "seed" money) the required field tests were begun at three universities in 1973. What return will those who invested in this project receive? Little beyond the personal satisfaction that they may have helped bring an environmentally sound product to the market. As a natural product, once it is registered, anyone can market it. The situation is analogous to that in pharmaceutical manufacture, as mentioned earlier. Testing is expensive, and the market potential must be there in terms of profit appropriability and sales volume before a firm will invest. Natural remedies do not fit these categories. For example, despite establishment publicity to the contrary, controlled tests have proven the efficacy of vitamin C in alleviating cold symptoms (Anderson *et al.* 1972). But since it is unpatentable, firms will not rush to market vitamin C for this purpose. Sales increases are a result of Linus Pauling's publications, not advertising. Another example is the antidote for mushroom poisoning that has been discovered in Czechoslovakia. It is not marketed in this country because of the limited demand (Culliton 1974).

Occasionally a larger-scale effort is made to develop biological control of a major pest. The Zoecon Corporation spent $8 million developing a hormone for use against mosquito larvae. The large market potential may justify this investment, but such ventures have been rare.

Since 1964 the state agricultural experiment stations have attempted to ease small-market-potential pesticide registration through a coordinating committee. The work has been poorly funded and scarcely adequate (NRC 1975).

We now turn to the buyers' side of the market. For free markets to function effectively, buyers and sellers must be well-informed. In pest control markets, suppliers are likely to be knowledgeable, but this is not true of buyers. The cost of pesticides is small, on the order of 5 percent of a farmer's total costs. The farmer is a comparatively small businessman without a large staff of experts. He must rely upon outside advice. When the factors involved in correct decisionmaking are complex, as in the case of pest control, the farmer is particularly vulnerable to an effective advertising and marketing program by suppliers.

If decisions made on the farm have effects which go beyond the borders of his land, a farmer is likely to be ignorant of them. Even if aware of external effects from his decisions, such as pollution, it is difficult or unlikely for him to take this into consideration in his decisions, since the cost is not borne by himself, but by others. That is why economists call this an external cost. The private cost to the farmer differs from the cost to society, or social cost. Many farmers are socially minded and would like to avoid damage to the environment. But their incomes are generally too low to allow discretion in this regard (see Chapter 9).

The economic optimum is achieved when the increment in benefit (marginal benefit) to society of further use of the good or service equals the increment in cost (marginal cost). Beyond this point, the additional cost is greater than the additional benefit. In the case of a product with negative external costs, such as persistent pesticides, the cost to society is greater than the benefits at the free market equilibrium. Referring back to Figure 4-2, recall that the socially optimum quantity of pesticide use, Q^o, is less than both the free market quantity with perfect information, Q^c, and the existing quantity, Q^e. The optimal amount may in fact be zero. The farmers use more than is optimal because of the forceful advertising by suppliers (Hildebrandt 1960). Thus, the existing markets fail to yield a social optimum because of external costs and also because of lack of information on the buyers' side of the market.

Private decisionmakers also fail to consider external benefits. A particular case of some interest occurs when a product can be consumed to any degree without diminishing the consumption of others. An example is public information, and such a product is known as a "public good" because it can be consumed jointly by any number of consumers without diminishing the intensity or extent of supply. The knowledge of how to control insect pests through an understanding of pest biology and crop ecology is just such a good. Once such information is generated, anyone in the world can make use of it. There may be great benefit to mankind, but the private benefit is comparatively small. This is known as market failure because of the public-good nature of the product. An economic optimum is achieved only when the *sum* of the marginal benefits to all potential users equals the marginal cost of supply. The marginal benefits to a private investor will be less than this sum, so that private markets will undersupply such goods. Again, private investors must make a reasonable private return on their investments.

Comparison of Chemical and Biological Controls

The major alternatives to chemical pesticides are biological agents, resistant varieties, or detailed knowledge of pest and plant biology and ecology. The last group we have been calling broadly, "biological controls." Used in this manner, biological control includes the use of some manufactured chemicals, such as sex attractants. But they are environmentally benign chemicals, are specific to the particular pest, and require detailed knowledge of pest biology. In these ways they differ from chemical pesticides. Even though our definition of biological control is somewhat simplified, it is in accord with a real distinction, conforms to casual usage, and is not out of line with usage in technical literature. The distinction enables us readily to distinguish organic from conventional farming. Organic farmers reject the use of chemical pesticides, except for those extracted from plants, but most other methods of pest control are acceptable. Conventional farmers rely heavily on chemical pesticides. Table 4-6 lists the differences between these two classes of pest control methods. As we discuss these differences, some of the main reasons why organic farming is rare will become evident.

Research and development and marketing. The two types of control differ widely in their potential for private profits. As mentioned earlier, new chemical pesticides are patentable and have a large market potential because of their "broad-spectrum" capabilities, that is, their use against a large range of pests. In fact, this capability is selected for in choosing chemicals, though more selective pesticides would benefit the farmer and the environment (van den Bosch 1970). On the other hand, biological agents are generally not patentable (although production techniques and chemical attractants and hormones may be). And they are generally specific to a particular species or even subspecies. In fact, it is this specificity which makes them useful. The market potential is thus extremely limited. These two characteristics, non-appropriability of profit and limited market, combine to make it virtually impossible for a private firm to invest in biological control methods, particularly of the classical type. Thus it is not surprising to learn, as summarized above, that biological control research must rely upon public funding for the most part; and that private firms have invested heavily in chemical control research. Since public laboratories also work closely with private firms and receive a substantial amount of their funding from them, sympathies and experimental work tend to follow chemical lines to the neglect of biological methods.

With private profitability comes advertising. Consumer—that is, farmer—ignorance makes advertising particularly effective. During the growing season, 30 to 40 percent of the space in cotton journals may be pesticide advertising (NRC 1975). Chemical pesticides have been heavily advertised; biological controls have not. Beyond specific product advertising, the general public has been subject to a more general kind of attitude-

Table 4-6 Comparison of Chemical Pesticides and Biological Controls

Characteristic	Chemical Pesticides	Biological Controls	Method Favored[a]
R & D[a] and marketing			
R & D support	Large, private and public	Some, mostly public	C
Private profit	Patentable	Generally not patentable	C
Market potential	Large, broad-spectrum	Small, specific	C
Advertising	Heavy	Minimal	C
On the farm			
Application costs	Comparatively large annual	Small or zero	B
Visibility	High	Low	C
Timing of effects	Fast Positive action; negative effects later	Slow	C
Percent control	Complete at first	Generally only partial	C
Long-range planning and careful timing?	Not needed	Needed	C
Inter-farm coordination needed?	No	Often	C
Effectiveness depends on weather? climate?	Usually not much	Yes, often	C
Compatible with other modern technology?	Highly	Varies	C
Compatible with other stages of the food system?	Highly	May conflict	C
Safety in use	Varies	Absolutely safe	B
Pest resistance; obsolescence?	Yes	Most, none	B
Appeal to ego?	Yes	None	C
Externalities			
Damage to wildlife	May be large	None	C?
Danger to consumers	May be large	None	C?
Public good?	Generally not	Often	C

[a]C means Chemical controls favored; B means Biological. R & D is Research and Development expenditure.

development advertising. One popular slogan was, "The only good bug is a dead bug." A 1954 New York City postmark exhorted the public to "Fight your insect enemies," along with infantile paralysis and heart disease. The increasing distance between the average citizen and the living world of plants and the soil enhances the effect of jokes like, "The only thing worse than finding a worm in an apple is finding half a worm." Chemicals are a much cleaner way to deal with this level of life.

For a particular product, heavy marketing effort serves a dual purpose. Not only does advertising expand sales and profit, but the high rate of use results in pest resistance, which leads to rapid obsolescence of old pesticides and the need to switch to new ones by the time the patent runs out. Research and development typically takes about 6 to 8 years; patents last 17 years, leaving about 10 years of profitable sales under patent protection. So if the major pests have built up resistance in that time, there won't be much profit potential left. Advertising also builds brand loyalty so that consumption will continue even after the patent expires. This same process is at work in the pharmaceutical industry for similar reasons (see Measday 1971). This is not to imply that there is any conscious plot to create obsolescence, but to show how economic institutions and the nature of the goods lead to certain economic behavior.

Farmers rely mainly upon industry sources for pest control advice: pesticide dealers, labels, and advertising in farm journals (Beal *et al.* 1966; NRC 1975). Not only do the dealers have an obvious incentive to boost sales, but they are generally untrained in ecology, entomology, or any of the technical areas relevant to an informed pest control decision (van den Bosch 1970). The extension agents typically rely upon standard pamphlets, which can hardly consider the complexities of ecosystem management (Giese *et al.* 1975). Thus the simplicities of chemical control speak more persuasively than the complexities of biological control.

On the farm. Not only does the private market favor the introduction of pesticides; it also independently provides strong incentives for their adoption. These "on-the-farm" incentives are listed in the central portion of Table 4-6. Most of them favor adoption of chemical pesticides.

To begin on a favorable note, the yearly application cost of a biological control may be insignificant. The use of resistant varieties requires no adjustment on the farmer's part. Many cultural practices can easily be incorporated into normal farming procedures. However, chemical pesticides have many real and imagined advantages that weigh the balance strongly in their favor.

The effects of chemical pesticides are highly visible. They act quickly.

Multitudes of dead bugs are an impressive sight and a good selling point. Biological controls act slowly, may take a period of time to build up effectiveness—perhaps years. In the meantime, chemical control may render a potentially more effective biological control ineffective by killing off a predator. Chemical controls do have significant adverse effects on the farmer's costs, often requiring eventually increased pesticide expenditures because of pest resistance and predator destruction. But these effects are not easily associated with the spray program, unless one has an ecological sophistication generally lacking in farmers.

Excessive use of chemical pesticides may impose higher costs on neighbors due to decimation of beneficial insects or selection for more resistant species. This has occurred in southern California, where heavy spraying of cotton has increased pest damage to sugar beets. If, however, a region is homogeneous in crop type, that is, monoculture prevails, then use of chemical pesticides provides positive externalities. All farmers will be attacking the same pests, and spray drift will reduce neighbors' costs. This is another good example of the compatibility of the elements of modern agriculture, and their overall incompatibility with the alternatives.

Resistant varieties are vulnerable to obsolescence due to changes in pest populations, just as are chemical pesticides. But most biological controls are permanent. Some laboratory experiments have produced prey selection for resistance to a predator, but this has never been observed under field conditions and is not expected due to the complex nature of ecological niches (Huffaker 1971).

Chemical treatment usually brings rapid total destruction of the pest, while biological control methods usually do not. More often, the pest population is reduced to a low level with the latter, below the "economic threshhold," the point at which damage to crop makes a difference in profit. (A minor infestation may sometimes make a crop grow more vigorously; so may ending pesticide treatment.) Chemical pesticides support the user's ego, as he is able to completely dominate natural processes. Biological methods, on the other hand, attempt to work *with* nature; a certain humility is required.

Chemical pesticides introduce more certainty into the farm operations, a significant advantage since reducing risk is generally an important factor in farmers' decisions. The structure of federal subsidy programs reinforces this effect. Since the farmer's income is supported through a guaranteed *price*, his gross income is proportional to his output (net income more than proportional). His "insurance" program fails if his crop fails. Entirely different support programs are of course possible: income or output insurance could be provided (see Davidson and Norgaard 1973).

Cultural methods and introduction of predators and parasites all require considerable planning and careful timing. A mistake can bring disaster, or at least wasted effort, as has been the case with the use of ladybird beetles, praying mantis, and certain wasps for biological control. The praying mantis is popular among gardeners because it is visible. But being omniverous, it is comparatively ineffective. When ladybird beetles were first introduced commercially, they were often shipped in the wrong life stage. When released in the field, they immediately "flew away home." Now ladybird beetles can be obtained in the correct stage, so that they will establish themselves where released. A particular wasp species is often specific to a particular pest species; some attempts at biological control failed because this was not appreciated (DeBach 1974). It is clear that biological control is a very tricky business compared with chemical pesticides.

Non-chemical controls are sometimes dependent on the weather, introducing further risk. A wet spring makes cultivating weeds impossible. A dry spring in 1976 was hard on Maryland's parasitic wasps, and led to weevil outbreaks in the alfalfa fields (Feinberg 1976).

Another difficulty with use of non-chemical methods is the frequent requirement of adoption over a wide area for significant benefits to result. Chemicals can be used by an individual farmer whether his neighbor chooses to do so or not. (However, courts have recently ruled that farmers are liable for damage or contamination of neighboring organic farms from chemical spray drift.) Early planting of northern corn to avoid the southern corn borer requires coordination of all the farms of the region. An effective screw-worm fly eradication program covered the whole of the southern United States. When first introduced, one hundred ladybird beetles rapidly multiplied and ended the red scale infestation of one citrus orchard. Within a few years they had spread throughout California, with no human assistance whatsoever. In economic terms, the supply of biological controls tends to have very high fixed costs compared to variable costs, and very large economies of scale. So benefits are external to the farm, as well as to the firm developing the product. This is truly a product with a high degree of "publicness."

A more diversified agriculture helps maintain an ecological balance and reduces the probability of pest outbreaks. Or, if an outbreak does occur, it will be confined to a single field or strip of field. Hedgerows between fields have been eliminated in modern culture; they harbor insects as well as taking space. Thus their elimination makes sense for conventional agriculture, since insects are generally dealt with by extermination. The elimination of hedgerows also saves tractor fuel, since fewer turns are required. Organic farming welcomes hedgerows as a place for beneficial insects to maintain themselves.

Chemical pesticides also have the advantage of being more compatible with other stages of the food delivery system (see the next chapter). Agricultural marketing orders are rules agreed to by a majority of growers in a state and then enforced by the United States Department of Agriculture. They often require a high degree of freedom from evidence of pest damage, partially as a means of controlling production. The Food and Drug Administration regulations are strict regarding the presence of insect parts in processed food, not for nutritional reasons, but purely for purity's sake (insects are nutritious and are eaten by many peoples). Such regulations clearly favor a vigorous chemical pesticide program (Perelman and Shea 1972).

There is one characteristic of pesticides that has begun to have a negative impact on farmers' use: toxicity to the user. Two developments have begun to raise the health costs to the farmer using pesticides. The first is the increased difficulty of using the old organochlorine pesticides, due to increased federal restrictions and pest resistance. The replacements tend to be more toxic to the user. The second development is the unionization of farm workers, which achieved its first government support in California in the summer of 1975 (BW 1975). Farm workers will presumably desire to bargain for improved safety as well as wages. Biological programs pose negligible hazards to human health.

Market failure: summary. In sum, the differences between chemical pesticides and other, biologically oriented, controls are large and introduce strong incentives to develop and use the former at the expense of the latter. The failure of private markets to achieve an optimum was clear from the far higher rate of return on investments in biological controls.

There are large positive externalities in the development and use of biological controls. Lack of information on the part of farmers leads to a strong bias toward using chemical pesticides, an informational market failure. The major benefits from the use of pesticides accrue to the private agents involved: manufacturers and farmers. But significant external costs result, which the private decisionmakers are unlikely to consider. On the other hand, the development and use of biologicals has positive external benefits. The net result of this series of market failures is too much pesticide use and too little biological control. How much of a distortion in allocation of resources is present depends on the weight given to the damages of pesticides and to the potential viability of non-chemical farming. The former is virtually impossible to evaluate analytically; the latter is the subject of the later chapters of this study. If it can be shown that the actual loss in production from eliminating pesticide use is small, then estimating damage functions is less important. One of the purposes of this section was to show the large contribution that market failures have made to the current situation. Further, we have shown in this chapter the large technological potential for increasing the economic viability of organic farming through the development of biological controls. The higher costs of organic production are partially due to the misallocation of resources, including public research funds: overinvestment in chemical pesticides and underinvestment in the alternative biological controls.

5 From Farmer to Consumer

Market failures at the farm stage of the food system are reinforced by failures and distortions that arise in the free play of market forces within the food processing and retailing stages of the food industry and also between the stages. We may call these failures systemic or institutional market failures. Many problems arise because the purchase and preparation of food are also the purchase of health; that is, food and health are inevitably intertwined. Other problems arise as the food chain from farmer to consumer lengthens.

The Federal Role

The federal government has a vital interest in the nation's health, or it should have. A healthy people contributes to a strong and stable nation. Increasingly, the federal government pays for medical care, making medical costs a public matter (Shapley 1975). This role is becoming more accepted. When food industry leaders and consumers recognized the need for public confidence in the safety of the food supply, the Food and Drug Administration was established in 1906. The United States Department of Agriculture also has responsibility for supervising the safety of farm products.

In some respects, food is safer today than it was in earlier eras. Many past scourges, due to faulty growing, preserving, processing or preparation, have been virtually eliminated. Stomach cancer is a case in point. High rates for this disease in Africa are probably related to consumption of peanuts, which often are infected with molds (Burros 1976). These alflatoxins also affect many grains and beans. The use of antioxidants in bread may be responsible for a decline in stomach cancer rates in this country since the 1940s (Whelan 1975). Tuberculosis used to be passed through cow's milk. Food poisoning can easily result if meat and processed foods are not properly preserved. The danger is not always evident to the consumer, and the effects may not appear soon enough to make a clear connection.

The Food and Drug Administration has frequently been criticized by consumer groups for laxity in inspection for disease organisms, natural toxins, and unsanitary conditions. But today the main dangers are chemical residues and the intentional additives which include preservatives, flavoring and coloring agents, stabilizers, smoothing agents, and bulking agents; as well as the decreasing natural nutrient content (Hall 1974). Missing nutrients include vitamins, minerals and also crude fiber.

Market Failures in Food Processing and Marketing

The reasons food markets may fail to bring maximum consumer satisfaction are similar to those leading to failure at the agricultural stage. They include consumer ignorance, habituation, joint consumption, and differing economies of scale in advertising and appropriability of profits among different food products.

Joint consumption. Food industry spokesmen often assert that there is little or no connection between diet and health. Despite this propaganda, consumers do implicitly purchase better health or disease with their food (Williams 1971). Because consumers generally enjoy (or suffer from) food and health separately, they may not make the connection between the two in their minds.

Likewise, the farmer's need for pesticides is linked to his purchase of a fertilizer and use of cultural control. But again, the consumption is typically separate in time. These conditions are present at both farm and consumer stages and for similar reasons. The effect of joint consumption on human behavior is increased by the widespread ignorance regarding nutrition and health.

Ignorance. Nutrition is a complex matter that nutritionists and other researchers are still far from understanding. Consumers are often not even aware of current knowledge. With thousands of foods and chemicals being ingested, and many other environmental factors to consider as well, it is extremely difficult to make a precise connection between a possible cause and a particular health effect. Experiments done with animals may or may not be applicable to humans. As if there were not enough problems already, there are long lags between cause and effect. These lags make epidemiological studies very difficult. Even such a simple event as food poisoning may not be traced to the food if too many hours have elapsed.

These long lags, perhaps 20 to 30 years in the case of cancer, mean that the rate of discounting the future, or discount rate used in evaluating risks, is crucial for current decisionmaking. Since the body politic has a lifetime which extends beyond that of any consumer, and consumers may discount the future more than governments, a public interest may arise even if individuals are unconcerned.

When confronted with a new technology, prudence argues for either a "wait-and-see" attitude, or reliance on the advice of experts. Our society generally opts for the latter. However, in our rapidly changing food system and complex society, experts themselves are ignorant. Reinforcing this ignorance is the tendency for scientists to become attached to traditional modes of thinking and experimentation, a set "paradigm" which is continually tested and refined, but which may become increasingly at variance with new evidence. An example is the case of cholesterol and heart disease (Hall 1974). Cholesterol was originally proposed as a cause of atherosclerosis in 1913 by a Russian who found increased fatty deposits in the arteries of rabbits fed diets abnormally high in cholesterol. Despite massive research since then, however, no clear evidence has been found that positively links cholesterol intake and heart disease. Since then, evidence *has* accumulated implicating sugar and refined food. But the scientific community, through a self-reinforcing circle of experts, continues to investigate the old paradigm and promotes the low-cholesterol diet. Scientists become habituated, just like consumers. (See Chapter 10 for examples in agricultural research.)

Advertising. For the consumer, the enjoyment of food is immediate; the danger lies in the future and is more or less discounted. Combined with ignorance, this makes for potentially good returns to investments in advertising by food producers, provided they can appropriate the profits. Another factor also makes advertising worthwhile: habituation. Not only cigarettes, but all caffeine products, such as cola drinks and coffee, are addictive (Brecher 1972). But addictive or not, food habits are hard to change once established. Food companies recognize this; a disproportionate amount of their television advertising is beamed to children, mostly for processed food of little nutritional value (Gussow 1973). Habituation and ignorance are also characteristic of markets for farm chemicals, and the same reasoning applies. These conditions favor good returns to investments in research and advertising geared to product differentiation.

Natural vs. artificial in food and farming. Food means much more to people than nutrients. It means friendship, remembrance of earlier good times, a sense of well-being and security, and sensory pleasure. All of these things are marketable and none of them are necessarily related to nutrition or health benefits. Marketing of non-nutritive dimensions of food has increased rapidly in the decades since World War II, with urbanization; with increased reliance of consumers on the mass media to form tastes, rather than family traditions; and with the new food technology that can potentially simulate the qualities of natural food, or better yet, "improve" on them (that is, make them more commercially acceptable). Since "taste" is, to a large extent, simply a matter of chemicals, an artificial product that can be made cheaper than the natural can be effectively marketed. Non-dairy creamers, artificial desserts and "fruit" drinks, and even artificial fruit and meat and cheese and "tomato" paste have all been marketed with some success. In fact, once consumers have adjusted to the artificial product, they tend to develop a distaste for the natural product (Bralove 1974). The situation at the processing stage is fairly analogous to that at the production stage, where natural and chemical products also compete for the consumer's dollar; in the latter case, the farmer is the consumer.

The same features that led to market failure in the adoption of agricultural chemicals are present at the food marketing stage, and reinforce the distortions of the farming stage. In both cases, natural and man-made products compete. And profitability is far higher with the manmade, although at the processing stage this edge arises primarily because of artificial product differentiation rather than patents. Another factor, while present at the production stage, operates far more strongly at the consumer stage. That factor is economies of large-scale advertising and marketing. Even if natural and man-made foods were equally costly to produce, the latter would dominate the market because of these marketing advantages. Thus we can understand why, if natural foods and farming practices are so good for people and land, they are not widespread. The answer lies, as we showed in the previous chapter, in the nature of the products and in the institutional framework in which they are sold.

Product Differentiation

While food at retail outlets has become more differentiated, with thousands of processed foods to choose from, food at the farm has become more uniform. Farmers sell far more to processors and other intermediaries (about 99 percent of production by 1966) than directly to consumers or even to food stores (NCFM 1966a). Product differentiation has become a major competitive tool of food processing and retailing firms, contributing in some cases to significant market power. A prime example is the breakfast cereal industry, where profits are consistently high, 18 percent of stockholders' equity in 1964 (NCFM 1966b). Kellogg averaged 23 percent return on stockholders' equity between 1972 and 1975. Average rates of return in food processing have been only slightly higher than the manufacturing average in the 1970s, 14.4 compared to 13.3 percent, between 1973 and 1975 (BW 1976).

Since market power is desirable, generally being accompanied by the possibility of higher profit levels, the incentive to develop it, where practicable, is strong. While excess profits are not associated with product differentiation per se in long run equilibrium ("imperfectly competitive" markets), firms can make use of the large economies of scale inherent within research, new market development, and advertising to build a larger market share. By an annual influx of new products, potential entrants are swamped, and long-run equilibrium is not reached. Competition on the basis of artificial product differentiation and advertising is characteristic of concentrated consumer goods industries like food processing.

In 1974 and 1975, new product entries declined, mainly because of the recession. There was speculation that changes in consumer buying habits may be forcing a turn to less-processed foods. However, although processed food sales fell and flour sales (for home-made bread) rose in 1974, the same thing happened in 1932–1933, for similar reasons: lower consumer incomes (Sullivan 1976).

Market concentration in food processing is high. In half of the 30 major food industries, the top four firms had 40 percent or more of industry sales. In only eight of these industries is the concentration of sales among the top four firms less than 30 percent (USDA 1972). Market power of these firms is further enhanced by the much higher concentration in particular product lines. Much of this concentration of power is attributable to the economies of scale in product differentiation, particularly mass advertising.

Farm output as raw material. Artificial product differentiation is made possible by the new chemistry of food technology, which can effectively simulate flavor, color and other qualities. And a different set of demand requirements is generated for farm products. The ideal input to food processing is a homogeneous raw material which is easily manipulated. So farm products come to be viewed more as raw materials for food manufacturing than as food. The "real" foods become the hundreds of new artificially differentiated products introduced yearly by the food technologists (Hall 1974).

Product differentiation at the farm. Attempts at product differentiation at the farm stage have been discouraged by government regulations, in addition to food processing requirements. Health regulations have eliminated many small independent meat and flour producers. While some of these regulations have protected the consumer, in many cases they have made it unnecessarily difficult for the small farmer attempting to market a product differentiated by flavor, feeding method, or growing technique. Beef and chicken taste different depending on how they are raised. For example, beef reaches top flavor at six years and generally acceptable full flavor at three years. But beef slaughter begins as early as ten months in the United States. Average slaughtering age (currently about 18 to 24 months) has been declining, reflecting production economics on large feed lots (Root 1975).

Grading of produce is generally on a simple, superficial basis, such as marbling in beef or size in eggs. Further differentiation has even been made illegal in some states. As mentioned earlier, in Maryland egg cartons cannot specify how the eggs were raised. This obviously denies the producer an opportunity to develop consumer loyalty, and assists in mass marketing of standardized agricultural products. "Quality" regulation may hamper the producer. Organic citrus, for example, cannot be shipped out of Florida in bulk because of chemical treatment requirements.

In the fresh produce market, the economies of scale in handling produce, inventory control, and advertising discourage variety. Thus, the number of apple varieties offered in supermarkets is quite limited compared to what one might have found a generation ago in apple-growing regions. We may choose Red Delicious all year round, rather than Mac-Intosh in the fall and York in the spring. With its surface waxed, the Red Delicious apple still looks appealing in the spring, though flavor and texture have deteriorated. Yorks improve with age (Root 1975).

Evidence of fraud in marketing "organic" and "natural" foods prompted proposals within the Federal Trade Commission to ban the use of these words in food marketing (FTC 1974). Such a move would have furthered the trend toward uniformity and market regimentation in the food industry, to the benefit of food processors and at the expense of farmers. There are, of course, alternatives to banning non-dangerous products: definition of terms and enforcement of labeling requirements. The Federal Trade Commission staff in fact offered reasonable definitions of organic and natural foods in its proposed ban. As of this writing, the health food industry pressure has forced a withdrawal of the proposal.

Resonance within the System

The market failures at the different stages of the food industry complement each other and their effect is multiplicative. There is a kind of resonance within the food delivery system, as effects of artificial substitutes ripple back and forth within the system. Chemical pesticides and drugs and manufactured foods can be patented, and thus marketing and research costs are recoverable. Biological and cultural controls are public goods. There are large economies of scale in manufacturing, distributing, and marketing manufactured chemicals and food. Organic fertilizer is just lying around in the barn: Who is going to advertise that? Artificial foods can be invented, manufactured and marketed for less than natural foods, taking advantage of the economies of scale in mass advertising and product development, as well as substitution of cheaper chemicals. What is the purpose of advertising organically raised carrots? Anyone can raise one in his backyard! The incentives for substituting chemical technology for natural processes thus exist at all stages of the food industry: farming, processing, retailing.

Under such circumstances, the standard economic models of consumer welfare maximization break down. These models assume that the market is responsive to consumer taste. But today the reverse is true:Tastes are generated by the system under the impetus of food technology and marketing economics. Market development and demand creation are just as much a part of the food industry as other consumer goods industries.

Under the present system, it is the technological imperatives that legislate taste and values, and humans are manipulated to support that technology (see Mishan 1971). Since such sales maneuvers as food advertising to children on television are regulated by public policy, then public policy must be held responsible, by omission if not by commission. Media intervention could help to redress the imbalance. Health and nutrition education could be given free time to balance advertising for "junk food," food with little nutritional merit. The same case can be made against the marketing of pesticides and manufactured fertilizers. A requirement for counteradvertising could open up farm journals to biological control information side by side with the slick pesticide copy. Governments need not be helpless giants, but may offer alternative·value systems.

Systemic Market Failure

The linkages between chemical and food manufacturers build strength through complementarity and mutual reinforcement. On the other hand, the linkage between farmer and consumer has been weakened to the point of practical nonexistence. The farmer has no direct connection with consumers, either personally, spatially, or socially. The welfare of consumers has become a completely external matter to the farmer in modern agribusiness, and the consumer seems altogether indifferent to the plight of the small farmer.

Compared with earlier eras, farmers are more separated spatially and emotionally from consumers. They are also separated by the intermediate stages of the food processing industry. The more steps there are between producer and consumer, the more alienated they become from each other. And the more likely it is that goals will be set within the intermediary stages or subsystems rather than for the system as a whole. The farmer who raises food for himself and his family or for his cattle has a far greater incentive to be concerned with its quality, than the one who is raising food for a large corporation. Corporations do not eat food. The industry may set quality standards, but generally only two or three grades at most. Highest qualities, where the small farmer can enjoy a comparative advantage, are dropped.

Farmers purchase most of their food at the supermarket like the rest of us. Looking at the system from the other side, consumers are alienated from farmers and farm life. Thus they tend to make purchase decisions purely on the basis of price or appearance, neglecting the impact their decisions have on farmer and animal welfare.

This alienation within the system leads to an emphasis on quantity at the expense of the high quality ranges. Federal subsidy programs reinforce this tendency. The system is self-perpetuating: selection will favor those entrepreneurs for whom monetary rewards are most important relative to other dimensions of satisfaction (Chapter 9).

We may call these system-induced failures to internalize effects on other stages of an industry system, systemic market failure. Or, the failures could be called vertical market failures because they occur between the vertical stages of an industry.

Systemic market failure also occurs because food processing firms do not take into consideration the effects of *their* actions on farmers. The drive for artificial product differentiation and the concomitant desire for a homogeneous raw material contribute to the movement toward large-scale, mechanized and chemically oriented agriculture. The resulting side-effects are not felt by the food processing firms involved.

6   Energy, Resource Use, and the Food System

The United States food system has been criticized for its large use of energy compared with the systems of other nations and other eras. Agriculture produces energy—food energy—as well as consuming energy. Some critics have pointed to a decline in energy output per energy input. Questions of equity have also been raised. Should one nation, or one group of nations, at one time in human history, consume the whole world's stock of readily exploitable, non-renewable energy resources? This is part of the overall criticism of modern agriculture's use or misuse of resources. First we will look at energy consumption in the food system and at possible ways to measure efficiency. Then we will look at the questions of pollution and equity. Dissatisfaction with the present state of affairs has led to the suggestion that other criteria be used to replace or supplement the traditional criteria for resource allocation. None of the proposed approaches offers a fully satisfactory method for handling the problems inherent in modern agriculture. The approach of organic farming appears to be an attractive alternative.

Energy in the Food System

One of the important functions of agriculture is the transformation of the sun's radiant energy into stored chemical energy in the plant's carbohydrates and protein, the process of photosynthesis. Only about 0.2 percent of the incident energy is converted to stored energy (primary conversion efficiency) (Leach 1975). This stored energy is then available to creatures who use the plants for food. Energy is the capacity to do work. It may be stored and released from storage, that is, transformed from one form into another; but it is not created or destroyed. (Even "atomic

93

energy" is a release of potential energy stored in the nucleus of atoms.) These transformations are never 100 percent efficient; there is always some loss to the system in the form of heat. Most of the sun's incident energy is used to heat up the earth, and is re-radiated into space, rather than stored in plants.

Renewable and non-renewable energy sources. Traditional agriculture used the energy of human and animal labor in addition to direct sunlight, but human and animal energy comes from energy stored in food, derived from incident solar energy within the preceding year or so. Thus a steady-state system is maintained, in which the food system operates entirely on the incident flux of solar energy. Not only their food system, but the whole energy budget of traditional societies is limited to the incident flux of solar energy. Their main fuels are wood and animal oils.

Solar energy has a large potential as an energy source, if we can learn to use it better. An incredible amount of energy reaches the earth annually from the sun, some $87,969 \times 10^{16}$ kilocaries, about 14,000 times the amount of fossil fuel and other commercial energy used in the whole world in 1976 (adapted from Holdren and Ehrlich 1974, assuming a 2.5 percent present growth rate in world energy use). Tilled lands capture about 1 percent of the incident energy, forests 0.2 percent, and pastures about 0.1 percent (deWit 1967; Loomis et al. 1971). There would appear to be some room for increasing the efficiency of capture of solar energy by plant life. If population can be stabilized, a new steady state is theoretically possible at an energy level comparable to current United States levels, relying only on annual plant production (Chancellor and Goss 1976).

Modern societies have learned to tap the stored solar energy, trapped over millions of years and now lying in coal beds and oil and gas pools in the earth. Modern technology, including agriculture, runs on these fossil fuels. But it was the discovery of the vast oil fields of Texas and Oklahoma in the 1930s that signaled the changeover to today's energy-intensive society. Later, in the 1940s, even larger stores were found in the Mideast. Prices for petroleum products were stable and declining in the 1950s and 1960s, reflecting the large supplies relative to demand. In the United States, a quota system and other restraints kept supply restricted. Prices, though comparatively low by recent standards, were still several times production cost (Adelman 1970).

Since 1970, however, fossil fuel prices have risen, most rapidly in 1972 and 1973. These increases have focused public attention on the dependence of modern society on energy, particularly the non-renewable energy sources. During the previous era of comparatively cheap energy, it was only natural for profit-maximizing firms and utility-maximizing consumers to substitute energy for other inputs and commodities. Many of these substitutions are in the investment or durable goods classes, so that they take many years for full adjustment. Examples are large cars and poorly designed and badly insulated buildings.

The recent high energy prices are not caused by a shortage of energy resources.* High prices have been set by a very effective cartel, the Organization of Petroleum Exporting Countries (OPEC) (Adelman 1970). Thus, a full adjustment may not be necessary, if potential weaknesses in the cartel materialize and/or alternative energy sources rapidly appear, such as the new oil fields being developed all around the world. (See, for example, BW 1976 and Nossiter 1975.) In the meantime, the "energy crisis" remains: high prices and/or shortages at previously prevailing low prices. And this maladjustment raises the issue of our comparatively extravagant use of energy.

The energy efficiency of modern agriculture. Fossil fuel resources have been particularly useful in agriculture. Petroleum is a far more convenient fuel for farm equipment than coal, and natural gas is convenient for crop drying and for use in manufacturing nitrogen fertilizers. Machine harvesting requires a higher moisture content and thus more energy for drying. The total energy used in agriculture, in addition to incident solar energy, may be called "cultural" energy (Heichel 1973). In modern societies, less than 1 percent of the cultural energy comes from animal and human labor. The ratio of food energy in the crop to cultural energy used in production has been called "energy efficiency" (Leach 1975), or more neutrally, "energy ratio."

Critics of modern agriculture point out that the energy ratios of primitive and traditional agricultures are much greater than those of modern systems. This has been used as an argument against conventional agriculture by proponents of organic farming. In primitive agriculture, the energy ratio is always greater than one, often much greater. That is, more food energy is produced on the land than human, animal and fossil fuel energy (cultural energy) consumed to produce it, assuming that some marketable product results. For subsistence cassava crop, for example, the energy ratio is more than 60 to 1!

In comparison, United States agriculture required, in 1963, 1.14 units of cultural energy, on the average, to produce 1 unit of food energy (Hirst 1973; 1974), an energy ratio of only 0.88. The overall energy ratio of the whole food system, including all direct and indirect uses of energy, from manufacture of farm inputs to household preparation, was about 0.15. The

---

*Nordhaus (1973) has constructed a model in which current petroleum prices do not appear unreasonable in the light of projected supplies and present costs of alternative energy sources. Be that as it may, the fact remains that a rapid increase in the price of crude oil occurred in the face of constant or declining production costs.

food system energy ratio has declined from about 1.0 in 1900 to about 0.1 in 1976 (Steinhart and Steinhart 1974).

These figures indicate that we put far more energy into our food system than we get out of it. But what meaning is to be attached to such figures? Are we to conclude that a native picking bananas off a banana tree is more "efficient" than a modern farmer? Surely few would advocate maximizing such "efficiency." We have here an implicit energy theory of value, with the attendant difficulties, to be examined presently. But first let us look a little more closely at the figures to see where all the energy is going.

Why the food system is energy-intensive. The energy ratio of United States corn production decreased from 3.7 in 1945 to 2.8 in 1970 (Pimentel *et al.* 1973). But this increase in energy use offset significant declines in other inputs, notably land and labor (Johnson 1974). So we are *still* producing more food energy in corn production than we put in, but we are using half the land area. Corn yield in 1970 was 8.2 million kilocalories per acre (Pimentel *et al.* 1973). But incident solar energy per acre is about 6800 million kilocalories per acre. Since yields more than doubled between 1945 and 1970, this much solar energy was saved by moving to more so-called "energy-intensive" production! Of course, it is fossil fuel energy that critics are concerned about. But it is not at all clear that the modern system is inefficient even on the basis of energy accounting (see Connor 1976).

Over 60 percent of the energy required in American agriculture is used directly on the farms to run machinery. The other large category is the energy required to make the chemical fertilizers, about 24 percent of the total (Fritsch *et al.* 1975). The average energy content of the major fertilizers, in terms of barrels of oil equivalent, is 12 barrels of oil per ton of nitrogen, 5 per ton of phosphate, and 3 per ton of potash. For a representative fertilizer application of 100 pounds nitrogen, 50 pounds phosphate, and 50 pounds potash per acre, an energy equivalent of 0.8 barrels of oil per acre is used. When energy prices go from $2 per barrel of petroleum to $8 as they did between 1972 and 1975, the energy cost of this fertilizer application should rise about $4.80 per acre (0.8 × [$8–$2]). Actually the energy cost of making fertilizer did not rise as fast, because nitrogen fertilizer production uses mainly natural gas, whose price has been kept artificially low by federal regulation. Fertilizer prices *did* rise rapidly in the early 1970s (Table 12-4). The rise was not due to energy prices but rather to a temporary shortage of manufacturing capacity to meet the upsurge in fertilizer demand as federal restrictions on acreage planted were ended (BW 1974a).

Even with higher energy prices, there is no guarantee that fertilizer prices will remain high, if technological change continues at its past rate. "With natural gas priced at $1.00 per thousand cubic feet (about twice the regulated price), the cost of producing nitrogen fertilizer with the 1974 technology would be less than the cost with free natural gas and the 1960 technology" (Johnson 1974). Nevertheless, only 40 percent of natural gas used today in nitrogen fertilizer production is burned for fuel; the remaining 60 percent is not burned, but incorporated into the fertilizer. Thus the potential saving from advanced technology is small (Davis and Blouin 1976). Interstate prices were raised in July 1976 for newly discovered (since 1 January 1975) gas, and for gas newly committed to interstate commerce. The new price of $1.42 per 1,000 cubic feet (up from $0.52) is close to the intrastate (unregulated) price of $1.55 (Rowe 1976). Since natural gas production is effectively competitive, the latter price probably is a pretty good reflection of 1976 production cost. An alternative technology is available for producing nitrogen fertilizer by making ammonia from coal instead of from natural gas, but the process requires 20 percent more energy. New technology can probably cut this back to zero percent in five or ten years (Davis and Blouin 1976).

One way to save on fertilizer is to use it more efficiently. Worldwide, only 50 percent of the applied nitrogen is absorbed by plants, only 3 percent of the applied phosphate. A 10 percent increase in efficiency is probably easily achievable. Also considerable potassium and phosphate is used where it is not needed; perhaps 20 percent could be saved by testing the soil first. Chemical fertilizers could also be replaced with organic materials (NRC 1975).

Lockeretz *et al.* (1975) compared the energy use on organic and conventional Corn Belt farms. On the average, organic farms used one-third the amount of energy consumed by conventional farms. Organic methods do not always save energy, however. Plowing is far more energy-intensive than using herbicides (see Chapter 4).

American agriculture uses a lot of energy partially because of its product mix. The average livestock and dairy farm has an energy ratio of about 0.3. Vegetables and fruits are also energy-intensive, when compared to corn and beans. The latter have energy ratios substantially greater than one (Heichel 1976). Differences between our country and underdeveloped countries would be much less if we corrected for our consumption of these high-energy foods. Obviously food has far more value to us than its energy content. Our agriculture surely cannot be faulted on the basis of efficiency for providing a high percentage of high-protein and vitamin-rich foods. Equity, however, is another matter, to be dealt with presently.

Comparison of food with other sectors of the economy. As mentioned earlier, the energy ratio of the American food system is about 0.1, which appears rather low. But the purpose of the food system is not to produce energy, but food and the resulting human satisfaction. If we want to look at the efficiency of the food system, we must compare it with other sectors of the economy. When we look at the energy used per dollar of sales, the best measure of consumer satisfaction, the food system turns out to look pretty good. Compared to value produced, the energy used in food is substantially less than the average for the economy as a whole.

Direct and indirect energy use in raising and processing food amounted to about 8 percent of total energy use in 1970, and, including refrigeration, 10 percent (Table 6-1). This use compares favorably with the percent of Gross National Product (GNP) spent on food in 1970, about 14 percent. Critics in environmental magazines seldom make such a comparison, perhaps because it might appear to imply that food production is *more* efficient than other sectors of the economy. Thus, it can be argued that the agricultural sector is comparatively efficient and that we could save energy by shifting resources into the agricultural sector (Martin 1974). More commonly, the figures cited are 12.8 percent of our energy used in production, transportation, processing and household consumption of food. Actually the sum total of all food-related energy use comes to about 17 percent, if garbage disposal and shopping costs are included. In making comparisons with other sectors, an amount of energy for waste disposal would also have to be added.

Adjustment to high energy prices. Since prices of energy have risen recently, and adjustment takes time, we are of course using more energy in the food sector now than we "should" be, presumably meaning than we would in long-run equilibrium. But the same is true of other sectors of the economy. Thus, high energy prices and/or shortages do not necessarily mean that

Table 6-1   Energy Use in the Food System Compared with Percent of GNP Spent on Food

Energy Used In	Food Energy: Percent Total Energy Use (1970)	Food Expenditure: Total Expenditure (1970)	Percent (GNP) (1975)
Raising	3.1		
Raising and processing	8.1		
Raising, processing, storing	10.0	13.9	13.8
Raising, processing, storing, transporting, home consumption	12.8		
Every phase, including garbage disposal and shopping	17		

Sources: Steinhart and Steinhart 1974;   Percent GNP from CEA 1975.

there will be large changes in agriculture. That depends on how easy it is to make changes in agriculture compared to other sectors of the economy. (In economic terms, it depends on the comparative elasticities of substitution for other inputs and products in production and consumption, respectively.) It is not at all clear that the burden of adjustment would fall to agriculture.

Food demand is relatively stable (inelastic) in the short run, so that adjustments in other sectors of the economy would be expected first in any event. And adjustments can be made. People may well prefer to drive smaller cars than eat less food. The potential for saving energy in non-food sectors is rather large and, in many cases, can be achieved with little impact on lifestyle (see OEP 1972). Better insulation of homes and commercial buildings could save 5 percent of total energy use within a decade. A substantial portion of the remainder still needed for heating buildings could be provided by solar energy. American automobiles average about 13 miles per gallon; their European counterparts, slightly less than double this amount. Automobiles consume about 16 percent of the nation's energy. If our cars were as efficient as the European, we would use 8 percent less total energy. These are two examples among many potential savings in the non-agricultural sectors.

Private industry will gradually make adjustments to higher long-run energy prices. But these adjustments may be easier to make and less costly to society in non-agricultural sectors. The impact of energy supply on agriculture was investigated at Iowa State University, using their large-scale model of the agricultural sector (Dvoskin and Heady 1976). The model predicts that a doubling of energy prices would lead to only a 5 percent decline in energy use in agriculture, and a roughly 13 percent increase in production costs. If the agricultural sector were forced to cut energy use by 10 percent, however, production costs would rise some 55 percent, as farmers were forced to substitute other more costly inputs. If energy is more costly, farmers will use less nitrogen fertilizer, but more herbicides and more energy in transporting crops to market. While these models have limitations from the point of view of our study, the results do show how essential energy is to the efficient functioning of American agriculture.

Much of the recent rhetoric of environmentalists about energy waste in agriculture appears wishful thinking. While there is a large energy component in the manufacture of agricultural chemicals, the case against their use does not lie in their possession or lack of energy efficiency (see Chapters 3 and 4). The real case for energy conservation is based on equity and damage to the environment.

Energy and equity. With about 6 percent of the world's population, the United States accounts for over 30 percent of the world's current energy use. Our per-capita energy consumption is 230 kilowatt hours per person per day compared to a world average of 45 and around 9 in India (Starr 1971). Since we are blessed with abundant fossil fuel reserves, we can probably sustain this level of energy use, or even increase it, for at least a couple of hundred years. It is possible that we may be able to continue consumption at high levels virtually indefinitely with the development of fusion power or efficient solar conversion. On the other hand, we may not. If everyone in the world used energy at the same rate that we do, world fossil fuel reserves would last only a matter of decades rather than centuries. The high consumption of fossil and other fuels in the United States and a few other Western nations is depriving both the rest of the world's population and also future generations of the benefits of consuming a proportional share of the world's inheritance. The same issues arise with other aspects of modern agriculture, such as the destruction of wildlife and the depletion of natural soil fertility.

These are primarily ethical rather than economic issues, particularly the question of how to share resources among the present world population. Various rationalizations have been proposed for justifying an unequal distribution of income and wealth (see Musgrave 1959). But the burden of proof would seem to lie upon those who would favor inequality. Certainly, "Might makes right," or "Whatever is is right," have little moral basis. A more equal distribution of income could well result in *more* rapid depletion of resources, so that an equal temporal distribution of wealth would conflict with a desire for equal intertemporal distribution of resource use. The proliferation of nuclear power plants and the accompanying bomb material and potential for blackmail may provide an impetus to egalitarianism among the rich nations in the near future. The issues raised by intergenerational equity are more complex and have more interesting dimensions. The following section will explore these issues.

Future Generations

Decisions made in the use of agricultural land affect the potential food production capabilities of future generations. Many processes are essentially irreversible. Each year our rich prairie soils yield up an increment of nitrogen which is lost in crops and to the atmosphere—a kind of soil mining. Overuse and misuse of heavy machinery can compact the soil below the top layers, making it impervious to plant roots. Excessive irrigation may raise the salt content of soils to the point where they are unsuitable for major crops. Plowing steep hills, neglecting cover crops, overgrazing, neglect of climatic factors, and decline in humus can result in wind and water erosion, even to the point of permanent destruction of a region's agricultural potential. Such was the fate of earlier civilizations in the Near East and North Africa (Osborn 1948). A new dimension is added with nutrient runoff and persistent pesticides, which may lead to biological destruction of lakes and the permanent loss of some wildlife species, respectively (see Chapter 4). Fossil fuels are a non-renewable resource, increasingly used by modern agriculture.

Conventional analysis of resource use compares the present value, the difference between the discounted expected future benefits and costs, for alternative uses of resources, including conservation. Generally future generations are weighted less heavily than the present generation, that is, a non-zero discount rate is used. Any finite resource will then be consumed eventually. This has led some critics to propose a zero discount rate as the only fair approach. Even with a zero discount rate, it may not be optimal to conserve resources for future generations, since technology is continually evolving, and new resources and more efficient means of using the old constantly appear. Technological optimists will advocate resource depletion, while pessimists would favor conservation. Krutilla (1967) developed a new argument for conservation within the conventional framework, based on an increasing relative abundance of substitutes for mineral resources and environmental goods.

With the recent publicity over depletion of energy resources, classical conservation has taken on a new urgency. The failure of private and public decisionmakers to stop environmental decay and rapid resource depletion has stimulated a variety of suggestions for supplementary or alternative methods of evaluating resource use. These will now be briefly mentioned, so that the potential contribution of organic agriculture in resource allocation may be better appreciated. The main suggestions are minimum throughput (for example, of energy); no-growth or steady-state economy; and equal consumption between time periods. All have some useful and some unsatisfactory aspects.

Minimum throughput. The concept of "spaceship earth" and the revulsion against the maximum consumption society have suggested the goal of minimum consumption, or minimum throughput (cf., Boulding 1966). While minimizing consumption has a ring of reasonableness about it, it cannot bear being carried to its logical conclusion. Even minimizing energy flow makes little sense, since we can increase energy flow and consumption by technology, without damage to the environment or depletion of resources. Specifically, we may be able to increase the photosynthetic capacity of plants, or harness solar energy through solar cells (cf. Chancellor and Goss 1976). We do not really live on a "spaceship earth," that is, on a closed system. Incident solar energy over the entire earth is thousands of times the annual consumption of fossil fuels, as explained earlier.

Stationary state. The concept of a stationary or steady-state or no-growth society has gained favor, particularly since the famous Meadows *et al.*

(1974) *Limits to Growth* (cf. also Daly 1972). They graphically showed the consequences of allowing resources and population to get out of balance when combined with a neglect of increasing future demand and negative feedback on the resource base due to pollution or depletion. This overshoot of resource use, and the ensuing disaster phase of population collapse, present a compelling picture. It is, however, a picture well known to biologists, with or without computer models (Hardin 1972). Nevertheless, when such a fate might occur, or whether it will occur at all, depends critically on the model's assumptions. If we are more optimistic about technological change, if prices are allowed to change and adjustments are made to the changes, or if humanity learns from its experience, entirely different results arise from the model (Ridker 1973; Beckerman 1972; Boyd 1972). Past experience with resource depletion and technological change is actually quite encouraging (Barnett and Morse 1963). Even with energy, the future is not entirely bleak. A few short generations ago no one dreamed of nuclear power. How can we know what the future may hold?

Ridker (1973) has pointed out that neither maximizing growth nor minimizing growth has much to recommend it as a goal for society. Many people feel that a certain amount of growth may be useful, even necessary, to increase the well-being of humans. Growth need not be purposeless nor heedless of its side-effects, though that has often characterized our recent past.

Equalizing consumption. The idea of equalizing consumption among temporal periods is appealing as an ideal for allocating resources. Such an idea appeals to feelings of intergenerational equity. In its simple form, this ideal has the fault that what is of value to one generation may not be to the next. There is no sense in conserving something that future generations will not desire. Should buggy-whips have been conserved for drivers of horseless carriages? Conversely, some goods, like natural environments, may become even more valuable to future generations, and so ought perhaps to be preserved for that reason (Krutilla 1967). A more general formulation of equalizing consumption has been suggested by Georgescu-Roegen (1971). He points out that economic activity tends to increase entropy, that is, to disperse ordered aggregations, particularly mineral deposits. It seems clear to him that it is only fair to allow each generation its own share of increasing entropy. But what if there are an infinite number of generations? Perhaps each generation should make no changes in the entropy, or at least minimize entropy changes. Stated that way, however, the proposition makes little sense, since entropy change is minimized only by using no resources at all. Perhaps a reinterpretation is possible, however, and we will return to the issue presently.

Even assuming constant tastes, can intergenerational equality really be recommended without qualifications? Ancient Greece exploited a lush and fertile land. Would we prefer to have good soil in Asia Minor today, or the legacy of democracy and philosophy from the Golden Age? Perhaps we could have had both, but sometimes choices must be made. Thus, Brubaker (1975) suggested that a shift to a steady-state economy in the present may doom future generations to a perpetual state of energy poverty. A full investment of our fossil fuels in a crash program to perfect fusion power might release almost unlimited supplies of clean energy. (There is a chance, of course, that the investment might not pay off, and future generations might be *more* impoverished.)

How much maldistribution of income should be tolerated? Rawls (1971) proposed that it should be tolerated up to the point where the least well-off individual ceases to be made better (maximin principle). That is, inequality is all right if it benefits the poor. But what if the least well-off are benefited less than the most well-off? Human happiness is partially a matter of invidious comparison, that is, we are least happy when our wealth differs most from that of our neighbors. So we are back again to equality with its attendant difficulties.

Perhaps a reinterpretation of the entropy criterion would be acceptable. If we put back as much useful information or order as we take out, we have not inconveniencd future generations. This is Brubaker's trade between fossil fuel now and fission power in the future. In fact, we may improve things. Viewing entropy in this way, human beings are not simply agents of increasing entropy, but can use their (solar-powered) energy and ingenuity to increase information and order and decrease entropy. The earth is not a closed system, so that we can presumably improve the lot of future generations through judicious investments. Just such investment produced the fossil fuels in the first place, and is part of the drive behind the evolution of civilization. From this point of view, the equity issue is not that we use a large percentage of the world's energy resources in America, but that we have so little to show for it. Our use of energy for big cars and electric can openers is unlikely to bear fruit for future generations. The high consumption of resources would appear to imply a concomitant burden to make some positive contribution to the evolution of civilization.

While perhaps intellectually satisfying, the above rule's import for practical decisionmaking is less clear. What is the entropy value of the invention of the laser? What we need is a way of internalizing the costs of future generations. The indefinite commitment of one person or family to one piece of land is one way. This is a key feature of organic farming.

Energy and the Environment

Virtually any use of energy has some impact on the environment, both currently and for future generations. Even increasing use of solar energy means less reflected energy. The resulting warmer earth would melt some of the polar ice, raising ocean levels. Aside from this free (and priceless) incident solar radiation, our energy (cultural energy) comes primarily from fossil fuels: coal, petroleum, and natural gas. Natural gas has negligible impact on the environment; petroleum and natural gas are our most versatile fuels, especially in agriculture. But they are in comparative short supply domestically. Though large reserves exist in the Mideast, adequate for many decades, there are political hazards in relying on such an unstable region for a large share of our energy supply. Petroleum production, transportation, refining, and use involve considerable adverse impact on the environment. Oil spills and leakage from off-shore oil wells and from tankers may induce permanent damage to wetlands, perhaps to wider regions of the oceans. Most American air pollution is a result of the use of fossil fuels, including coal. Air pollution causes lung diseases, particularly in cities, and may lead to irreversible changes in the earth's climate (cooler or warmer, depending on whether particulates or carbon dioxide dominate).

The United States has substantial coal reserves, enough to satisfy our energy needs for a few hundred years at current consumption rates. The environmental price of production is high, but in some cases can probably be substantially lessened by appropriate legislation. Coal is either surface-mined, or deep-mined; currently about half of our production comes from each. Deep mining may lead to some acid drainage and land subsistence, but the main problem has been danger to the miners themselves, in the form of explosions and lung disease. (Since United States steel firms and European firms have exemplary safety records in their coal mines, worker injury does not appear to be inherent to deep mining.) The main danger of surface mining is the loss of land to other uses, a danger which is minimal when there is adequate water and the land is fairly level. With strong and strictly enforced legislation, strip-mining could be confined to these areas with little environmental impact.

The major alternatives to fossil fuels are nuclear power and solar power. The latter received little federal research attention prior to the mid-1970s. It is possible that with further research work and mass production of receptors, solar power can fill a substantial portion of our heating needs.

Nuclear power has the potential for providing large energy supplies, to satisfy domestic energy demand for hundreds, perhaps thousands, of years. Nuclear energy is released when nuclei of small atoms are stuck together or those of large atoms are broken apart. The former process, fusion, has yet to be proven technically feasible, much less economical. The latter, fission, is the basis for the current burner-type reactors and the experimental breeder reactors. The breeders, which generate fuel as they run, have a potential for substantially expanding energy production. Fission reactors eliminate the air, water, and land pollution (most of it) associated with conventional energy production by fossil fuels. However, new hazards are introduced: radioactive pollutants.

The dangers from nuclear reactors arise primarily in three ways: reactor failure, theft of fuel in transit to reprocessing or storage, and leakage from waste-storage facilities (Kneese 1973). Reactor failure is generally agreed to be the least of the problems. Yet, though the estimated probability is small, the possible damages could run above $1 billion for a single failure. A close call at the Brown's Ferry, Alabama, reactor gave cause for alarm or relief, depending on the perspective (BW 1975). Fuel, particularly that for the breeder, can be used to make nuclear bombs, thus opening the door to terrorist activity or blackmail if these materials are stolen during transit. Nuclear waste is not degradable into safe material by any known means, and must be kept isolated from human beings for thousands of years, perhaps as long as a million years. A significant release of waste material to the environment, such as by blowing up a large waste storage facility, could end human life on earth. Yet no satisfactory means of storage currently exist. Reliance on nuclear power thus poses an increasingly grave risk to humanity, especially as plants and fuel spread around the world to less stable societies.

None of the energy alternatives offers an unmixed blessing. Since modern agriculture is energy-intensive, compared to the alternatives, including organic farming, a changeover to alternative agricultural methods would contribute to alleviating the pressure on our environment and our finite energy reserves.

Rights of Non-human Life Forms

Much of the effect of human activity on animal and plant life occurs through agriculture. Farm machines and chemicals have a great impact on the quality of life of animals and plants, both commercial species and others, whether targeted as pests or not. Plowing a field is one of the most destructive operations that human beings engage in, in terms of numbers of life-forms killed.* The extensive use of energy in agriculture has a great impact on the environment, both directly in the operations that are energy-intensive, and indirectly through the effects of energy production itself. Even if one believes in using plants and animals for food, and it is rather difficult to avoid at least some exploitation of other life forms, there is still the ethical question of the ways we treat animals. Just because we *can* get more eggs out of a mechanized chicken house does not mean we *ought* to.

---

*This statement refers to the conventional farmer's moldboard plow, which buries the living upper layers of soil. Organic farmers usually use a chisel plow, which stirs, but does not mix, the soil layers.

To put the matter more vividly, consider the possibility of producing ideal babies efficiently in test tubes. This is close to a technical possibility today, and will surely be done unless some moral restraint is imposed.

Traditional economic welfare analysis considers only the pleasure or displeasure derived by human beings from the way other life forms are treated (Westman 1977). Nature has value insofar as it gives utility to man: man is not just the measure, but the measurer of all things. Land, animals, plants, even human beings themselves, are inputs into an economic system, whose goal is purely to satisfy the desires of human consumers. This approach is inherent in even the "new conservation" developed at Resources for the Future (Krutilla 1967; Fisher and Peterson 1976). If natural features are preserved, it is because they have utility to humans, either in the present or in the future. Pollution is ideally dealt with by taxes or other measures designed to raise private costs up to full social costs (to humans). What if the market value of off-shore oil is greater than the value of all the fish and other sea creatures that live in the area? Then conventional economic analysis would argue for oil production, whether or not the ocean life nearby was destroyed. Of course, the argument runs, it would be better to avoid pollution. But if that is a risk we have to run to get at the oil, so be it.

The conventional approach is characteristic of modern "agribusiness," but was not always the view of farm leaders. Henry Wallace, then Secretary of Agriculture, wrote in the *Agriculture Yearbook of 1938*:

The social lesson of soil waste is that no man has the right to destroy even if he does own it [the soil] in fee simple. The soil requires a duty of man which we have been slow to recognize. . . . The Earth is the mother of us all.

The literature of organic farming picks up this theme. Man is more than the economist's "labor," and land, animals, seed, are more than mere "inputs" (see, for example, von Jeetze 1975). All these elements have inherent value, whether they are used in the economic system or not.

Interspecies equity. If plants and animals have inherent value, is there any way to compare this value with the value of other species, in particular, with that of humans? How can we compare the demand of a fish for its life with the demand of a human for oil? If we could solve the problem of interspecies equity, perhaps the result could be transformed into a solution to the intergenerational equity problem. For it is precisely a lack of respect for the value of our contemporary animals, plants and minerals that will affect the welfare of future generations. The value placed on the damage to natural features depends on the distribution of income in society and, in addition, on what, if any, rights or effective demand are assigned to natural objects themselves.

Legal, biological and animal welfare writers have been attempting to provide alternatives to the conventional economic approach. Stone (1972) argued that natural features should be recognized as having inherent rights, as a logical extension of society's gradual recognition of the rights of slaves and women. Former Justice Douglas (1972) picked up the theme in his dissent from the Supreme Court Mineral King decision. Women do not have rights because it pleases men to think so; the same is now argued for other life forms. Acceptance of these ideas would make animals and natural features easier to defend in court. A character in one of Dr. Seuss's (1971) stories announces, "I am the Lorax; I speak for the trees." Who, indeed, has the right to speak for the trees? If these rights could be assumed by environmental groups, their position in court would be greatly strengthened.

The question remains, however, as to what *value* to place on these rights, a question of distribution of income. For example, at what point do human desires for a house take precedence over a tree's (supposed) desire to remain in its present condition? In one court case, environmentalists attached an arbitrary value of $1 per fish. Why not $100? Or $0.01? Such arbitrary assignments are not terribly convincing.

In recent years God has often been castigated for telling man to "have dominion over the fish of the sea and . . . over every living thing that moves upon the earth" (Genesis 1:28). Our environmental decay is then seen as stemming from this attitude of lording it over the rest of creation (Moncrief 1970). Nevertheless, to quote Him a little more fully:

And to every beast of the earth, and to every bird of the air, and to everything that creeps on the earth, everything that has the breath of life, I have given every green plant for food. (Genesis 1:30)

These are some pretty clear qualifications to man's "dominion." The implication is that these fellow-creatures have some right to *their* food, as man has to his own. (Even if they have no rights of their own, trees are required by animals.) In other words, a kind of God-given right to life for animals is found in the same place as the commandment to rule the earth. Two suggestions for valuing rights of other species are animal liberation, or equal rights for animals, and net energy analysis.

Animal liberation. Some writers argue that animals have not *some* rights, but rights *equal* to those of human beings. Singer (1975) defines "speciesism" by analogy with sexism and racism, as the prejudice that humans are of more value than other life forms which can also experience pleasure and pain, namely, the higher animals. Pigs and chickens and cows have an equal right to life, and so should not be eaten or otherwise exploited, but allowed to live out their lives in peace. Some environmentalists go further. Snyder (1974), writing in the Wilderness Society magazine, argues that we should assign rights proportional to the biomass, or mass of living substance, independent of quality considerations. He refers to Eugene Odum, who apparently believes that, "There is more information of a higher order of sophistication and complexity stored in a few square yards of forest than there is in all the libraries of mankind." Further, "Man may not be necessarily the highest or most interesting product" of evolution.

While everyone is entitled to his point of view, it appears unlikely that this one will have much appeal to members of the human species. It is also not clear that animals themselves, if they could do so, would opt for liberation. There really *is* a difference between the master-slave relation and that of master-dog. Domestic animals would not last very long in the wild. Whether they should be treated as appendages of machines is another matter. Again, some middle ground would appear more appropriate than either no rights for animals or equal (or greater!) rights.

Man alone among the species of the earth has been endowed with the ability to unfold the hidden capacities of the universe: those of the mineral, plant, and animal kingdoms, as well as of his fellow human beings. Indira Gandhi (1972) recalls the ancient Indian Emperor Ashoka who "defined [a] king's duty as not merely to protect the citizens and punish wrong-doers, but also to preserve the animal life and forest trees." The image of man as the farmer or gardener is best suited to this middle path: "The Lord God took the man and put him in the garden of Eden to till it and keep it" (Genesis 2:15). Man's role is to care for natural resources, to "husband" them, to assist in bringing forth their best qualities, which might not be possible without man's assistance (cf. Dubos 1976; McHarg 1969). It is precisely this middle way that is characteristic of organic farming.

Net energy. Howard Odum (1971) advocates valuing all creatures and commodities on the basis of the total energy required for their production. Since he proposes to measure efficiency by the energy ratio, or net energy gain, the method has become known as "net energy." The difficulties with this concept as an absolute evaluation of production efficiency were discussed earlier in this chapter. The net energy method makes a lot of sense when comparing energy programs; for example, deciding whether to go ahead with shale oil development (BW 1974b). If it takes as much energy to get the oil out as the energy value of the resulting oil, clearly the game is not worth the candle. This "net energy analysis" shows that the net energy produced would be too small, even if current market prices signaled a go-ahead. But it is not clear that this approach is equally applicable to all situations. What Odum is really proposing is an energy theory of value (cf. Huettner 1976). In the long run, all energy sources may be interchangeable and all resources have a cost expressible in energy extraction cost. But over any reasonable decision horizon, there are generally other factors in limited supply. Only a few short decades ago, in the 1930s, petroleum was so plentiful relative to demand that price reflected virtually no scarcity value at all. It is hard to believe that human potential can be measured simply in energy.

As an example of the application of energy analysis to evaluating natural objects, Odum (1971) raises the question of the value of trees in a particular recreation area. The market value of the wood was $64 per acre, and this was the value assigned to the trees by the engineers planning to cut them. A more sophisticated analysis would, of course, include recreational value considerations. Odum, however, calculated that the total energy flux or throughput required to produce such a stand of trees and the related ecosystem was about 40 kilocalories per square meter per day for 100 years (the energy flux passing through photosynthesis). Current (1970) costs put the value of this energy at $590,000 per acre! (And a non-zero discount rate would produce a far higher figure.) Since this is so much higher than the puny human demand of $64, the trees should clearly be spared.

The logical extension of such thinking would appear to be that hardly any natural feature should ever be disturbed. Who could afford to build a house at a price of $590,000 per acre for wood? The economic fallacy is that, while there has in fact been a lot of energy going into (actually through) the trees, it is energy without opportunity cost, that is, it has no other use at present. Thus, it may more properly be assigned a value of zero. It would be more appropriate to look at the replacement cost of the natural features in the same economic terms in which demand for lumber is calculated. Along these lines, Cumberland (1975) has suggested the requirement of purchasing and preserving an equivalent natural system to compensate for any destruction. This would force a full comparison of opportunity costs.

The other fallacy in the net energy valuation method is that, if trees are assigned a wealth (self-demand) equal to their total energy flux during production, the same favor should be done for human beings, else we are comparing "apples and oranges." In terms of energy input, a 30-year-old human being is worth about $180,000. A human being requires about one acre per year to feed, with a similar photosynthetic throughput to the trees, but he has lived 30 years instead of 100. So $0.3 \times \$590,000 = \$180,000$. This doesn't include imports and fish. In comparison, the input of cultural energy is miniscule, about ten times the human daily caloric intake, or 30 kilocalories per acre per day or about 0.01 kilocalories per meter squared per day.

The $180,000 figure is at least of the same order of magnitude as what Odum calculates for the trees. Human beings also can consume a lot of energy in their other activities. According to the Odum logic, the more energy throughput, the higher the value of the human being. In other words, we are back to maximizing a rate of *flow* rather than a *level*, with all the attendant difficulties pointed out by advocates of a steady-state economy.

Whether or not we can find an energy value of human beings comparable to that of trees, this whole approach neglects the crucial features of the situation: the unique place of mankind in the evolution of the world. We *are* in fact at the top of the evolutionary ladder and we embody a great sweep of biological evolution far beyond that achieved by trees. This is not to belittle trees, but to try to put things in perspective. In addition, we embody the accumulated wisdom of past civilizations. If a comparison of the relative biological and cultural energy expended in producing trees and people were made, the value assigned to people would have to be far higher. Such a relative valuation would place man and other species in perspective. Man *is* the measure of all things. While it may be unfair to assign no inherent value to other life forms, it is also unfair to assign a value on physical terms which are applied in the same manner to man. An appropriate task for biologists would be to design a measure of evolutionary effort expended in producing a given species. On this basis perhaps a scale of self-worth or self-demand could be derived with which to value other life forms in comparison to human demands.

Ethics. The fact that such a variety of criteria are being proposed to supplement or replace traditional welfare analysis testifies to the ferment in current social thought. All of the alternative approaches do have one thing in common. The issues are dealt with at a very abstract level, far removed from actual human relations. It is in fact just this abstraction of human decisionmaking from the concrete level of human interactions with other humans that is a large part of the problem. The welfare of these others is not internalized, but decisionmakers are alienated from nature, from other human beings, and from future generations. The chain of interconnectedness, the "chain of love" (Passmore 1974), has been broken. In economic terms, the welfare of others enters only very marginally into our value system. We say that the effects are external to the decisionmaker. Or, alternatively, that our discount rates are high: inter-temporal, inter-personal, and inter-species.

   The other side of the problem is the lack of a clearly defined system of ethics. Resource decisions are not ethically neutral (Nagel 1972). Adam Smith (1776), the father of economics, recognized that there was nothing about free markets that would guarantee that individuals would act morally. He relied upon public pressure on businessmen to keep abuses from going too far. Today, in a far larger society, dominated by corporations and other more or less impersonal institutions, the personal relations Adam Smith relied upon have been strained by spatial and institutional distances (Chapter 5). The emotional ties are no longer there. This is increasingly true in agriculture, as we move toward larger economic units, more distance between farmer and consumer, farm and regional specialization, and large-scale corporate farming. An organic farming system overcomes many of the problems associated with both traditional and alternative resource use criteria. Man again assumes his role as husbandman.

PART TWO

Alternative Agriculture: Organic Farming and Organic Food

7 Alternative Agriculture

Types of Alternative Agriculture

Four main types of alternative agriculture are represented on commercial-scale farms in the United States and Europe: organic or biological, biodynamic, French intensive, and ecological (COBL 1977).

Organic farming. None of the names in use to describe alternative forms of agriculture is entirely satisfactory. The term "natural" is often suggested, but is now associated with unprocessed (rather than refined) food, not with a farming method. Perhaps the word "biological" would be better (Coleman 1975). In practice, these words are used interchangeably with the commonly used term, "organic."

Modern organic farming had its origin in England where a type of agriculture emphasizing feeding the soil through compost was introduced by Sir Albert Howard in the 1930s (Howard 1940; 1945). The work has been carried on by Lady Eve Balfour and the Soil Association of England (Balfour 1975). The word "organic" is used in the traditional sense of pertaining to living organisms, or having the character of living creatures. The approach is holistic, rather than analytic. Land, farmer, food, and consumer compose a whole system. Consumer health is achieved by eating whole (not refined), fresh, and organically raised food.

The food system begins with the soil, and that is where organic farming places its focus. Conventional farmers often think of themselves as feeding the plants with certain nutrients. Organic farmers seek to feed the plants *indirectly*. They feed the soil life with compost and other natural materials, and the microbes in turn feed the plants. The situation is analogous to that in human nutrition. We know that humans need certain vitamins. This does not mean, however, that they must all be eaten. If the bacteria in the intestines are fed properly (for example, with roughage), these bacteria will manufacture vitamins for their human host. Just so does the organic method seek to feed the soil life in order to feed the plant.

Balance is a key theme, not only acid-alkaline balance, but a balance of all nutrients in appropriate ratios. Although chemical fertilizer can be applied in a balanced manner, organic farmers believe that only through the intermediary action of the soil microbes can a plant be fed in a truly balanced manner (Bizet 1974).

Organic farmers avoid the use of highly soluble, quick acting, chemically manufactured fertilizers and pesticides that are produced with chemical processes (not derived from natural materials by physical means). Use of other artificial (manufactured) chemicals is also rejected, such as hormones and antibiotics (cf. OSDA 1974), although antibiotics may be used for medical purposes.

The use of the word "organic" has led to some confusion. The branch of chemistry that deals with substances found in living creatures became known as "organic chemistry." The current scientific definition includes all substances that contain carbon. This category also includes many compounds that are rejected by organic farmers, such as many common pesticides and the nitrogen fertilizer, urea.

Organic farmers reject chemical fertilizers not simply because they are chemicals, but because they feed the *plant* rather than the *soil life*. Thus crushed rock phosphate is used in preference to the more soluble chemically treated "superphosphate." Crushed limestone, calcium carbonate, is all right, but not the more soluble, faster acting hydroxide or calcium oxide. Even though potash is generally obtained from simply crushing rock, this mineral is more soluble, and so is generally avoided. Potassium is ideally obtained from organic sources only. Wood ashes are satisfactory supplements (Bizet 1974). According to some advocates, the ideal organic farm would not need any importation of fertilizer once any natural soil deficiencies were overcome. In practice, organic farmers make liberal use of whatever approved materials are available.

A distinction can be seen between the forcefulness of the organic and conventional approaches. The organic grower tends to a more gentle approach which seeks to stimulate the life of the soil and plant; the conventional approach leans toward a more forceful intervention that will drive the plant toward maximum production. Some organic growers even have an ambiguous attitude toward natural hormones, such as those derived from seaweed.

In England, the Soil Association publishes a journal and has set up an advisory service for farmers that provides them with information on organic techniques. The association also has set up a company that licenses growers and assists in marketing. About 15,000 acres were being farmed organically in 1972 (Bizet 1974). On the Continent, a cousin known as "biological" agriculture is practiced. In 1972, between 25,000 and 50,000 acres were farmed in this manner in France by members of the main organic farming organization there, Nature et Progress. Perhaps another 25,000 acres are farmed biologically by farmers who are not members. Biological agriculture methods vary according to a number of schools, but principles are similar to those described above as organic (see Cadiou *et al.* 1975). The use of seaweed products is a distinguishing characteristic. The major marketer of processed seaweed fertilizer estimates that over a million acres of farmland use its products under its biological farming supervision, but this figure may be on the high side (Aubert 1972).

In America, the leading advocates of organic farming have been Rodale Press (Emmaus, Pennsylvania) and the Natural Food Associates (Atlanta, Texas, headquarters). Rodale publishes *Organic Gardening and Farming*, a monthly magazine with tips on organic techniques and general natural food information aimed mainly at home gardeners. Other periodicals in the health and environment field such as *Compost Science* and various books (e.g., Rodale 1961) on organic farming and natural living are also published regularly. Rodale's other major magazine, *Prevention*, is a leading advocate of vitamins and other food supplements, as well as of organic food. Since vitamins may be viewed by their users as at least partially a substitute for eating wholesome food, some conflict of interest is present. In fact, many *Prevention* articles end with the admonition that one should take vitamins since most people don't get enough in their food. A megavitamin approach to human nutrition is really much closer philosophically to that of standard agriculture than European organic farming. The British organic approach, theoretically accepted by the Rodale people as well, is to build the whole organism rather than import large amounts of specific nutrients (Mellanby 1976).

No services comparable to those provided by the Soil Association of England have been available in this country. A number of regional associations have sprung up in recent years, however, that are beginning to fill the need for advice on farming methods. Presently numbering about twenty (OGF undated), these organizations, such as the California Organic Growers (Halcyon, California), The Soil Association (Minnesota), and the Natural Organic Farmers' Association (Vermont and New Hampshire), are publishing newsletters, coordinating purchases and marketing, and forming a network of information-sharing. Some are attempting to promote regional self-sufficiency to the point of encouraging locally grown and adapted seed, and a return to the use of animal power.

The Rodale people set up an organic produce certification program in 1971 and turned it over to the growers two years later. A few state associations have set up functioning programs; most have not. The state of Massachusetts requires certification of sellers and distributors of organic food (Johnson 1974), and Oregon has established labeling standards for organically raised and processed food (OSDA 1974).

With few exceptions, all this organizational activity is privately funded. The same goes for research, though of course much general agricultural information is applicable to organic farming as well as conventional. Rodale has set up an experimental farm. But all in all, the organic grower in this country has had to fend for himself as far as advice peculiar to organic farming is concerned.

Table 7-1 gives the numbers of organic producers registered with *Organic Gardening and Farming* in 1975 in the eastern United States. Note that over half of them market fruit and vegetables only. These producers are mostly small market gardeners catering to a local population, rather than full-time farmers. Most of the animal and grain producers also raise and sell vegetables in season. Thus they maintain the tradition of a diversified farm, selling its surplus. The total number of United States producers registered at that time was 839 (OGF 1975). This figure cannot be taken as representative of the total number of organic farms nationally. Many of the producers on the list are only part-time growers. And many organic farmers are not on the list. There are only 33 registered producers in Minnesota, but Larry Eggen, president of the Soil Association of Minnesota, estimates that there are over 300 more or less organic farms in southern Minnesota averaging about 400 acres in size, about average for that region. This is about 0.3 percent of the 118,000 farms in Minnesota (USDA 1975).

Bio-dynamic agriculture. A second type of alternative agriculture was inspired by a series of lectures given by the Austrian philosopher Rudolf

Table 7-1   Registered Organic Producers, Fall 1975,
             Eastern United States

State	Animal Products	Feed Grains	Vegetables and Fruit Only	Total
Delaware	0	0	1	1
Maryland	1	2	10	13
New Jersey	8	1	13	22
New York	17	12	33	62
Ohio	3	19	19	41
Pennsylvania	25	30	45	100
West Virginia	0	1	3	4
Total	54	65	124	243
Percent of Total	22	27	51	100

Source: OGF 1975.

Steiner in 1924 (Steiner 1958). It is known as biological-dynamic agriculture or simply bio-dynamic, the meaning being something like "life power" (Greek *dynamos* meaning power). The movement is much stronger in Europe than in America. Standards for growers have been set up there and products are marketed under a trademark. Today there are about 200 to 300 bio-dynamic farms in Germany, five-sixths of them run under contract with the bio-dynamic marketing organization. Supervision covers production, processing, and storage. Much marketing is on a regional basis. In Britain there are only about a dozen farms, half of which supply institutions. A one-year training course is now offered at Emerson College (Koepf 1976). In the United States, too, there are only a handful of 100 percent biodynamic farms. Nevertheless the influence is greater than these numbers would indicate, particularly in the area of composting. The American society, the Bio-dynamic Farming and Gardening Association, markets a "compost starter," a formula of bacteria and herbal extracts, that is widely used among organic farmers to initiate a controlled decomposition process in compost.

Bio-dynamic research is carried out in Europe by the national associations at research stations in Sweden, Germany and Switzerland. Results are published in the periodical *Lebendige Erde* (see von Wistinghausen 1977; Koepf *et al.* 1974). Some university research has also been done on test plots, and a partially state-funded experimental farm was set up in Switzerland in 1976 (which will also test other biological methods). In America, biodynamic research was carried on for many years under the leadership of the late Ehrenfried Pfeiffer (1938; 1962) and the association, which publishes a journal, *Bio-Dynamics*. Research in this country has focused on composting and non-chemical treatment of pests (Philbrick and Philbrick 1963; Philbrick and Gregg 1970).

Bio-dynamics is a way of life. The theology and social philosophy of Rudolf Steiner imply a certain relationship to society and to the land. Ideally, a bio-dynamic farm would be owner-managed and self-sufficient. There would be diversity in crops and at least two kinds of animals to provide balanced manure. A farmer should make a life-long commitment to his own piece of the earth, with which he must establish a close personal relationship. This personal relationship to his soil and plants and animals is important in productivity and quality. A farm should be a self-contained ecosystem. Outside interference is suspect, not because it is poisonous per se, but because it is from outside. Even such environmentally beneficial methods as imported predators may signify a less than perfect relationship between farmer and his land (Grotzke 1976).

Bio-dynamics lacks the confidence in "leaving things to nature" that is often found among organic buffs. The bio-dynamic goal is not to do what is natural, but to do what is best in terms of its philosophy. For top quality, man's strong intervention is necessary, but we must learn to do what is appropriate for working *with* nature (Pank 1976). Some bio-dynamic farmers are not as rigid in their abstinence from agricultural chemicals as organic farmers generally are.

Bio-dynamic farmers see themselves as participants in a mystical process of healing a mistreated earth and soil that have deteriorated in natural fertility due to years of neglect. One is reminded of monks in a medieval monastery praying for a degenerate society: If there are effects, they are not necessarily visible to the naked eye. However, crystallization methods have been developed that are used to distinguish food raised by different methods.

To stimulate life in the soil and in plants, bio-dynamic farmers use a series of herbal preparations on the plants and soil and in their compost. The extracts are so dilute that obvious physical effects appear unlikely. Still, significant increases in yield and quality have been observed. The approach is, in a way, analogous to that of homeopathic medicine, in which extreme dilutions are used to stimulate the body's natural defenses or life energy. The use of these preparations is a major distinguishing feature of bio-dynamic farming (Linder 1975). The old peasant practice of planting by the phases of the moon and planetary positions is appreciated, if not followed in large-scale operations (Grotzke 1976), and an effect on production has actually been documented (Chapter 10).

French Intensive Method. Developed by French market gardeners near Paris toward the end of the last century, the French intensive method involved the intensive use of a small area of land. Plants were placed close together in deeply cultivated, highly fertilized, raised beds, surrounded by fresh horse manure to protect against early spring frosts. Recently the method has been wedded to bio-dynamics and imported into California (Jeavons 1974). The approach flourished in a region where land prices were high and when transportation was still relatively costly. Despite recent increases in fuel costs, it is questionable whether there is as yet much potential for commercial farming. Research continues, and advocates believe that the yield will continue to increase to the point where returns will be commercially competitive.

Each raised bed covers about 154 square feet including paths so there are about 290 beds in an acre. Four hours per bed are required for initial preparation, which involves hand-digging to a depth of 12 inches and loosening the soil down another 12 inches, a total depth of two feet. This is 1,160 manhours of hard labor per acre. The time could be shortened by the use of subsoiling machinery, but such operations would presumably violate the method's principles. In following years, digging is, needless to say, easier, but must be repeated yearly. Yields per acre, once the garden is established, are impressive. Three to five times the conventional averages have been achieved, even higher for some vegetable crops (Jeavons 1976). Because of the large amount of labor, return on labor was less than $3 per hour in 1972, perhaps twice that with the higher yields achieved since then (Jeavons 1972). However, the compost is assumed to be free, and returns apparently consider only current year's labor, neglecting the initial investment.

Eco-agriculture. The ecological agriculture, or eco-agriculture, movement is closest to the mainstream of American agriculture. The guiding light came from William Albrecht, a soil scientist and professor at the University of Missouri, whose research focused on the dependence of plant and animal health on soil characteristics (Albrecht 1975). The message is carried by a monthly newspaper, *Acres, U.S.A.*, which first appeared in 1971. Eco-agriculture is thus the youngest alternative, at least as a formal movement. The readership is mainly farmers, in contrast to *Organic Gardening and Farming*.

The timing is of interest. The late 1960s saw the increasing restriction of organochlorine pesticides due to public pressure and decreased effectiveness. Their replacements are generally less persistent in the environment and the foodchain, but more toxic to the user, the farmer. The adverse effects tend to be quick and visible rather than subtle and long-term. The substitutes also tend to be more toxic to bees and beneficial predators, and can also exert harmful physiological effects on crop plants (USDA 1970).

Furthermore, 1970 saw the passage of the Occupational Safety and Health Act, which requires a hazard-free environment for all workers. Employers must keep records of work-related injuries and be available for periodic visits by federal inspectors (Wilson 1972). Since pesticide users tended to be more lax with hired help than with family members, implementation of the law tends to take away the advantage large-scale farmers had of exploiting worker ignorance. Increasing militancy and success of farmworkers' organizations has also hampered the large growers and made them more sensitive to farmworker health. All these developments have led to a transfer of costs of pesticide side-effects from society to the farmer. With costs internalized, the time was ripe for a movement such as eco-agriculture.

The ideological soil of ecological agriculture is grassroots populism. While there is concern for pollution and poor consumer health, much of the ire is saved for the influence of giant corporations on farmers (Walters 1975). There is an appeal to populist economics, which sees increased input use causing dependence on the industrial sector, overproduction of low-quality food, and resulting low prices for farmers. The farmer has been the victim of the corporate supersalesman and the university "Dr. Expert" whose advice has guided the farmer into high-cost production, high debt, and low profit. There has been a conspiracy of oil companies, chemical companies, and government advisors. This theme of conspiracy of other sectors of the economy to keep natural resource prices artificially low is also found in the steady-state economics of Herman Daly (1972). Daly also ties low resource prices to high throughput and high pollution rates.

Eco-agriculture advocates note that farmers have suffered from toxic pesticides, along with consumers and wildlife. The use of pesticides can be virtually eliminated if proper soil conditions are restored. This requires detailed soil testing, not just for the traditional few major elements and acid-alkaline balance, but for many elements, including the so-called trace minerals. The testing must evaluate the balance of these nutrients and the soil's capacity to hold and release nutrients. Fertilizer should be insoluble, but available to the plants by being held out to the root hairs, so to speak, by the humus in the soil. Chemical fertilizers may have a place, depending on the soil's capacity. Building humus, or adding humates, is thus a key feature of the fertilizer program. Balanced soil leads to healthy soil life, to healthy plant life, to higher quality crops, and to healthy animals living on the crops. All this leads to independence and healthy living for the farmer.

Reports from various sources indicate that at least some farmers are getting the message. Besides articles in *Acres, U.S.A.*, a survey of Nebraska organic farmers disclosed that many had changed over within the past decade (NLR 1975). Many Amish farmers come close to realizing the ideal of eco-agriculture. Being both frugal and in a close relation to their farmland, they tend to use only the minimum amount of imported chemicals. They are more likely to ask the extension agent's advice on a particular pest infestation than to simply carry out a spray program (Schwecker 1975).

Economic rationale of eco-agriculture. Of all the alternatives, the eco-agriculture approach appears to have the best prospects in this country. The appeal is in a language and philosophy that farmers understand and appreciate. From a social cost point of view, the hard line on chemical pesticides and the soft line on fertilizer makes some sense. The damage from introducing a hazardous chemical appears to be directly proportional to the amount. Some biologists believe that one molecule can cause a mutation; carcinogens appear to be additive. Assuming that residues are proportional to the amount used, even a small amount would presumably increase the health hazard by a corresponding amount (Carper 1970). On the other hand, small amounts of chemical fertilizers are likely to have only a limited effect upon the environment, depending on external effects of production and also on the extent of erosion. Soils have a certain capacity to absorb or tie up fertilizer. But as amounts of soluble nitrogen are increased, a certain limit is exceeded, depending on soil conditions; and more and more is lost to surface and ground water (Welch *et al.* 1972).

The main features of costs and benefits of fertilizer use as a function of application rate are shown in Figure 7-1. As in Figure 4-2 analyzing pesticide use, the upper portion shows total costs and total benefits, measured as yield times price, the total value product. The lower graph shows marginal or incremental costs and marginal value product (that is, the slopes of the upper graphs). Farmers probably use too much fertilizer, as well as pesticides, so that existing use, Q^e, is greater than the use in markets with perfect information, Q^c. (Actual use varies widely.) The social optimum is even less, because of the pollution generated after a

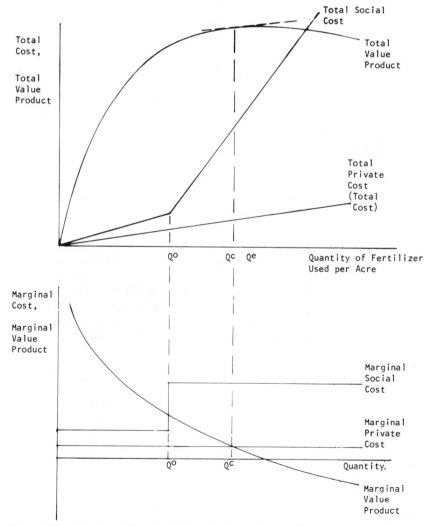

Q^o = Optimal Quantity

Q^c = Quantity in Perfectly Competitive Markets

Q^e = Existing Quantity

Figure 7-1. Total and Marginal Value Product and Cost for Fertilizer Use

certain critical level of use. But note that this critical level is very likely to be the social optimum and, in practice, may not be much less than the amount actually used (see Chapter 3). This coincidence of the social optimum and the critical level arises because of the shape of the cost curves. (Note that we are considering pollution effects only.) Note the differences between the curves in Figure 7-1 and Figure 4-2. Total social cost of fertilizer use is small until a certain critical level is exceeded. With pesticides, on the other hand, costs rise regularly from the start.

A consideration of benefits reinforces the difference between fertilizer and pesticides. The benefits of using small amounts of fertilizer are large. Pesticides, on the other hand, exhibit a threshhold effect, and their total value has a sigmoid form (Carlson 1971). Or small amounts may even have a negative effect if beneficial predators are affected more than the target pest. Excessive amounts of either chemical yield negative returns (Figures 4-2 and 7-1).

Thus, for levels of application where fertilizers are most beneficial, damage is minimal. The reverse is true of pesticides. As benefits increase, social costs also increase. So the double standard of eco-agriculture makes economic sense. A minimum amount of pesticides must be used before any benefits accrue; but such use will be accompanied by some increase in human and/or environmental damage. A small use of fertilizer, on the other hand, will have a comparatively large impact on crop production with negligible environmental damage. In other words, eco-farmers are seeking maximum productivity while at the same time minimizing adverse impact on humans and on the environment.

Pesticides and organic farming. Organic farmers do use some highly toxic chemicals, some not of plant origin, for particularly difficult jobs, such as copper fungicides in grape production. Mined sulfur dust is a common "organic" fungicide. Similarly, Stoddard's solvent, a light oil, one of the light "fractions" of petroleum distillation, is used to kill weeds among carrots. If no weed-killers are used, a great deal of hand weeding is necessary. A few purists do hand weed, but most use the herbicide. Organic farmers generally believe that Stoddard's solvent is ecologically sound because no noticeable harm is done to soil life and no allergic or other adverse reactions appear in humans who eat the food. In any event, Stoddard's solvent is not absorbed by the carrot and other members of the carrot family (King 1966), and the critical time for use is early in the season. Much the same could be said about other agricultural chemicals. But for an organic farmer to resort to chemicals, the benefits must be very high.

A related issue is the toxicity of natural pesticides themselves. In some cases natural poisons are more highly toxic than commonly used chemical pesticides. Nicotine is more toxic to warmblooded animals than many of the organochlorine pesticides. And strychnine has a toxicity comparable to that of parathion, a common organophosphorus pesticide that is highly toxic to humans. Sometimes natural pesticides are extracted from plants using poisonous chemicals that may leave residues. Strychnine is extracted from *Strychnos nux vomica*, by using benzene as a solvent (Martin 1968).

Organic Agriculture

In 1976 an International Federation of Organic Agriculture Movements was formed. Headquarters are in Oberwil, Switzerland, at the new Research Institute for Biological Husbandry. A newsletter reports activities and research on a worldwide basis. Their research group's first international conference was held in Switzerland in October 1977 (IFOAM 1977).

Although working together, the alternative agriculture schools do differ in philosophy, goals and constraints ideally imposed. All assert that quality is more important than quantity, and lay claim to generating high quality food, though not necessarily outstanding in appearance. There is a general rejection of chemical pesticides and an emphasis on building a healthy soil. In the light of the continuum of practice and philosophy, it is understandable that organic farmers' organizations in this country are currently involved in some debate over what exactly organic food *is* and what practices ought to be required, recommended, or rejected (see, for example, Harnish 1976). The main area of disagreement is fertilization.

The American organic movement seeks high levels of physical nutrients in plant and human nutrition, the megavitamin approach. What is natural is good, and the more the better. This is, however, not necessarily true. Natural mushrooms may be poisonous; natural soil conditions may be inhospitable to crops; and natural sewage sludge may contain poisonous heavy metals. An "organic" farmer used 25 tons of chicken manure slurry per acre; as a result, the soil contained so much nitrogen that his crops grew too lush and fell over (OGF undated). This is really land disposal of feedlot waste, not crop growing. The nitrate content of such crops is often at toxic levels (Wilkinson and Stuedemann 1974). The implicit goal of such an approach is to maximize production under the constraint of using only substances derived from natural materials by non-chemical means.

Other approaches are more holistic, believing that quality life can be obtained with *less* nutrients under proper growing conditions. The eco-agriculture approach may be characterized as seeking to maximize animal or human feed value under the constraint of zero release of potentially toxic substances into humans or the environment. The farmer must also show a profit. At the other end of the spectrum are bio-dynamics and European organic organizations that believe that some kind of non-material quality of the food may be as important as actual nutrient content.

The differences among the alternatives are far less than their differences with conventional agriculture. First, with regard to the use of chemicals, the eco-agriculture approach is the most flexible, yet the constraints of zero release and limited dependence on giant corporations means drastic reductions in chemicals used, particularly pesticides, and a very wary, conservative outlook toward chemicals in general. Although some farmers may use chemical fertilizer and consider themselves ecofarmers, for the most part the main manufactured fertilizers, NPK, are replaced by manure, soil amendments, and crushed rock. In particular, strong, fast-acting nitrogen fertilizers like anhydrous ammonia are avoided. Some farmers may use chemicals to supply trace minerals, while others use only seaweed. The difference does not appear large. Out of this confluence we may construct a composite "organic agriculture" that will be used throughout this study and, in fact, has been implicitly assumed in the previous chapters.

A general definition of organic food is food "which has not been subjected to [chemical] pesticides or artificial [chemically treated, fast-acting] fertilizers and which has been grown in soil whose humus content has been increased by the addition of organic matter" (Leverton 1974; also see Johnson 1974). Organic farming is the raising of such food. The main characteristics are the constraints of zero use of chemical pesticides and artifical fertilizers. Ecological agriculture may allow judicious use of either, and presents a middle ground. But it is a middle ground that lies far closer to organic farming in philosophy and practice. The purpose of this study is to examine the feasibility of organic farming as the term is generally used, that is, zero use of chemicals, rather than zero release. Since organic farmers also use chemicals on occasion, the differences between organic and ecological are in degree, not kind.

Organic farming also requires regional diversity because of the need for manure fertilizer and crop rotation. Also, many advocates believe that crops should be produced and consumed locally. This belief is based on considerations of freshness, and attunement to a local natural environment. Thus, monoculture is rejected for reasons of consumer taste as well as more practical considerations. A bias is introduced against large-scale industrial farming for that reason and also because large economies of scale are less apparent in mixed farming.

Organic Farming and the Critique
of Conventional Agriculture

In earlier chapters we identified a number of market failures associated with conventional agriculture. These failures arise from the fact that conventional agriculture need not take account of its effects on the environment (except as forced by law); from hidden dimensions of food quality; and from the distribution of resources among the present inhabitants of the world and between us and future generations. Critics of conventional agriculture have also questioned the role of man as both exploiter (of other creatures) and exploited (treated as an input to the system rather than as purely an end in himself). Organic farming provides an alternative which meets most of these criticisms.

Pollution. Organic farming avoids the use of the major pollutants from conventional agriculture: large quantities of nitrogen and phosphate fertilizers and chemical pesticides. Furthermore, replacing these fertilizers with human, animal and food processing wastes has the effect of indirectly reducing their burden on the nation's water. Farm and regional diversification also reduces the environmental impact of such runoff as does occur. Since less energy is used in crop production, the environment benefits indirectly from less energy-related pollution. Regional diversity also means less energy required in the transportation stage. However, the restriction on pesticide use may mean *more* regional specialization with some crops.

Food quality. Since organic farmers avoid the use of chemical pesticides, hormones, and antibiotics (except for specific illnesses), residues from these substances are no longer a danger. Excessive nitrogen fertilization is improbable with a diversified organic agriculture, so that high nitrogen concentrations in food are unlikely. Fresh, organically raised, locally produced food has a higher nutritional value than preserved, chemically raised, imported food. Organic fertilization may add some other quality dimension to food that is lacking when chemical fertilizers are used. The closeness of farmer and consumer tends to overcome the alienation of spatial and vertical distance down the marketing chain, so that the consumer's welfare is more likely to be considered in farmer decisions.

These values must be balanced, however, against the increasing possibility of damaged appearance due to insects and possible lower yields.

Temporal and intergenerational equity. Since less cultural energy is used in production and also. in transportation, organic farming's impact on the resource base is reduced. In fact, the goal of organic farming is self-sufficiency, with any energy needed on the farm coming from solar and wind power, or from farm sources (cellulose, methane). These circumstances would maximize intergenerational equity, in the sense of minimizing non-renewable resource use during each generation. There is a second impact on future generations that is produced by the close contact of man and land. When land is viewed as merely an input into a production function, conventional economic analysis implies that it may be optimal to destroy the resource base if this maximizes near-term profits (unless a zero rate of discounting the future is used). Thus it is "economical" to overgraze, neglect contour plowing, and allow the natural fertility to decline. When an enduring relationship between man and land is established, a sense of responsibility grows that extends beyond profit maximization (see McCarthy 1973). Further, if a man believes that a piece of the earth is going to be the means of livelihood for his children and their children, as well as for himself—that is, this is one piece of earth that belongs to him and to his family forever (as in the entail system)—he is more likely to establish a regime of steady or even increasing fertility, rather than profit maximization. Organic farmers take pride in leaving the earth a little better than they found it (cf., Pfeiffer 1947).*

There is another side to the matter of temporal equity, however. A turn to organic agriculture in the developed nations would in some ways benefit them at the expense of the underdeveloped. This shift in benefits would occur because the former, which include the major food exporters, would benefit from less environmental damage. Also the agricultural sector would benefit from any higher prices resulting from lower output, since the overall demand for food is comparatively insensitive to price (inelastic demand). For the same reasons, underdeveloped nations would suffer relative loss in welfare, paying higher prices for food imports, and perhaps be driven to use more chemicals to grow their own.

Man's place in the universe. In organic farming, man is viewed as seeking to bring forth the potential of each natural feature, plant and animal. Man has a preeminent place in creation, not as exploiter, but as husbandman. Through his close relations with soil, plants, and animals, humans obtain a sensitivity for an appropriate value and place for each element. These values are constantly weighed in the human mind, acting as an analog computer if you will, seeking to bring all into a harmonious and productive relationship. Likewise, man himself is not viewed merely as an input to the industrial system. The organic farmer believes that living and working as he does is good for the soul, good for his own life and for the lives of his family members. Within this context of human values, there is a role for machines, but not a preeminent one. In the words of the Indian Coomaraswamy (undated, quoted in Schumacher 1973), "The craftsman himself can always, if allowed to, draw the delicate distinction between the machine [which eliminates the human element] and the tool [which enhances a man's skill and power]."

---

*This same principle could be applied to our public lands. Each citizen could be given the ownership of his own particular piece of land, but with no rights of exploitation, only of preservation and enjoyment. Though rights of exploitation were still held by the public through government agencies, the private ownership would be a means of focusing attention on the implications of particular decisions. You would feel far differently if you knew that *your* acre of national forest was going to be clear-cut, than simply knowing that *some* was.

It must be emphasized that a simple return to traditional farming practice is neither organic farming nor a solution to our ecological problems. Lands that once supported great civilizations are now virtual deserts. Parts of America, too, suffer from worn-out or eroded soils.

The return to a smaller-scale, family-type farming structure would encourage a repopulation of the countryside. Many city dwellers would be only too happy for the opportunity. Nevertheless, we cannot castigate large-scale farming for forcing people off the land because it breaks up human relations and institutions, and then in the next breath advocate mass migration in the opposite direction. A policy that aimed toward stabilization and gradual population dispersion might be appropriate, however.

8 Retail Markets for Organic Food

Organic food is being produced and consumed in this country in quantities which are only a very small percentage of total food consumption. Retail prices of organic food tend to be far higher than prices for conventional food, giving an impression that organic food is expensive to produce. In this chapter we will first look at the growth in organic food sales and the main features of the health food industry which supplies it. We will note why retail prices of organic food are far higher than those for conventional food, and show why this is not related to production cost. Then we will look at the consumer's side: why some consumers purchase organic food, why the demand has grown, and why it is unlikely to continue to grow at past rates.

Organic Food Sales and Prices

No estimates are available of the amount of organic food sold directly to consumers from farms, farm stands and farmers' markets. Some data are available on food sold by so-called "health food" stores, from a recent industry survey. In the spring of 1976, an industry magazine, *Health Foods Business*, took a survey covering 4 percent of independent stores, and also checked responses against those of 850 stores connected with large retail chains which were not included in their summaries (HFB 1976). The independent stores' total sales for 1975 were estimated at $550 million. This compares with another estimate of $600 million for 1974 total industry sales (Colamosca 1974), up from an estimated $100 million in 1970. In the late 1960s, industry sales were growing at an annual rate of 30 percent a year. Sales more than doubled between 1970 and 1972 (Wright 1972), and the number of stores increased from 1200 in 1968 to 3000 in

1972. Since then the growth rate has declined to its earlier pace. Growth tends to come in spurts, associated with consumer fads, superimposed upon a steady upward climb. Recent interest has been associated with increased ecological awareness of the early 1970s and periodic revelations of chemical residue incidents.

Organic food sales and margins. Average health food store sales, markups, and gross margins are shown in Table 8-1, together with margins for similar items in supermarkets. In wholesale and retail trade, "markup" refers to the difference between retail price and cost of goods purchased as a percent

Table 8-1 Health Food Store Sales, Markups and Margins Compared with Supermarket Margins

	Health Food Store			Supermarket
Product	Sales (percent total)	Markup (percent cost)	Margin (percent sales)	Margin (percent sales)
Non-food				
Vitamins	39.5	85	46	
Books	5.1	54	35	
Cosmetics	3.7	64	39	
Appliances	2.7	59	37	
Miscellaneous	0.9	89	53	
Total Non-food	51.9			
Food				
Nuts	8.0	54	35	23
Herbs	6.0	56	36	
Grains	5.7	52	34	
Snacks	4.5	54	35	23
Fruit (mostly dried)	4.4	52	34	22
Dairy	4.0	48	29	17
Juices	3.5	52	34	19
Meats	3.4	47	32	21
Baked goods	2.3	43	30	20
Produce	1.4	45	31	35
Other groceries	3.8	54	35	
Diet foods	1.3	52	34	25
Total food	48.3			
Total	100.2			
Average		65	39	
Average food		52	34	21

Sources: Health Food, HFB 1976; Supermarket, PG 1975a.

of purchase price. Gross margin is the same difference expressed as a percent of selling price, so that gross margin is a smaller quantity. Gross margin is frequently simply called margin, and is distinguished from net margin or profit (NCFM 1966a). In the health food and organic food business, however, the terms have been amalgamated, so that what health food stores commonly report as "markup" is really gross margin. Thus in the issue of *Health Food Business*, from which Table 8-1 is taken, the average "markup" is reported as 39 percent. This figure is really the average gross margin, however, the average markup being 65 percent (39 / (100 . 39). It is certainly understandable that, burdened as it is with comparatively large margins, the industry would seek to have the smaller figure associated with the word "markup." Some would call it misleading. At any rate, the words will be used in this study in their generally accepted meanings.

Some 40 percent of health food store sales are vitamins; slightly less than half of sales are food products. Margins vary considerably, being highest on vitamins and lowest on produce and baked goods. Gross margins for health food stores are generally higher than for supermarkets, although margins for produce are lower. In health food stores, produce is carried as a service to customers or as a loss leader, depending on the perspective.

Most food items in health food stores are sold as "natural" foods, which is not the same thing as organic food. The word "natural" means that no chemicals were added in processing, but implies nothing about how the food was grown. In the Washington, D.C.,area, much of the grain and grain products (baked goods, snacks) are organically raised. Some fruit and juice and most of the produce are organically raised, but most nuts, herbs, dairy products and meats are differentiated primarily on the basis of processing rather than farming method. (Meat is raised without hormones.) To produce a sale in a health food store, it is necessary to differentiate your product from comparable products in the supermarket. Often "unfiltered" or "unpreserved" is sufficient for processed foods. The added cost of using organically grown produce would not attract sufficient increase in consumer demand to make it worth the trouble and/or cost. Most conventional stores carry some type of whole grain bread. Thus, effective differentiation requires "organically grown" on the label. A rough estimate of between 10 and 20 percent of health food sales is labeled organically grown (produce, 1.4 percent; baked goods, 2.3; grains, 5.7; dried fruit, 4.4; some other groceries, 3.8; some snacks).

Is food labeled "organically grown" really raised in that way? Only the farmer knows for sure. Fraud is admittedly a problem in the industry, particularly with the sales boom of the early 1970s. Laboratory testing can sometimes detect chemical residues, but such testing is expensive and cannot offer positive proof. Some consumers are allergic to residues. But in the absence of a strict certification program, most people cannot tell the difference between two products with identical taste and external appearance. (Organic food consumers often claim their food tastes better, but this may reflect freshness.)

The situation is complicated by a common practice among organic produce dealers. Dealers often "fill in" with the "best available" produce, including conventionally raised produce from the local commercial wholesale market. This practice exists because retail health food stores need a steady supply of produce. The poorly developed organic produce markets cannot presently supply this year-round demand. Of course one of the reasons for weak demand at the farm level is just this practice of filling in! As long as health food consumers are satisfied with conventional produce in off-seasons, there will be no development of organic sources in Mexico. Health food store patrons often place a high value on appearance. If organic celery doesn't have broad stalks, it doesn't sell. If top quality organic produce is not available, retailers may prefer commercial substitutes. While wholesalers report that they make it clear when substitutions are being made, retailers and consumers often express ignorance of the practice. Thus, except for freshness, much food purchased as "organic" is identical to that found at nearby supermarkets. Because of the practice of "filling in," we should be conservative in estimating sales of organic food. In highly developed markets with certification programs, as found in most grain and bean markets, mistaken identity appears less of a problem.

Taking everything into consideration, we may estimate commercial organic food sales through health food stores to be about 10 percent of $600 million or $60 million in 1975. This is about one-sixth of one percent of total United States food sales of $38 billion in 1975 (USDA 1975a). This estimate is biased downward because it does not include sales through natural food stores, which have also been increasing rapidly since the early 1970s. These stores are generally run by members of the so-called counterculture, with their primary motivation being service rather than profit. No estimates are available of their sales, but in some areas they probably are comparable to those of the traditional health food stores or greater. On the other hand, organic food carries a higher price tag than conventional food, so that percent of sales overstates organic food's share of production.

Prices. Some organic food is sold at prices comparable to those of conventional food, particularly in season produce. But most prices are higher, often twice as high or more. In 1972, the United States Department of Agriculture surveyed organic and natural food prices in the Washington, D.C. area. A "market basket" of 29 food items was found to cost $21.90 at the health food stores, and $11 for the comparable conventional food in a supermarket. Prices in the health food section of a supermarket and in a natural foods store were somewhat less than in the health food store, $20.30 and $17.80, respectively (USDA 1972). The health food store price is a better reflection of the actual cost of such foods to the consumer, however. The organic foods section was a comparatively new addition for supermarkets, and markups were lower to stimulate sales. The natural food stores are run by counterculture people who take lower incomes than their skill could demand elsewhere, in order to bring what they consider to be high-quality food to the people they wish to serve. Since part of their salary is in satisfaction, the prices are lower. These stores also choose low-rent areas and much food is sold in bulk, so that overhead costs are not comparable to those of supermarkets. Natural foods stores generally don't have the high profits from vitamins to subsidize the other lines.

Since the health food stores are not selling all organic food, their prices would presumably be even higher if they were. A reasonable estimate of the difference between organically raised and conventionally raised food at retail thus appears to be about twice as much. This large difference is responsible for a widespread belief that it is far more expensive to raise food organically than conventionally. This, however, is not a valid conclusion. Most of the differences have little to do with farm production costs. The main reasons for the differences are scale economies in processing, transportation, and retailing, and brand loyalty or quality differences, particularly at the processing stage.

(1) Processing costs. Small-batch processing and small plants characterize the natural foods industry. For example, the largest eastern producer of organic apple juice processes a maximum of 23,000 cases per year, compared to over a million for a nearby commercial competitor (Tap-an-Apple vs. Lehigh). Economies of scale in food processing depend on the industry. Table 8-2 shows the increased production costs for firms with plant capacity a given percent less than the minimum efficient scale (scale at which unit costs reach a minimum) for five major food processing industries. The increased cost associated with small plant size varies from 1 to 16 percent. Smaller plants than those considered in this survey could be at even greater cost disadvantage.

(2) Transportation costs. The markets for organic food are small and scattered, necessitating shipments of small quantities. Table 8-3 shows the cost per 100 pounds of shipping processed food from Harrisburg, Pennsylvania, which is near a number of organic foods processers and wholesalers, and Washington, D.C. The cost to ship 500 pounds is almost ten times the cost to ship a full truckload of 40,000 pounds, a difference of almost 5 cents per pound. For example, a case of canned tomatoes, shipping weight 30 pounds for 24 cans, would cost a Washington, D.C. store about $6.30 at Walnut Acres in Pennsylvania, but the shipping charge would be about 7 cents per can (assuming at least 300 pounds were ordered), which

Table 8-2   Production Cost Increases for Food Processing Firms with
            Capacities Below the Minimum Efficient Scale

Industry	Minimum Efficient Scale (million $ sales per year)	Percent Increase in Production Costs at Given Percent of Optimum Size	
		25 Percent	10 Percent
Meatpacking	6 to 40	0.5	1.0
Poultry dressing	0.1 to 60	3.1	5.3
Fluid milk	0.2 to 8.8	3.2	7.5
Frozen vegetables	1 to 8	12.0	
Bread products	0.1 to 8	16.0	

Source: NCFM 1966b.

Table 8-3   Truck Shipping Class Rates
            Harrisburg, Pa. to Washington, D.C., June 1976

Weight Range (lbs)	Shipping Cost per 100 lbs ($)	
	Not on Pallet	On Pallet[a]
Minimum charge	15.10[b]	
Under 500	5.50	
500 to 1,000	4.61	
1,000 to 2,000	3.65	
2,000 to 5,000	3.31	
5,000 to truckload	2.53	
Truckload		
24,000	0.89	0.83
36,000	0.76	0.71
40,000	0.72	0.66

[a]Shipper loads and unloads if on pallet.
[b]If special pickup, an additional charge of $2.50 is made.

Source: Mid-Atlantic Conference Motor Carriers.

would make up some 14 percent of the retail price. ($6.30 / 24 = 26¢; 26¢ + 7¢ = 33¢; 33¢ × 1.53 = 50¢ selling price.)

When shipping by truck from California, the difference between large and small shipments is even greater, as can be seen from Table 8-4. This time, the cost difference between shipping 100 pounds and the largest shipment is over 10 cents a pound, 14 cents if the shipper loads and unloads.

Much fresh produce is shipped from California to eastern states. Since organic produce is not waxed or otherwise preserved, much must be flown. Air freight accounts for 14 cents per pound (June 1976, up from 11 cents in March 1976), or about 27 percent of the price of a head of lettuce. Truck freight costs about two-thirds of the air-freight cost (ERS 1976; Table 8-4).

(3) Quality differences and brand loyalty. The health food industry is dominated by a few food processors with strong brand loyalty developed either over many years in the business and/or through strong positive associations in the consumer's mind with purity, wholesomeness, and supernutrition. Consumer demand is made more inelastic by the small percentage of a consumer's budget that is spent in health food stores. The average purchase is a little over $8 (HFB 1976), so that the average food purchase runs about half as much or $4. This is only 20 percent of the average consumer's food budget of about $20 per week per capita (USDA 1975a), and even less compared to the higher food budgets of the middle and upper income health food customers. Prices reflect the high demand for certain brands. For example, between 1969 and 1971, the price for Tigers Milk Cookies jumped from 69 cents to $1.19 per package (Lichtenstein 1971). Retail prices for organic peanut butter are given in Table 8-5. Even after deducting a transportation cost difference of 7 cents per pound from the national brand prices, they are still higher than the local brand, Apocalyptic. To be fair, however, it must be noted that the national brands may in fact offer higher quality, for example, using fresher, higher quality peanuts, with a higher probability of being truly organic.

(4) Small-scale retailers. Most of the health food stores are small "mom and pop" operations, reflecting the low level of demand for these foods. Even when demand is high enough for larger scale operations, small scale still seems to typify the health food retailers. The average store has 1,200 square feet, about two-thirds selling area, one-third storage; and sales of a little over $140,000, compared to average sales in large supermarkets of around $5 million (PG 1975a). On the average, each health food store has 2.5 competitors (HFB 1976). Sales per square foot of selling area average $180, about the same as that of supermarkets, $175.

From Table 8-1, we find the gross margins of health food stores averaging 39 percent. Gross margins of supermarket chains average 21

Table 8-4   Truck Shipping Class Rates, Los Angeles
            to Washington, D.C., June 1976

Weight Range (lbs)	Shipping Cost ($)	
	Minimum Charge	Rate per 100 lbs
0 to 99	2106.00	∞ to 21.30
100 to 149	2473.00	24.73 to 16.60
150 to 200	3157.00	21.00 to 15.80
200 to 500		15.20
500 to 1,000		14.00
1,000 to 2,000		12.59
2,000 to 5,000		11.42
5,000 to 10,000		10.48
10,000 to 20,000		10.27
20,000 and over (on pallet)[a]		6.87

[a]Shipper loads and unloads.

Source: Consolidated Freightways.

Table 8-5   Retail Bulk and Jar Peanut Butter Prices, Washington, D.C.
            June 1976

Brand and Origin	Natural Food Store		Health Food Store Jar ($/lb)	Supermarket Jar ($/lb)
	Bulk ($/lb)	Jar ($/lb)		
Deaf Smith (Texas)	1.10	1.38[a]	1.42[a]	1.32[a]
Erewhon (Mass.)	1.10	1.50	1.56	-
Walnut Acres (Pa.)	0.99	1.50	-	-
Apocalyptic (Md.)	0.79	0.97[b]		
Shedd's	-	-	1.63	-

[a]Per pound based on 1.125 pound jar.
[b]Plastic container instead of glass jar.

Source: Survey by author.

percent; independent supermarkets, who do not have their own warehousing facilities, average 19 percent (PG 1975b). Health food stores' margins are far higher. Even if non-food items, mainly vitamins, are eliminated, margins of health food stores average 34 percent, more than half again as large as independent supermarkets.

From an efficiency point of view, it is not fair to compare the small health food store with supermarkets. A better comparison is with convenience stores, whose gross margins run about 29 percent (PG 1975b), still much less than the health food store's 39 percent. The higher gross margin is not necessarily a reflection of excessive profits. There are no significant barriers to entering the health food business. Stores are highly differentiated by the personnel, however. Consumers are presumably getting what they pay for: personalized service, advice, and perhaps inventory control for freshness (cf. Colamosca 1974). In a market where consumers do not trust expert advice (in fact, that is why they are *in* the market), confidence in a knowledgeable proprietor is crucial.

Not only do organic foods carry higher margins at retail, but these margins are usually on top of the wholesaler's margin. Supermarket chains have integrated backwards into wholesaling, which contributes only about 2 percent to their gross margins. Independent wholesalers have gross margins that range from about 5.5 to 8.0 percent, with an average of 6.6 (PG 1975b). But organic food wholesalers commonly have a 25 percent gross margin. This makes the total markup between farm or processor and consumer to be 84 percent for food products $(1.33 \times 1.39 \cdot 1 = 0.84)$.

Health food stores and natural foods wholesalers do some food processing (rebagging of bulk items) and some direct buying from producers. But so do supermarket chains. Still, the higher markup at wholesale also does not necessarily mean excess profits or inefficiency. Organic wholesalers do more of their own transporting of food products than their commercial counterparts do. And inventory control and spoilage loss may be more of a problem if preservatives are avoided. The point we wish to make is not that organic merchants are charging excessive amounts for their services. They may well be only covering their costs. What should be clear is that retail prices of organic food do not give a very good impression of production costs.

(5) State marketing orders. Federal law allows growers associations in a region to set standards for marketing produce grown in their area. These "marketing orders" may include requirements for chemical treatment. Such requirements forced a large organic date grower out of business in the 1940s. Present citrus marketing orders for Florida make it impossible to ship citrus out of state in larger than one or two box quantities. Eastern consumers must buy in individual boxes, or pay the higher freight from California.

In conclusion, while prices are generally much higher for organic food, this premium is not primarily a reflection of higher production costs. Rather, the high consumer prices are a result of higher transportation, processing and retailing costs, plus some brand loyalty. Production costs may be higher, but most of the retail difference can be accounted for by these other factors.

Eco-food. The above conclusion would appear to weaken the argument for an intermediate-priced food line using ecologically sound growing techniques, but not fully organic methods (Fryer and Simmons 1972). Such a product line would be differentiated from both conventional and organic food, a suggested label being "eco-food." One supermarket chain *is* already marketing a kind of eco-food. Contracting directly with growers, the Swiss Migros chain now offers two lines of food side-by-side in their stores. Introduced in 1977, their "Migros Sano" line is priced the same as conventional food both at farm and at retail. (Eco-growers do get purchase priority.) Of domestic produce, about 35 percent of their apples and 70 percent of their vegetables are grown in this manner (Palasthy 1977).

Since most shoppers are still insensitive to the quality dimensions of interest to health food consumers, one of the main effects of introducing another line of non-conventional food would be to fragment the market for organic foods and raise distribution, processing, and retailing costs. If the cost differential was really a matter of production costs, eco-food might make some sense. But with the large economies of scale in distribution, further market fragmentation is more likely to raise prices than lower them. The whole of conventional agriculture could, however, be turned over to producing "eco-food." This is more of a viable policy option than encouraging product proliferation in a market already burdened with the higher costs of moving small quantities. (For a similar argument relating to marketing cigarettes, see Tennant 1971.)

The Organic Food Consumer

The demand for conventional food is primarily a matter of price (Colamosca 1974). Quality, particularly appearance and avoidance of signs of deterioration, are important. But most supermarkets have a policy of keeping only good-looking produce on display, so that factor is for the most part eliminated from consumer choice.

Some organic food consumers are, on the other hand, virtually insensitive to price; that is, their demand for organic food is almost completely price inelastic. These are the few individuals, making up a minority in a minority, who have recognized allergic reactions to chemical residues. Most consumers, however, have some sensitivity to price, as there are alternatives, namely, conventionally raised food. The quantity demanded is then a function of both the price and the degree to which the product meets the purchaser's standards of quality.

The organic food consumer perceives food as jointly consumed with other goods and services, particularly medical care (believing that natural is healthier), environmental quality, farm animal welfare, farmer welfare, probably in that order (cf. Darling 1973). For the organic food consumer, food is a differentiated product, along these other quality dimensions. In addition to being organically raised, organic food often has two other quality dimensions that differentiate it from conventional food: freshness and physical proximity of the grower.

Organic food must be preserved by cold, heat, drying, physical isolation from pests, and/or traditional processing methods like canning or pickling. Or else food must be consumed quickly. While chemical preservation may prevent deterioration in appearance, flavor is another matter. It is commonly thought by organic food consumers that organically raised food has a better flavor. Flavor is largely subjective, however. Consumers in general now prefer canned tomato juice to bottled because of the tinny flavor added by the cans. Likewise, some consumers of conventional food may have grown to prefer the flavor changes induced by chemical pesticides, or the bland taste of watery vegetables. Further, it is virtually impossible to separate production methods from freshness, for commonly available foods. Thus, consumer experience is not necessarily a good guide here. Perhaps it is better to describe the second dimension as flavor rather then freshness, keeping in mind that opinions about flavor are often subjective.

Locally raised vegetables and some fruit are available in most regions in season. Such produce is often not available at local health food or natural food stores. These stores find that the dependability of a year-round supply of produce from California outweighs the less dependable in-season low price of local suppliers. Local organic growers are also affected by the upsurge in home gardening, especially for such crops as tomatoes, lettuce and squash. Dependability is the same reason given by supermarket chains, an ironic twist to the organic food market. Thus, during summer months, organic food consumers often have the choice of either California (probably) organic or local non-organic produce. California has well-developed organic food markets. So it is possible that the dependence on California produce is a transitional characteristic, due to small scale and underdeveloped local markets in other parts of the country. California may have a comparative advantage for organic food production, however. Much of the land is irrigated, allowing easier control of weeds, the great bane of organic farmers.

Consumers can, of course, search out their own local supply sources, and many do. Most of the regional organic food organizations are composed of both farmers and consumers, and one of their main functions is an informational one, linking potential buyers with potential sellers. Generally, farmers and gardeners are listed by address and food products offered. (Information on these groups is available from Rodale Press, Emmaus, Pennsylvania.)

Critics often imply that organic food consumers have fallen victim to irrational fears. About the least pejorative term applied to them is "natural food buffs," implying a taste for a rather exotic item, such as model railroads or Ming vases. To imply that the purchase of a differentiated product is somehow irrational because it costs more displays a paradoxical lack of trust in the consumer's own judgment to know what pleases him most, that is, what mix of goods and services maximizes his utility. It is only human to laud consumers when they make judgments that we ourselves would have made, and condemn other decisions as "irrational." But if differentiated products bring satisfaction, this justifies their production. Further, there *is* a rationale for organic food consumption, based for the most part on considerations discussed in Chapters 3 and 4.

While it is more efficient from a production economics point of view for the economy to generate standardized products, this does not necessarily maximize consumer satisfaction. It would be cheaper to clothe the American population in green pajamas like the Chinese Communists, but it would hardly maximize consumer satisfaction. Likewise, there are consumers who prefer organic food and are willing to pay a high price for it. The attempt to portray organic food consumers as irrational can be viewed as either a prejudice against differentiated products, a promotional ploy of purveyors of conventional food, or a lack of understanding of the issues. In a free society there is no reason to discourage consumption unless it involves a threat to the consumer's well-being, with which he is incapable of dealing. All consumers are presumably rational in the sense of acting in their own best interests as they see them. Heavy smokers may be killing themselves, but the current pleasure outweighs the threat to future well-being.

The annual per capita expenditure on food is about \$1,000 (CEA 1976). If solely organic food were purchased, a consumer would spend on the order of twice this amount, or \$2,000, assuming the same or similar food items were purchased. Most health food consumers are on the continuum between these extremes. Their satisfaction is highest, given their available choices and incomes, when they purchase some of each kind of food. Economists like to show this situation by a diagram, such as Figure 8-1. Point P represents consumption of F_o^* units of organic food and F_c^* units of conventional food (units in pounds, cans, crates). Each consumer is assumed to have tastes for organic food which can be described by sets of purchases between which he is indifferent, called indifference curves. The health food consumer has a set of indifference curves, $\{IC_H\}$, for which the highest level of satisfaction for a \$1,000 food budget, Budget Line 1, comes at point P. F_c' is the amount of conventional food that can be purchased for $1,000, and is the optimal consumption pattern, P', of the conventional food consumer with indifference curves, [IC_c]. The health food consumer may wish to increase his food budget to Budget Line 2, in which case he will probably increase his consumption of both organic and conventional food, finding a new optimum at P''.

Purchasing organic food is not a matter of irrationality. It is just as rational as any other purchase. In this case, a weighing of risks of future illness against current satisfactions is made. The decision of whether or not to smoke cigarettes involves similar considerations.

Demand Growth

With demand for organic food growing at 30 percent a year, it might appear that there is little need to be concerned about side-effects of conventional farming. After all, at this rate, we would soon all be eating organic food. Advocates of organic food have cited this high growth rate as evidence that we are rapidly becoming an "organic America," as the Rodale people are fond of putting it. A 30 percent rate is indeed rapid. A simple mathematical calculation shows that, if that rate were to continue, in 23 years, half of our food would have to be organically raised; and in 26 years, 100 percent.* But it appears highly unlikely that such a heady growth rate can be maintained, especially if we explore the basis for such growth.

Perhaps the least controversial quality dimension of organic food is the comparative freedom from chemical residues. The wide use of chemicals in modern society virtually guarantees that no food will be entirely free from contamination. However, organically raised food does not receive a direct application, so on the average a lower residue burden is fairly assured. Where certification programs have been set up, periodic testing for residues may be required, and standards are set below those of United States government agencies. We will now develop a model of consumer demand based on the technical characteristics of these residues.

As explained in Chapter 4, while considerable testing is required before a chemical can be used in the food system, the complexity and expense of

---

*Assuming population growth continues at about 1 percent a year and per capita food consumption increases about 1 percent a year, reflecting increased consumption of high-input foods such as meat (USDA 1975b) and technological progress sufficient to keep prices relatively constant, the food market would grow at about 2 percent a year. Since organic food currently makes up about 0.0017 of food sales (assuming natural food and farm sales to be equal to health food sales, and recalling that volume share is about half sales share), after n years, organic food sales would make up X in the relation: $0.0017 (1.30)^n = X (1.02)^n$. When X = 0.5, that is when organic food is 50 percent of food sales by volume, n = 23.4 years.

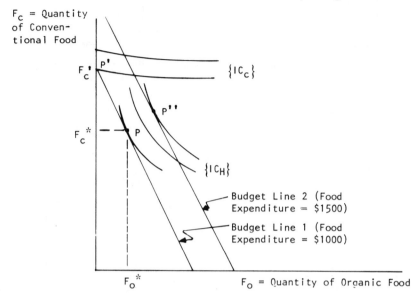

F_c = Quantity of Conventional Food

F_c' P'

$\{IC_c\}$

P''

F_c^* P

$\{IC_H\}$

Budget Line 2 (Food Expenditure = $1500)

Budget Line 1 (Food Expenditure = $1000)

F_o^* F_o = Quantity of Organic Food

Figure 8-1.   Consumers Maximizing Their Utility by Purchasing Organic and Conventional Food

obtaining complete knowledge regarding long-term effects make it virtually impossible to know ahead of time what these effects may be. Short-term toxicity can be established, but whether a chemical causes cancer or may interact with other chemicals to cause cancer is often not known. Some known carcinogens and teratogens are still used in agriculture under certain circumstances or at small concentrations.

Two characteristics are of importance. The first is that the effects are believed to be cumulative, that is, they are proportional to the total exposure; and the effects do not generally appear until a long time has passed, perhaps twenty years or more (Cornfield 1977). These facts have two implications for consumer demand. Consumers are unlikely to give much consideration to the potential danger at first. And while we are waiting for the epidemiological information to come, our sense of deprivation decreases as the day of reckoning approaches. Thus, a consumer who desires to avoid risk may increasingly seek to avoid residues in order to hold his options open. This is known as "option demand" (Krutilla *et al.* 1972).

These factors help account for the rapid increase in demand for organic food in the late 1960s and early 1970s. The theory also, however, implies that this rapid growth should not continue unless clearcut evidence emerges in the next few years linking agricultural chemicals and cancer, at the rates of application currently in use. An example may clarify the situation. The water supply and the air of Duluth, Minnesota, have been contaminated with asbestos-like fibers for about 20 years (Carter 1974). Some scientists believe that an epidemic of lung and stomach cancer may break out soon. A prudent person might drink bottled water in the meantime to (1) reduce his risk if there is a problem, and (2) retain the option of choosing between expensive water and cancer once the data are in and analyzed.

In Appendix A, the following formulae are derived, which link the marginal disutility, MD, of consuming food which may contain residues of poisonous chemicals, to the consumers' rate of discounting future discomfort, r, an interest rate; and to the activity strength of residues, a:

$$MD = \frac{a(1+r)}{r} \left(\frac{1}{1+r}\right)^{T-P} \qquad P < T \qquad (8.1)$$

$$MD = \frac{a(1+r)}{r} \qquad P > T \qquad (8.2)$$

Here P is the present time and T is the time at which the evidence is expected to be obtained that would establish whether or not there has been a real danger. The marginal disutility of consuming food with residues is presumably directly related to consumption of organic food. From Equation 8-1, it is seen that the marginal disutility of consuming food with residues increases each year at the rate that consumers discount the future, when we have not reached time T. Since the agricultural chemicals which are of greatest concern were introduced after World War II, the rapid increase in demand for organic food in the late 1960s and early 1970s is understandable. Once the critical time, T, has been passed, however, the information is available, and demand growth from this motivation ceases (Equation 8-2).

For those who are averse to risks, and consumers of organic food are in this category, there is also a value in keeping their options open. The cost of keeping the option of avoiding an increased probability of cancer in the future is assumed to be the same each year, namely, the increased cost of organic food. But the value of the option increases each year, as the day of reckoning approaches. (Actually, the probability of knowing of harmful side-effects increases each year, but increases much more rapidly after a period of time, say 20 years.) The reason is the same as before, because the increase in probability lies in the future and is thus discounted. The rate of increase is thus also the same, the rate at which future discomfort is discounted. And again, once it becomes highly unlikely that new information will be obtained implicating chemical residues in human illness, the growth in demand will cease. In fact, if new chemicals were not being introduced annually, demand would fall off, reflecting the decline in value of the option.

In the real world, new chemicals are introduced regularly, and no one knows exactly when we can be certain that no new information will be produced. Thus a steady-state, a relatively stable level of demand, should be achieved in the next few years unless some dramatic new publicity provides a large stimulus to demand. However, in such a case, presumably the government agency responsible would act, as in the past, to take such a substance out of the food supply.

The preceding discussion implicitly assumes that organic food consumers are well informed about the risks involved. It explains the portion of demand growth arising from consumers who already make some purchases of organic food on a rational basis. Growth also takes place from new consumers. Perhaps the low level of demand for organic food is a matter of ignorance. This seems doubtful, except in the sense that we are all more or less ignorant of the effects of agricultural chemicals. Most consumers know that there are finite risks involved in chemical use. First of all, chemical residue hazards are often described in the media, as are the dangers of smoking cigarettes, which provide a good analogy. Despite widespread acceptance of the dangers of smoking, cigarette sales continue to increase. Food may not be addictive, but eating habits are also deeply ingrained and slow to change. Despite possible risk, most people prefer to continue eating conventional food.

If prices of organic food were to drop closer to the prices of conventional food, demand would increase, although the rate of increase of demand would not. But prices will not fall significantly unless demand increases to the point that economies of scale in marketing come into play. In fact, some of the supermarkets that got into the organic food business in the excitement of the early 1970s have been disappointed by sales that did not rise as fast as expected (Colamosca 1974; PG 1976). This confirms that price is not as important to organic food consumers as other factors. In other words, demand is insensitive to price.

9 Organic Farmers and the Choice of Production System

Consumers of organic food do not make their decisions solely on the basis of price. The same goes for producers: profits are only one factor entering into a farmer's choice of production method. To be sure, profits are important. But profits alone are not sufficient to explain the decisions of conventional farmers, much less those of organic farmers.

Goals of Farmers

Surveys of farmers generally agree that, in addition to a desire for high income, the average farmer is guided by the following values (Breimyer and Barr 1972):

(1) Most farmers are quite receptive to new technology.

(2) Though willing to go into debt, most desire a sizable equity in their land.

(3) Farmers prefer to remain independent proprietors, buying and selling in free markets.

(4) Farmers prefer to avoid risk. Risk can be avoided by entering into contracts with buyers or suppliers (contract vertical integration), a practice that has become more and more common. Apparently most farmers find avoidance of risk more important than remaining independent.

(5) Farmers are reluctant to become involved in group action, though approving collective bargaining in principle.

(6) Farmers reject economic justice achieved through a redistribution of income, but rather advocate what they believe are fair prices for farm production. The latter are known as "parity" prices. (A parity system would link prices of agricultural products to those of industrial products. A

favorable base year is used for the standard, so that parity prices are comparatively high.)

(7) Farmers "have a genuine love of the land, a respect for it, and a desire to protect and preserve it. This attitude is not mercenary; it has roots that are almost religious. It extends to an acceptance of measures relating to what is now called ecology, which includes the older idea of conservation but extends beyond it to environmental protection and preservation" (Breimyer and Barr 1972).

Thus a model of farmer behavior based exclusively on profit maximization will be simplistic and inaccurate. For example, a recent study of conventional farmers in California found that aversion to risk had to be included if their behavior was to be satisfactorily explained (Lin *et al.* 1974). Farmers are willing to take lower average profits over the long run if they can be assured of a steady income. Aversion to risk accounted for a good deal of the diversity of traditional farming, and the removal of risk through crop supports smoothed the changeover to monoculture (see Johnson 1967; Dillon and Anderson 1971). Some farmers embrace organic farming as an attempt to secure long-term profitability.

Is it inefficient not to maximize profits? Organic farming is often a hobby of part-time or gentlemen farmers, and discounted by some critics for this reason. However, the generalization that "real" farmers cannot afford to farm organically, even if it were true, would only confirm that as income falls, monetary considerations must become more important. In general, the less one has of something, the greater the marginal value relative to other goals. For the farmer, money means a lot if he is poor, and farmers' incomes have tended to be below average. Thus farmers have had to emphasize the monetary dimensions of job satisfaction: income and risk. They have little possibility of trading off income for other values. Economists have traditionally assumed that maximizing profits or income is the same as maximizing job satisfaction. While this may be a good approximation when incomes are relatively low and desires for purchased goods and services high, this simple assumption becomes less meaningful as incomes rise and an individual achieves more discretion. Economists have now developed more sophisticated models of an entrepreneur's behavior, which include a variety of satisfactions in addition to money, including prestige and security (see, for example, Simon 1959; Williamson 1963).

But would an intelligent, rational, educated farmer avoid the methods that would bring him the highest monetary return, perhaps modified to avoid some risk? Isn't it somehow irrational to use a technology, such as organic farming, if it does not maximize income? The contrast with physicians, another group of individual entrepreneurs, may help clarify the situation.

Physicians are intelligent, rational, and highly educated. Yet they do not maximize their incomes. They do not choose the organization of their firms that would minimize cost. They would maximize their efficiency in treating patients, and also their profits, by increasing the average number of staff from two to four and by practicing in groups rather than alone (Reinhardt 1972). While average staff size has been on the increase, most physicians continue to spend more than the minimum efficient time with their patients and avoid group practice. Many work only twenty hours a week. Despite their image of wealth, many physicians could make more money if they really wanted to. Apparently they prefer to substitute other kinds of job satisfaction, such as individualism and providing what they believe is the highest *quality* care.

The situation in which the average family farmer finds himself is precisely the opposite of that of the physician, with regard to financial rewards. Farm incomes have been lower than average for decades. During the 1960s, farm incomes were about 20 percent lower than incomes of other workers. Farm incomes did rise faster than those of other workers in the early 1970s, until income parity was virtually achieved (USDA 1975). (Since then, farm incomes have fallen, however.) Higher incomes, if they continue, may provide some discretion that farmers did not have before. The low incomes over the years have forced farmers to bring the profit motive to the fore, together with the correlative desire to limit risk, at the expense of other satisfactions. Maximizing profits has been highly compatible with adopting the new technologies, but has conflicted with other values, particularly the desires to maintain independence, avoid debt, and protect the land. It is these latter values to which the eco-farming and organic farming movements appeal.

Low prices and incomes have also undercut one of the main incentives for conservation: the desire to pass on high quality land to the next generation. The younger generation leaves the farm. The older remains until retirement and then sells in a strictly monetary transaction. In this way, land is transformed into a commodity.

Organic farmers' goals. Despite financial and promotional pressures, and the many advantages of the conventional techniques, a few farmers have resisted the trend. Some avoided conventional techniques because of a lack of access to capital or due to ignorance, but many have made a free and conscious decision to do so. A growing number tried the chemicals, then changed back to organic or ecological farming. The switch back, or forward, if you prefer, is made more difficult because loans are generally available for changing *to* conventional farming, but not for changing *away* from it.

At times, the adoption of organic farming has been made on the basis of financial advantage. The surge in demand for organic food in the 1970s brought higher prices and some new entry based on profitability. With higher chemical fertilizer prices, and with increasing federal restrictions on some of the cheaper pesticides, farmers are more receptive to the alternatives. Strict environmental regulations could encourage further changeover to organic farming. For the most part, however, those who have chosen to farm organically have done so in spite of financial incentives rather than because of them. Even though they might not make a lot of money, they are proud to feel they are leaving the earth a better place.

For some farmers, organic farming continues a tradition of natural methods and involves a conscious rejection of the trappings of modern society. The Amish reject the use of heavy machinery, though they do use horse-drawn machinery. Except for the Old Order Amish, most Amish will use chemical fertilizers and pesticides in moderation. Large families provide the labor, and the practice of frugality as a virtue lowers the money income requirements. Many young people of the counterculture or back-to-the-land movement also reject what they view as an unnatural way of living, and choose to avoid machines and chemicals.

One of the main reasons cited by organic farmers for changing over from conventional farming is a desire to improve family health (Wernick and Lockeretz 1977). Some farmers and their families have experienced allergic reactions to pesticides, or perhaps a child was poisoned, or cattle became ill. Such farmers express a sense of relief that they can allow their children to wander freely about the farm again. There is a clear trade-off in the minds of these farmers between health and farming method. In a more positive vein, organic farmers tend to believe that organic food is the best that they can feed their families, and thus operate their farms organically to provide a convenient and reliable family food supply (Buck 1975). Since these incentives are missing from large-scale corporate farming, this is one reason that organic farms are almost invariably family farms.

For many organic farmers, more important than family health is livestock health. In a survey of French organic (biological) farmers, 18 percent said they changed over from conventional methods out of concern for health and nutrition of themselves and their families, but 68 percent cited a desire to improve the health of their livestock (Bates 1976). Testimonials of lowered incidence of disease and death are common among organic farm reports.

Some farmers see their work as part of a spiritual relation to the land and the related plants and animals. They respect nature, and attempt to work with it. This feeling is widespread among farmers (value 7 above). The prevalence of this attitude of reverence for the land and for life indicates a substantial reservoir of farmers who would be happy to change over to organic farming, or at least approximate it, if they could achieve what they feel is a fair income level for their families.

A slightly different motivation has appeared among newer organic farmers, out of the environmental movement of the 1970s. A farmer who is deeply concerned about pollution and consumer well-being may be willing to sacrifice some other goals to satisfy his desire to do good to his neighbor. A West Virginia organic farmer, a former government statistician, derives deep satisfaction from treating the land right and bringing good food to the people in Washington, D.C., where he has a fresh produce stand. For himself, however, he prefers the hoagies at Eddie Leonard's across the street.

Beyond a reverence for life, organic farmers frequently have a deep religious faith. Organic farmers are innovators, or at least individualists. In standing up to ridicule, many farmers draw the strength they need from their faith.* In fact, some have chosen their farming techniques because of what they regard as the direct guidance of God. One Iowa organic farmer speaks in awe of the tornado that left his house and land virtually untouched, while destroying many of his neighbors' farms.

Because organic farmers are less motivated by monetary considerations, they may be willing to settle for a lower income than conventional farmers. Thus the monetary cost of producing organic food, when measured by farm prices, may underestimate the supply price required by growers who consider only monetary rewards. Farmers who treat farming purely as a business have become more dominant in agriculture, since they are favored by the direction of technological change (see next section). Nevertheless, most farmers still hold other values to be important.

While organic farmers may in fact sell their production at a premium, the premium may not provide a fair return on the resources employed. Higher resource cost may also simply reflect inefficiency. If we take a broad view of job satisfaction, the price of organic food *is* a good measure of present production costs. These farmers are producing both food and personal satisfaction. If we believe the opinion surveys, there is a large reservoir of farmers with sympathy for a more ecologically sound approach, provided they can be shown that the income sacrifice is small enough. This leads us to one of the great paradoxes of modern agriculture.

---

*Organic farmers often leave their land fallow one year out of seven, in accordance with the Biblical injunction of Exodus 23:10-11 and Leviticus 25: 1-7. As the seventh day is the day of rest for people, so the seventh year is the year of rest for the land. Giving the seventh year to God is to demonstrate that man is really only a steward of the land; the real owner is God. The Bible also has something to say about farm ownership and size. After seven times seven years comes the fiftieth year, which is called the Year of Jubilee. According to Mosaic Law, when the year of Jubilee arrives, all rural properties—houses and lands—must be returned to the original owners or their heirs (Leviticus 25:8-28). Since Old Testament times the devout have believed that natural disasters and wars are the result of not observing these divine laws. The exile of the Israelite nation from its homeland for 70 years is interpreted in the Old Testament as punishment for working the land for that many fallow years (II Chronicles 36:21).

The adoption of conventional agricultural techniques has led to greater production and to lower cost production. This might be expected to improve farmers' profits. However, just the reverse has actually happened. The bumper harvests flooded the market and forced prices down. There is a limit to how much consumers can eat, so increased food production translates into a more than proportional fall in prices. The farmer gets locked into a high volume, low margin (net return) production system.

Some farmers recognize that one way to break out of this trap is severe environmental restriction, which would help to cut back quantity and raise quality. If severe limitations on chemical pesticide and fertilizer use would raise prices and incomes, why don't farmers embrace such legislation? Because, while *individual* farmers suffer from larger crops in the aggregate, they benefit from their *own* large harvest. Furthermore, farmers who are in business today have made their investments based on the present institutional arrangements. Any changes in these institutions would benefit some farmers more than others. Those who would benefit most would be the smaller, poorer, traditional or organic farmers, poorly financed and poorly organized. Those who would benefit least, or even lose, are the large, highly mechanized, specialized farmers whose soil has lost its natural fertility and who must rely upon chemicals to keep profits and production high.

Choice of Production Method

A production function relates the inputs of an economic system, such as agriculture, to the outputs, such as food. That is, it tells how much will be produced for various levels of the required labor, materials, land, machinery, fertilizer, pesticides. Generally, we think only in terms of some physical output such as bushels or tons of, say, corn or cucumbers or milk. But sometimes there are also other products, or byproducts, which are produced concurrently as joint products with the food. In particular, agricultural production yields not only food, but environmental quality, consumer health, farmer satisfaction, income distribution between generations and among nations.

We will now describe an economic model of the choice of production system. For simplicity, let us consider the case in which two products result from agricultural activity: food and environmental quality. The second variable may be assumed to include all dimensions of interest other than gross (nutrient) production. For a given level of food production, society will have a maximum level of environmental quality achievable, and vice versa, for a given set of resources committed to the agricultural sector. In the short run, and even over a period of several years, the major resources are relatively immobile in agriculture. If we consider the resource base to be fixed, these situations, a set of output and corresponding environmental quality levels, define the "production possibility frontier," f, in agriculture, shown in Figure 9-1.

The evidence examined in earlier chapters indicates that society is not currently producing on the frontier, but somewhat inside, at a point such as P, with a large production of food, F*, and an amount of environmental quality, E*, which could be expanded to E′ with little or no loss in production. Market failures account for this inefficiency, particularly faulty information provided to farmers and high private profitability of conventional techniques contrasted with the positive external (social) benefits of the biologically oriented technologies.

The fact that society has chosen, through public policy and through consumption decisions, to emphasize the quantitative dimension has implications for the market value of agricultural inputs. The choice of a point such as P or P′ indicates a high valuation of food quantity relative to the environment. In such a situation, those inputs will be rewarded, and those input industries will expand, which are comparatively more essential for producing high levels of production. The reverse is true of inputs and industries which favor environmental quality. In fact, until the last decade, environmental quality and other non-quantitative outputs of food production have received a comparatively low priority, a low valuation in terms of public research funding and consumer expenditures.

Technological change pushes the frontier outward from the origin: with the same resource endowment, more goods and services can be produced. Technological change in conventional agriculture and its supplier industries has made it possible for us to produce more food, but there has been a concomitant lessening of our ability to maintain environmental quality. The change is shown diagramatically in Figure 9-2. The production possibility frontier changes from f^1 to f^2. (Actually, resources are gradually being withdrawn from agriculture, so that f^1 is pulling back toward the origin. That is, with the present commitment of resources to agriculture, we could produce less food and other services with the technology of earlier generations.) Individual farmers confront a similar change in option sets. For society's options reflect those of its members. Farmers whose personal preferences and resources are compatible with the new techniques benefit more than those whose do not. The preferences of the former are shown schematically by the utility- or satisfaction-indifference curves (constant satisfaction contours), $\{IC_c\}$. To such a farmer, gross yield, and by implication, monetary reward, are far more important than other considerations. The system will select in favor of the survival of these types. On the other hand, those for whom other values weigh heavily will be selected against. The preferences of such an ecologically concerned farmer are indicated by indifference curve set, $\{IC_e\}$. Conventional technological change has not benefited him. While he could produce more

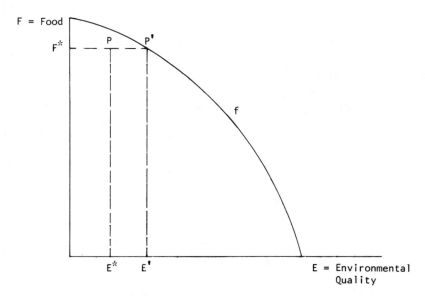

Figure 9-1.   Trade-off Between Food and Environmental Quality:
A Production Possibility Frontier

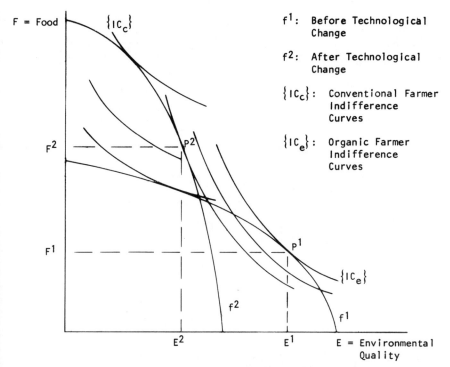

Figure 9-2.   Production Possibility Frontiers Before and After Technological
Change in Agriculture which Favors Output over the Environment

by adopting more of the new techniques, he would be even more unhappy. With the options shown in Figure 9-2, such a farmer is happiest at point P^1, producing an amount of food, F^1, and an amount of environmental quality, E^1. He does not adopt the new system. The best he could do under the new system would be the combination of F^2 and E^2 at P^2. But this point is on an indifference curve that is closer to the origin, indicating that such a position makes him worse off than at P^1. The loss of both monetary and other satisfactions drives such individuals out of farming. However, the larger incomes are only temporary to the early adopters of new technology. Prices fall as output expands. Thus, an ecologically motivated farmer will lose both monetary income and the satisfaction of maintaining the environment. Such individuals may well find greater satisfaction in other jobs, and are selected against. Still, attitude surveys indicate that the vast majority of farmers desire to protect their land. But the sacrifice in production to achieve environmental quality often appears to be too great. And it is large under the conventional agricultural system.

Meanwhile, other technological change has been occurring along biological lines, which allows expanded production without sacrifice of environmental quality. In fact, the environment may be enhanced by the replacement of harmful chemicals. Such a change is shown by the

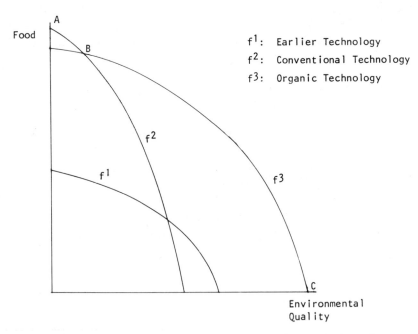

Figure 9-3.   Production Possibility Frontiers for Agriculture's Technological Options

movement from f^1 to f^3 in Figure 9-3, where f^3 is a production possibility frontier for organic farming. Precise methods of crop coordination in time and space and other cultural and ecological controls of pests have been devised. Alternative production also makes use of some technologies in common with conventional production, such as resistant varieties. However, to a large extent, as we have argued in earlier chapters, these two systems are distinct and internally consistent. Society's choice is more between two systems than between the various shades between. The market segmentation into two types of food reinforces this distinction for the farmer.

The overall production frontier for society when confronted by two different systems would be the outermost portions of the curves in Figure 9-3, line ABC. Since not all farms nor regions need follow the same system, however, some combination may be preferable. Since there are large economies of scale and clustering economies in pest control and marketing, combinations of systems will lead to some increased cost.

Decisions on which production system to adopt are made on the farm level. On the one hand is the conventional system with comparatively high use of manufactured inputs that have a concomitant environmental burden both directly in use and indirectly, at other stages, from the extraction of raw materials to the manufacture of machinery and chemicals. The private cost to farmers and consumers as eaters is comparatively low. On the other hand is the organic system with higher private costs, but with less dependence on industrial inputs and less environmental impact. The question thus arises: What price in increased production costs would have to be paid by us as a society if we encouraged a wider use of the organic farming option? Would large-scale adoption of organic farming doom the nation to hunger or starvation, not to mention the rest of the world, dependent as it is on our grain surpluses? This is the oft-repeated gloomy prediction of agribusiness leaders. Or would the trade-off be more modest, as in the movement from point A to point C in Figure 9-3? In the latter event, a national policy encouraging organic farming might become more reasonable, as concern over environmental damage and energy shortages increases.

PART THREE

Organic Farming Production Costs

10 Methods of Estimating
Production Costs

In earlier chapters we have addressed the output quality dimensions of environmental purity, producer satisfaction, consumer health, and income distribution. We have yet to deal explicitly with cost. Organic farmers and consumers believe that gross yield (in bushels or tons per acre or per manhour) is less important than quality; that, in fact, people and animals can live with better health on less food if it has been raised organically. The evidence in chapter 3 indicates that any yield loss under organic farming will be partially compensated by higher nutrient content. The evidence on consumer health is less clear. Part 3 of this study will explore the production potential of alternative agriculture in terms of gross yield without attempting adjustments for nutritional quality. Readers will have to make their own adjustments, based on their personal evaluation of the insufficient evidence on nutrient content and consumer health. An analysis of the extent to which expansion of the organic farming sector would cause production costs to fall or rise—that is, the question of economies or diseconomies of scale in the organic farming industry—will be found in Chapter 13.

Four methods have commonly been suggested for estimating production costs under a system of organic agriculture. These methods are retail food price comparisons of organic and conventional food, agricultural experiment station plot data, national production in earlier eras, and adjustments in the conventional system. The first, retail prices, has been dealt with in Chapter 8. Retail prices of organic food are far higher than those of conventional food, but possible differences in production costs are largely outweighed by the higher costs of handling small quantities of food. So retail prices give no indication of production cost differences. The other three approaches will now be explored in turn. Each is deficient. For that reason, we turn to two other more satisfactory methods in the next two chapters, namely farm prices and production costs of functioning organic farms.

National Production in Earlier Eras

Conventional agriculture has posted some impressive yield increases when compared with production in the 1930s and earlier. Corn yield per acre increased 240 percent and yields of other grains over 100 percent (Table 1-1). Some of the fruit and vegetable crops showed increases in yields of over 300 percent. If we assume that the yields of the 1930s represent what we can expect from organic farming and compare them with current yields, we might well conclude with Earl Butz (*cf.* Chapter 1), that a "return to organic farming" would be disastrous. Such a conclusion is invalid, however, because the comparison is invalid. Farming in the 1930s was in some respects organic farming, in others not. In any event, many changes have taken place since then which make modern organic farming more productive. Many of the developments in conventional agriculture are also useful in organic farming.

First of all, much farming in the 1930s was hardly organic farming. Most of the basic feed and grain crops were raised using only manure and previous crop residues for fertilizer. But many of the fruit and vegetable crops received heavy treatments of the old pesticides such as arsenic.

But second and more important, organic farming today is not simply a reversion to methods of earlier eras. Organic farming is a highly developed method of using ecological and biological knowledge, much of it acquired since the 1930s (Chapter 7). There has been much progress in understanding and applying biological and cultural controls (Chapter 4). Recalling Figure 9-3, the suggestion that a changeover to organic farming is a movement away from production possibilities set f^2 back to f^1 is simply an expression of ignorance regarding the existence of alternative modern production possibilities with organic farming, f^3.

Finally, much of the technology developed for use by conventional agriculture can be appropriated by organic agriculture. While some organic farmers prefer open pollinated corn, many organic farmers make use of the hybrid varieties. If the plant doesn't know where the nitrogen comes from, as the conventional farmers are fond of saying, then hybrids will grow as well with heavy manure application as with heavy chemical fertilizer. Actually, varieties could be developed which were better suited to organic farming. Again, much of the new machinery can be used and is being used by organic farmers. Some mechanical fruit harvesting, which requires auxiliary chemical use, cannot be adopted. But the standard field crop machinery can be used as well by organic as by conventional farmers. To put the situation in perspective, we will briefly explore the contributions of the main factors to the yield increases of the major crops over the last few decades.

Yields have increased much more rapidly since 1960 than in preceding years, particularly corn yields. Thus, it is convenient to look at the yield changes for two periods: from the 1930s to 1960, and from 1960 to the present.

Heady and Auer (1966; also Auer and Heady 1964) investigated the factors contributing to yield increases for the major grain crops and soybeans, cotton, and hay between the years 1939 and 1960. They used a statistical (multiple regression) analysis of yield data by state for the major producing regions. Since the use of hybrid varieties and the use of fertilizer are highly correlated, the authors constructed a yield response function for fertilizer use based on experimental plot data (from Ibach and Adams 1968). Yields were then corrected for fertilizer response before running the regression on the other factors. The percent of farmers adopting hybrid corn was modified by the effectiveness of hybrids in inducing higher yields, to obtain a hybrid yield index. Since overall yield is affected by the quality of land used for production, acreage changes for each state were also included in the model. Presumably, if less land is being farmed in low-yield states, overall yield will be increased. The effect of weather was included through an index based on the difference between actual yields and trend yields at state experiment stations. The results obtained by Heady and Auer are summarized in Table 10-1. Most of the increases in

Table 10-1 Factors Contributing to Yield Increases, 1939 to 1960[a]

| Crop | Per Acre Yield Increase Due to: | | | | Percent of U.S. 1960 Production Included in Study |
	Ferti-lizer	Vari-ety	Loca-tion	Other	
Wheat (bu)[b]	3.3	2.1	0.1	2.1	70
Corn (bu)	9.7	9.2	4.6	3.9	84
Soybeans (bu)	1.3	3.8	-1.4	0.8	84
Cotton (lbs)	41.8	32.5	-3.8	104.7	52
Oats (bu)	3.1	6.1	0.9	-5.6	86
Barley (bu)	1.4	2.4	0.6	0.1	32
Sorghums (bu)	3.1	6.7	1.0	7.6	85
Hay (tons)	0.18	-	-0.02	0.13	48

[a]Period begins with 1942 for oats and 1943 for soybeans and barley; period ends with 1961 for corn.
[b]Bushels.

Source: Heady and Auer 1966.

yield are a result of two factors: fertilizer and new varieties. For corn, these two accounted for over two-thirds of the yield increase; for hay, over one-half. Corn yields also benefited significantly from shifts from less productive to more productive land. The reverse is true of cotton and soybeans: yields would have been even higher for these crops had they been grown on the same land in 1960 as in 1939. The contribution of "other" factors includes thos of pesticides, improved cultural practices, better educated farmers, and mechanization (though the latter probably is associated with fertilizer and variety). Weather also played a role. Better weather in 1960 than in the late 1930s probably contributed to most of the other yield change in corn. Other studies of factors affecting yield increases over this period came to much the same conclusion regarding the main contributing factors and their importance (see Shaw and Durost 1965; Johnson and Gustafson 1962).

It should be recalled that fertilizer and new varieties are highly complementary and their use highly correlated. Thus, it is really the combination of fertilizer and variety that has led to the yield increases. This is of some consequence when we realize that most of the increases in fertilizer use can be explained by a relative decline in its price relative to the price of crops. Griliches (1958) showed this for the years 1910 to 1956. Thus we might conclude that the yield increases are mainly due to the high relative price of food compared with input prices, and the availability of new varieties which could take advantage of the additional fertilizer. A high relative price of food means more use of agricultural inputs because *their* value is higher. If chemical fertilizers were not used, other practices (such as cover crops and waste recycling) would have a higher value in agriculture than they did in the 1930s, and would be extensively used.

Since 1960 there has been a more rapid increase in yield per acre for the major crops. This increase has been associated with more rapid increases in the use of fertilizer. For example, before 1960 nitrogen fertilizer applications on corn were increasing at the rate of about 2.0 pounds per acre each year. Between 1960 and 1968, per acre nitrogen use on corn increased about 10 pounds per year (Thompson 1969a).

Perrin and Heady (1975) extended the earlier studies through 1971 for three major grain crops: corn, sorghum, and wheat. They used much the same approach, but had a more sophisticated weather index. They also restricted their analysis to only a few of the major states for each crop: Illinois and Iowa for corn, together making up 38 percent of the 1974 United States crop; Kansas and Nebraska for sorghum, 31 percent; and Kansas, Nebraska, and North Dakota for wheat, 30 percent. After 1960, new varieties had virtually no effect on yield. The use of fertilizer accounts for the lion's share of yield increases for corn and sorghum: over 30 bushels out of a 40 bushel-per-acre increase for corn, and almost all of the increase for sorghum.

Increased fertilizer use had a variable impact on wheat production: no effect in Nebraska, about four bushels' increase in Kansas, and about seven in North Dakota. Two of the major factors in increased wheat yield over the last few decades are the increasing practice of leaving land fallow (uncultivated) for a year between crops, which allows moisture to build up in dryland farming, and the increasing practice of not harvesting fields whose yields are uneconomically low. Increased fallowing may have contributed to an increased yield of five to ten bushels per acre over the last few decades. Currently about 8 percent of planted wheat acres are not harvested, but as high as 20 percent were left unharvested in the mid-1960s and again in 1972 (USDA 1975). Yield increase figures based on fallowing and unharvested acres are specious since more land is committed to wheat than is actually harvested.

The main reason for the increased use of fertilizer in the 1960s was the good weather. The good weather alone probably contributed to an increase of some 10 bushels per acre in corn and wheat production compared with yields in the 1940s and 1950s (Thompson 1969a, 1969b). But beyond that, it was the weather that led to the fertilizer use. Weather during the 1960s was not only better, but also more stable or predictable than in earlier decades. Large fertilizer applications need plenty of moisture during the growing season to be effective. In fact, if moisture is deficient, the crop may be harmed by the fertilizer. Thus, the good, stable weather guaranteed a good return on investments in fertilizer. Reliable weather also meant that crops could be planted closer together, thus allowing more plants per acre and better use of the fertilizer. Corn plants per acre increased 50 percent between 1945 and 1970 (NRC 1972). The last few years have seen a return to the unpredictable weather of earlier decades. If variable, drier weather continues, farmers will cut back on fertilizer use and plant density, other things being equal.

The fact that the relative price of fertilizer to feed grains continued to fall during the 1960s also encouraged increased fertilizer use. But the decrease of 16 percent in relative prices between 1960 and 1970 (USDA 1975) was small compared to the decline in the 1940s when the price of fertilizer halved while the price of other inputs doubled, relative to food prices (Griliches 1958).

For other crops, the situation is much the same as with grains. A combination of new, high-yield varieties with more fruit per plant, capable of closer spacing, more resistant to pests; increased fertilizer use; and better weather are the main contributing factors to high yields in the 1960s and 1970s. In some cases, the introduction of pesticides has made a larger contribution than in others. Fruit production has become heavily dependent on pesticides. Mechanization and education have also had roles, in many ways complementary to the other inputs. Because the factors work together, it is hard to say that the yield increase has been because of varieties and fertilizer rather than, for example, machinery and education. The machinery has been designed to harvest the new varieties, and the new varieties to go with the machines.

One factor that is missing from most of the lists of major contributors is pesticides. And this is the only input which organic farmers are prohibited from using. Organic farmers can use hybrid seed, machinery (for field crops), good weather, and increased levels of natural fertilizers. And they have been doing just that. So yields on organic farms have also increased over the years. The hybrid seed is not designed for organic farmers, so they may lose a bit there. And the organic fertilizers have been more expensive and less readily available. But yields in the 1930s are hardly good estimates of what production we could expect from widespread adoption of organic farming.

Agricultural Experiment Station Studies

The technology of standard farming practices has been thoroughly researched by facilities across the nation for many years. The situation is quite different in alternative agriculture. Controlled research has been sparse. Only in recent years have major agricultural research stations begun to test some of the claims. Much of the material in alternative publications is anecdotal in nature, in the form of testimonials rather than controlled studies. And reports of studies usually neglect statistical analysis and consideration of factors of little interest to the writer, such as the weather, which might have had as much effect as a particular natural technique.

The neglect of organic farming research is partly a matter of lack of funds. Major universities have gone into testing chemical products, sometimes working closely with the manufacturers, who often supply part of the research funding. Agricultural chemical suppliers have comparatively abundant funds available and a strong economic incentive for research and promotion (see Chapter 4).

The state agricultural experiment station research is generally carefully designed under known conditions, so that reliable comparisons between methods should be possible. Extensive studies of various agricultural techniques are carried out in neighboring plots. Unfortunately, for a variety of reasons, valid comparisons of conventional and organic techniques appear to be virtually nonexistent.

Why experiment station studies neglect organic farming. The neglect of organic farming by the state experiment stations is a result of incentives within the system, tradition, and the characteristics of organic farming itself and its claims, which do not lend themselves readily to empirical verification.

Complexity. Chemical systems and effects are far less complex than biological systems. Studies of organic methods must extend over many years to really test a system. These characteristics conflict with the desire and need of researchers to produce data quickly for publication. Chemical research can produce comparatively quick results that are also rather easy to interpret in terms of conventional wisdom. Such research leads to more funding and to promotions. These incentives are hard to resist.

Product quality research. Testing organic farming claims is inherently difficult because of the nature of the claims made. The primary claimed effects for organic food are in product quality, not in quantity. Quality is far more difficult to test objectively and is also subject to a good deal of personal taste variability. Some tests of quality have been made, such as the controlled experiments with kelp done at Clemson University, showing increased shelf life for fresh peaches (Senn *et al.* 1972); but such work has been rare (see Chapter 3).

Quality claims are made with regard to plant, animal, and human health. And the effects on health are said to be manifested not just in one generation, but more importantly, over two or three generations. It is hard enough to establish short-term effects in human diet. Refined foods have been common dietary elements for many years. Yet the epidemiological and laboratory studies linking such diets with common diseases are only now being carried out (for example, Bremer 1975). If the way we raise our food is as important as or more important than how we process it, we may not discover this from epidemiological evidence because processing and chemical use have increased concurrently. The claims for animal health and plant health are easier to test. But again, they are more complex than simple assertions of increased growth or yield.

Tradition. Scientists tend to stick to the areas of research that they are used to, from habit or taste. Patterns of thought are established, and scientists, like any group of human beings, find change difficult. Administrators may be even more conservative than scientists. Research funds are more readily available for slight modifications of previous research than for work that breaks new ground. In agricultural research, this situation is compounded by a lack of new funds. For example, when asked why the United States Department of Agriculture did not put more funds into alternative agriculture research, the energy coordinator of their Agricultural Research Service responded, "We are pretty well stuck with the complement of people we have, so there is some reluctance to redirect much of our program into energy research" (Wade 1975).

The attitudes in agricultural institutions are similar to those prevailing in medicine today. American medicine is oriented primarily along curative and allopathic lines, rather than preventive and homeopathic. For exam-

ple, while experts assert that up to 90 percent of cancer may be environmentally induced, the government's war on cancer is primarily an attempt
to find a cure (Greenberg 1975). Homeopathic medicine seeks a cure via
stimulating the body's own defense mechanisms; allopathic via overpowering the disease with an external force. Many forms of alternative
medicine are based upon a belief in a life force or living power which
inheres in living creatures and can be harnessed to promote health. Some
proponents of alternative agriculture also embrace a world-view that
includes a belief in this non-material life force. Techniques are designed to
enhance these effects. However, if one does not believe in the existence of
certain effects, one is unlikely to investigate them, or if one does so, it is
difficult to take an unbiased approach.

There is evidence of a break with the conventional approach in Europe,
surprisingly, at the Justus Liebig Institute, founded by and named for the
father of modern chemical fertilization. A recent PhD dissertation there
(Abele 1973) has proven a statistically significant increase in yield from
planting by the phases of the moon (for example, a 20 percent rise in carrot
yield) and also from using certain (bio-dynamic) solutions in such high
dilutions that any presently explicable physical effect is hard to imagine.
Such effects do not fit easily into the traditional modern world-view.

Another line of research that is at variance with accepted scientific
tradition has been taken by L. Kervran (1972) and others in French
government agencies. They believe that, under certain circumstances,
plants and animals achieve the goal of the alchemists. That is, living
organisms may transmute one element or nutrient into another, though
apparently they are more likely to turn sodium into potassium than lead
into gold.

Objective versus personal approach. The characteristics of natural materials
or conditions are more difficult to standardize than those of chemicals.
Some organic groups argue that techniques must be specific to particular
areas or even to particular farms. Such an attitude would not favor
generalized research, but specific research by the individual farmer or
community. (Research on this scale is apparently being encouraged in
Communist China.)

The alternative techniques may present a difficulty inherent in independent evaluation. Organic farming tends to operate by enlisting the aid
or building up the natural mechanisms in the soil, plant and animal. The
plant and the soil are intermediate agents in the productive system. There
is some (highly controversial) evidence that plants may respond to the
feelings of those working with or on them (Tompkins and Bird 1973;
Hawken 1975). If the plant is a constructive agent in the success of the
experiment, and the plant's contribution depends on the attitude of the
experimentor, the independent verification by non-sympathetic persons
may be impossible. Suppose an investigation is proposed into the question

of whether or not lions can be tamed. Would it be rational to recommend introducing some into the nearest university biology department office and observing the results? At the end of the day, we will have either dead lions or dead biologists, and what will have been learned? If we want to know if lions can be tamed, we must go and observe professional lion-tamers. The lion-tamers have their similarities to organic farmers. If we wish to know whether or not it is possible to raise food by working with nature rather than by overcoming her, the way to do it is really to observe the lion-tamers, the organic farmers.

Personal involvement of the researcher is not absent in conventional science. Successful scientists are committed to an independent, empirical form of knowledge (see Polanyi 1958). In alternative agricultural research, the involvement of the researcher may be more explicit. The knowledge obtained is to a large extent dependent on the researcher himself, on his involvement in the experiment.

Experiment station studies. After the preceding discussion, it may not be surprising to discover that we do not have very much to learn about organic farming production costs from experiment station research. Many stations have carried out studies, some over many years, testing a particular element of organic farming, for example, manure versus chemical fertilizer and herbicides versus cultivation. In experiments lasting 40 years, corn, oats, and wheat showed comparable yields when comparable amounts of nitrogen were applied, whether in manure or in chemical form (Thorne 1930). Slife (1973) raised corn, soybeans, and wheat continuously and in rotation, under two weed control programs: herbicide with one cultivation, and three cultivations without herbicide. The latter treatment resulted in a roughly 75 percent drop in profit per acre for continuous corn, a 10 to 20 percent drop for soybeans and the rotations, and no change for wheat, when compared with herbicides. While rotations did better than continuous corn and soybeans, cultivation was still markedly inferior to herbicide treatment. Interesting though the results may be, they unfortunately have little relevance to a comparison between conventional and organic farming. It may take three years, the full time of the rotation in this experiment, to establish favorable conditions for natural weed control. And organic farmers use additional methods to control weeds, such as a second plowing under in the spring and a winter cover crop.

Some experiment station work has been carried out with the stated purpose of comparing organic and conventional farming techniques. These studies have shown large yield losses under an organic regime, and some have been widely quoted. Unfortunately, the experimental designs often have serious flaws that make the results of little value for an unbiased analysis.

Beginning in 1971, the University of Minnesota Experiment Station carried out a series of experiments comparing corn and soybean yields with commercial fertilizer and with some organic soil amendments (Holcomb *et al.* 1976a; 1976b). The conventional plots received herbicides; the "organic" did not. In fact, there is no mention of weed control on the latter plots at all. Consequently, it should not have been surprising that yields on the "organic" plots were low, even below a check plot which received only herbicides.

A study at the University of Illinois compared yields for a number of crops, finding them far lower without the use of chemicals than with chemical treatment. They calculated production costs from the non-chemical yields. For example, they estimated that broccoli would cost $14.00 a pound if grown organically (Conterio *et al.* ca. 1971; ICES 1972). This conclusion was reached despite the fact that organic broccoli could be bought for about one-twentieth of that amount in natural food stores. The yield differences, which were widely publicized, were again mainly a matter of weeds. A rainy season kept cultivators out of the fields.

The standard method of testing pesticides often leads to erroneous conclusions. Crop yield increases of 50 percent with the use of pesticides are commonly reported (USDA 1965). Unfortunately, the "controls" are usually neighboring untreated plots or fields. The untreated plot not only suffers from pest infestation, but also from the strong bugs chased from the treated fields (DeBach 1974). The organic plots also often are handicapped by residues or predator suppression on the untreated plot, due to previous years' treatment (*cf.* Headley 1968). These experiments do illustrate the fact that the benefit from introducing a pesticide is not equal to the potential loss from giving it up. In other words, system changes are not reversible.

An attempt at a fair comparison of a number of alternative agricultural systems was begun at Cornell in the early 1970s. Experimental plots were established on land that had not been chemically treated for many years. The program came under fire from the dean of agriculture, however. The director resigned and the program was snuffed out before enough years' data had been obtained to produce reliable statistics (Buck 1975).

The future may be somewhat brighter. Under pressure from organic farmers' groups and possible energy and materials shortages, experiment station interest in serious comparative studies has picked up. The University of Iowa is now planning a five-year study of organic farming. The Department of Agriculture's Meade Experiment Station in Nebraska has begun a long-term study of chemical and organic methods, using rotations, legumes, and manure. A standard 100 pounds of nitrogen per acre will be used on each plot (Demmel 1976). And MacDonald College of McGill University, Canada, established a center in 1975 for the study of alternative food and agricultural systems, including soil-health relationships. A few preliminary results are available. The University of Maine ran trials on tomatoes, dry beans, and carrots under five treatments: French intensive, commercial, commercial with seaweed extract spray, organic, and organic plus seaweed mulch (Eggert 1977). Marketable (red-ripe, *i.e.*, pink) tomato yields were not statistically different (about 13 tons per acre) among the treatments, although the French intensive and organic had higher total yields, including green tomatoes. The marketable yield of dry beans was about a ton per acre for all but the organic without seaweed, which was about 25 percent lower. Commercial carrot plots had a 10 to 20 percent higher marketable yield (straight, single, and five or more inches long), though total yields were not significantly different.

Some relevant experimental work has been carried out in Europe, particularly that by W. Schuphan at the Bundesanstalt für Qualitätsforschung Pflanzlicher Erzeugnisse (Federal Institute for Quality Research on Plant Production) (see Chapter 3). Some interesting nutritional relationships were discovered, but the very large applications of compost to the organic plots make extrapolation to farm scale impossible. In general, the lower yield on organic plots was partially compensated for by higher nutrient content.

Quality results of the Swedish Agricultural College joint research with the nearby Bio-dynamic Research Station were discussed in Chapter 3. While organic potato yields were down 10 percent, this drop was more than made up by grading and storage losses in the conventionally grown crops. Bio-dynamic spring wheat and barley yields were 5 percent higher, a difference that is probably not of significance. A 20-year plot study at the Swedish Bio-dynamic Research Station used four-year rotations of wheat, hay, potatoes, and beets under eight different fertilizer programs. The organic hay yields were about 10 percent higher. Beet and wheat yields were slightly higher on the chemical plots (where 40 percent more nitrogen was applied). Potato yields were equivalent (von Wistinghausen 1977).

Experiments and farms. Even if enough experimental plot data were available, the application to working farms is never simple (*cf.* Davidson *et al.* 1967; Headley and Lewis 1967). The experimental plot may receive a higher level of management. Experiments may deal with higher pest infestations than normally experienced in the field. Quality changes may be induced by pesticide use, not measurable or measured. There may be externalities between farms or between plots, as mentioned above.

In conclusion, experimental tests of organic farming techniques have rarely been done in a sufficiently controlled manner as to allow generalization to farm-scale conditions. The evidence that is available points to similar yields for the crops studied.

Adjustments in the Conventional System

Earlier in this chapter, it was explained why organic farming is not a return to production of a previous era, that is, a shift from f^2 to f^1 in Figure 9-3.

This section will consider movements *along* f^2, that is, modifications of the conventional system in order to improve on environmental quality. In general, some other policy variables will have to be sacrificed. Increasing environmental quality means limiting the use of certain inputs, namely, chemical fertilizers and pesticides, or making their use more costly. Within the context of the conventional system, the sacrifice in output may be substantial. This does not, however, tell us what sacrifices would have to be made if we *shifted* to organic farming, that is, moved from production possibilities f^2 to f^3 of Figure 9-3. The system of organic farming is designed to enhance environmental quality, rather than crop yield.

In Chapter 4 we discussed the yield loss estimates of Pimentel under a pesticide ban (Table 4-4). These simple estimates and other similar ones do not allow for changes in product mix or in geographic location, which would surely occur under new economic conditions. They also rely upon experiment station studies that are to a large extent inapplicable to organic farming, as explained in the preceding section. Pimentel (1973) notes that a total ban on the use of pesticides would have different effects on different crops and regions. In some crops decreased yields may be augmented by simple substitution of land for chemicals. For others, such as apples and other fruit, he suggests that quality may be so reduced that no marketable crop would be produced. The availability and, presumably also the potential, of biological controls varies considerably between crops. As crop geographic patterns have changed over the decades with the increased use of chemicals, so a set of pesticide controls would also have locational incentives. Some regions are better suited by climate, soil, or other features, to the raising of crops without chemicals.

Computer models of the agricultural sector. Heady and co-workers at Iowa State University have investigated some of the geographical patterns of crop production using a linear programming model of the agricultural sector. The model uses between 150 and 254 producing and consuming regions for as many as nine of the major field crops: corn, other feed grains, soybeans, wheat, and cotton, plus silage, hay, and wild hay. The nation is divided into 31 consuming regions for animal and grain products, including exports. The model can include up to 12 livestock and dairy production activities. Regional data for crop response as a function of fertilizer use were taken from a Department of Agriculture survey (Ibach and Adams 1968) primarily based on experiment station data, but also on some farm data. The data were adjusted for a time trend of productivity increase. For an assumed state of production technology and demand, including exports, the model can calculate the least cost means of filling the demands. Transportation and production costs are minimized. Thus the results are not identical to existing patterns. Existing locational patterns reflect traditional crop patterns which may not minimize cost.

Brokken and Heady (1968) found that an efficient spatial arrangement of agricultural activities cut production cost 2.5 percent in comparison with existing patterns in 1965. The main reasons were a movement of cattle feeding and grazing to the Southeast and South; and of crops, particularly cotton, to the West. Most impressive is the decline in land required for crop production. When these changes in location are made, increased food production takes place on less land. And more beef is produced as well, responding to consumer demand for lower-priced production. Much of the less productive land is taken out of production. Surplus land increases by about 60 million acres to 163 million acres. This land is of a lower agricultural potential, however.

With a demand increase of 22 percent over the 1965 level, the model estimated that there would still be a surplus of 44 million acres (Brokken and Heady 1968). By coincidence, this situation corresponds closely to the conditions of 1974. The value of these crops produced in 1974 was $50,857 million. Deflated by an index of crop prices (CRB 1976), this figure becomes $18,600 million in 1965 dollars, about 22 percent higher than the actual 1965 production value of $15,346 million.

Not only may we conclude that the agricultural system has a good bit of slack in it (internal inefficiency), but it turns out that pesticides are used much more than is necessary because of this inefficient arrangement. As mentioned in Chapter 4, Dixon *et al.* (1973) estimated that 50 percent less pesticides would be used under the optimal conditions than were actually used in 1965. They simply took the Brokken and Heady rearrangement and calculated the pesticide use that would be needed to raise crops in their new geographical distribution. All this change is strictly within the confines of the conventional system.

Mayer and Hargrove (1971) used the Iowa State model to investigate the effects of limiting fertilizer use. They considered three cases: maximum fertilizer used per acre held constant at the average 1969 level for corn, 110 pounds of nitrogen; maximum nitrogen use of 50 pounds per acre and other fertilizers proportionately reduced; and a total prohibition on chemical fertilizer. The production function was assumed to remain constant for the first two cases. For the third case, some return to crop rotation and the crop mix of the early 1950s was assumed. At that time about half of the harvested land received NPK fertilizer, but at very low rates. In the first two cases, land substitutes for fertilizer until well beyond 1980.

In the third case investigated by Mayer and Hargrove (1971), the abolition of chemical fertilizer, acreage planted to corn increases substantially at the expense of other grains and, particularly, soybeans. Yields drop precipitously to 60 to 65 percent of 1969 levels, except for soybeans, where yields remain constant, since soybeans are less dependent on nitrogen fertilizer for good production. Production of major grains drops from about nine million bushels to a little over seven million bushels. This level would be more than sufficient for domestic use, but would require severe export limitations. Although in this third case Mayer and Hargrove allowed changes in the production system to adjust to fertilizer restrictions, their ban on phosphate makes it impossible to relate the results to organic farming. Recall that phosphate pollution is primarily a matter of erosion which can be controlled by sound agricultural practices. And organic farmers use the less soluble rock phosphate instead of super-phosphate. A similar model developed by Taylor and Swanson (1975) at the University of Illinois came to similar conclusions to those of Mayer and Hargrove.

In a related study, using the Iowa State model, Heady *et al.* (1972) projected agricultural land use and requirements in the year 2000, given the assumptions that productivity would continue to improve at past rates, that export demand would also grow modestly, and that domestic population would increase to 280 million. Cropland available for meeting export demand amounted to 51 million acres under these assumptions. Then the model was modified to satisfy constraints on fertilizer and pesticide use. When nitrogen fertilizer was limited to 50 pounds per acre, about half the present use, only 13 million acres were available for export, that is, 38 million more acres were needed for crop production. Banning all insecticides on cotton and corn had less impact: Only three million acres would be required to grow these crops under the optimal geographic arrangement.

An aggregate production function approach. Headley (1968) estimated the marginal product of agricultural pesticides, chemical fertilizers and other inputs using a Cobb-Douglas production function and state data for output per farm. Another model using output per acre for 59 crops gave similar results. Marginal value products were compared to input costs to obtain estimates of marginal productivities which, for pesticides and fertilizers, came out to a little over $4 per $1 invested for both. The marginal product of land and buildings came out about 7 percent, near the interest rate at that time. Two high input correlations mar the results, however, and indicate that the pesticide figure may be spurious. Labor is highly correlated with pesticides ($\rho = 0.77$), and "land and buildings" are highly correlated with machinery input ($\rho = 0.83$). The model yielded a marginal product of labor of between $1.40 and $4.20 per day, which was below the existing farm-labor wage rates at the time. On the other hand, the marginal product of machinery came out as $2.40 per $1 annual expenditure. Thus, the latter may be picking up some of the contribution of "land and buildings," and some of the measured pesticide contributions may belong to labor. The inputs in these pairs are highly complementary. Aside from these problems, the apparent productivity of pesticides and other inputs may be purely imaginary, reflecting crop differences and weather differences between regions. Recall that much pesticide use is in regions where the treated crops should probably not be grown. What we have here is an interesting mathematical exercise.

In a related study, Headley estimated marginal products of herbicides, insecticides, and fertilizers for 10 regions of the United States (Langham, Headley, and Edwards 1972). Wide variations between regions appeared, ranging from as large as three orders of magnitude for insecticides to a factor of four for fertilizers. The same problems as noted above apply for the most part to this study.

Langham, Headley, and Edwards (1972) calculated marginal rates of substitution and an "elasticity of substitution" of land for insecticides, e, for the 10 regions and for the nation, from their regression coefficients for marginal products. This elasticity is defined as the percent change in one input divided by the corresponding percent change in another input, holding output constant. The (point) value of e varied from -2.7 for the Appalachian region to -327 for the Southeast. For the United States as a whole, e was -6.5. Langham *et al.* then suggested that this elasticity estimate of -6 to -7 implies that a 12 percent increase in cropland harvest (approximately the amount of farmland in retirement at that time) would correspond to a reduction of insecticide use of 70 to 80 percent. This result was apparently obtained by simply multiplying the point elasticity by the percent change. Note, however, that the correlation between input variables works to overestimate the marginal product of pesticides and to underestimate that of land. Thus, both errors are additive, pointing to an overestimate of the marginal rate of substitution of land for pesticides; that is, they indicate that more land is required to compensate for a reduction in pesticide use than is actually the case.

The actual response would, however, depend on the production function. Chapman (1973) notes that if a Cobb-Douglas function of the form $Y = AX_1^{a_1} X_2^{a_2}$ is assumed, where X_1 equals land used and X_2 equals pesticides used, then the marginal rate of substitution is a_2X_1 / a_1X_2 and $e = a_2 / a_1$. For a 12 percent increase in land use and no change in any other parameters, insecticide use would decline to $(1/1.12)^{6.5} = 0.48$ of its initial value, a decline of 52 percent rather than 70 or 80 percent.

However, in the case of pesticides and fertilizers, is a Cobb-Douglas form for the production function really satisfactory if large changes in the inputs are envisioned? Studies of crop response as a function of pesticide and fertilizer use show not only diminishing marginal product but eventually negative marginal product. This allows a good fit for a production function of the form $Y = aX - bX^2$, where a and b are positive constants (Heady 1952; see Figures 4-2 and 7-1). For such a function, it would be easy to substitute farmland for chemicals at high application rates ($e = -\infty$?!). But at low application rates, chemicals may be highly effective and substitution may be far more difficult ($0 < e \leqslant 1$). Because of the overuse of farm chemicals, it is reasonable to suppose that there is much more flexibility in substitution of land for chemicals at the present usage rate than if the rate were substantially reduced. Thus, aside from the questionable economic basis of these estimates, the model does not appear to come very close to approximating the real world.

Limitations of previous studies. All of the studies reviewed have one thing in common: They begin and, for the most part, end with the technology of conventional agriculture. The linear programing models of Heady and others offer the most insights since they allow full interregional adjustments in crop production locations. Still, even if large changes are envisioned, such as outright banning of chemical pesticides, the current state of technology is still assumed. The one study which allowed for changeover to alternative technology, by Mayer and Hargrove (1971), put a restriction on fertilizer use that made the results inapplicable to organic farming.

Modern agriculture is a system of interrelated parts, many of which are dependent upon each other. The inputs to an agricultural system exhibit a high degree of complimentarity (*cf.* Headley 1968). While not being exactly a fixed production function technology, there are certainly limits to the extent of a satisfactory adjustment within the confines of the technology in use. For example, it would be most difficult to operate close-confinement animal husbandry without antibiotics.

If alternative methods of production are available (for example, organic agriculture), then when the relative advantage of conventional and organic methods changed sufficiently, a point could be reached where changeover to the alternative technology would begin. The discounted increase in income stream, adjusted for uncertainty, would have to exceed the cost of changeover, and also compensate for the loss (or gain) of satisfaction which might occur if a change in technology were made. Referring to Figure 9-3, a point would come when movement along f^2 would be more costly than a shift over to f^3.

Furthermore, changed ground rules will change research priorities. No one knows what will happen when a technological challenge is set. But surprises are often in store, and research can frequently rise to the occasion of developing new methods which are no more costly to use, or are even less costly, than those replaced. Thus, to anticipate realistically the future cost of environmental controls on the basis of the present technology, is virtually impossible. For example, in 1863, the British Parliament required a 90 percent reduction in hydrogen chloride emissions from alkali plants. Within five years, the emission reduction was exceeded, and new processes had been developed which turned the reclaimed wastes into profits (Squires 1970). In agriculture, we are already seeing chemical controls being wholly or partially replaced by non-polluting biological controls, at least partly in response to restrictions (or the threat of restrictions). Farmers are also using agricultural consultants to obtain the same yields with less chemical use (cf. Hall, Norgaard and Willey 1975). A high tax, or a tax that increased rapidly after a certain minimum use per acre, would encourage the trend.

Pesticide and chemical fertilizer use is not reversible. Benefits from increased use do not equal losses from decreased use, particularly in the short run. Soil conditions change, predator-prey relations change, pest resistance changes; with the result that yields may be lower after removal of chemical controls than before application. On the other hand, yields may be larger than prior to chemical application because of residual positive effects.

In conclusion, with large changes in pesticide or fertilizer use, there would be technological, structural and geographical changes. These changes may be described as at least a partial shift to different production functions (cf. Headley and Lewis 1967).

Production Costs of Organic Farms

Previous investigations have focused on marginal policies of limiting chemical use or have assumed the continuation of current agricultural technology. Many of the studies assume a continuous production function and/or that the same production function would apply to the changed situation, but this will depend on the technology of the alternatives available. Some aspects of the situation approximate a series of fixed coefficient production functions with a significant cost of changing over from one to another. The conventional and organic methods are to some extent incompatible, so that marginal substitution is often difficult or impossible (*cf.* Davidson and Norgaard 1973).

It would seem appropriate to investigate production possibilities under alternative agricultural methods. It is, even now, possible to grow marketable fruit, vegetables, grains, and beans without the use of any pesticides or manufactured nitrogen fertilizers. It is possible to obtain high quality. Costs may be higher, and input mix different. Conclusions may be different when the perspective is that of the commercial-scale organic farmer, than when the perspective is that of the grower using standard techniques.

Since organic growers have already imposed upon themselves the "no-chemical" constraint, they are presumably doing everything they can to control pests by other means, or at least some of them are. When we recognize the likelihood of technical change in agriculture along non-chemical lines, cost estimates from organic farms must be recognized as potentially overly high. Nevertheless, these estimates may give some realistic indication of the costs of limiting chemical use in the current state of ecological knowledge.

The approach in this study is to look at the cost structures of organic farming. Cost estimates will now be presented for growing the major crops under strict non-industrial chemical regimes, that is, organic farming on a commercial scale. Estimates of these production costs can be obtained from (1) a comparison of farm prices of organic and conventional commercial farm crops (Chapter 11); and (2) the production costs of modern organic farmers, compared to those of conventional farmers (Chapter 12). From the latter we will be able to obtain some estimates of differing input requirements, particularly labor requirements.

The approaches taken here are not without their faults. Nevertheless, we are now actually dealing with the alternative systems we are seeking to understand. It is felt that these two approaches, coming from the two sides of production cost and market price, will complement each other. The results should be of greater validity than estimates from one side alone.

11 Estimating Production Costs of Organic Food from Farm Prices

Price differences between organic food and conventional food may be used to estimate production cost differences if these differences are measured at the farm. Such differences must be adjusted, however, to account for the presence of any excess (or deficiency of) profits over the long-run value of the resources. Such excess profits may arise because of strong brand loyalty, a temporary excess demand in an expanding sector, and barriers to entering an expanding sector. The most likely divergences from competitive markets will tend to overstate the additional cost of producing organic food. In the last section of this chapter, comparisons will be made between prices of organic and conventional food.

Effectiveness of Competition in Agricultural Markets

Conventional markets. Prices in the mid-1970s can be taken as a good measure of long-run production costs for most agricultural commodities, at least when comparing alternative production systems. For conventional agriculture, we will assume long-run equilibrium in a competitive market structure for most major crops: grains, beans, field fruit, vegetables. There are hundreds of thousands of growers. While there are only a few buyers for some products and some regions, there is considerable flexibility in changing from one crop to another, at least for many of the larger farmers. Brand loyalty and barriers to entry are minimal at the farm level. Government price supports were well below market prices in 1973 and 1974 for most crops. In the case of production requiring considerable investment in plant and equipment, or a long period of investment before making a profit (such as fruit trees), or requiring large feed inputs, temporary market imbalances can be large, and may extend over a period of years. Even here, however, presumably an average over a number of years would give a good estimate of long-run costs. To the extent that farm prices and profits in conventional markets are artificially low due to buyer power, our estimates of increased cost of organic food will be biased upwards.

The period 1972 through 1974 saw a rapid increase in prices of basic food commodities, not primarily because of production cost increases, though there were some large increases in production costs, but because of abnormally high foreign demand caused by bad weather in many of the major crop-producing areas of the world. The United States also had some poor harvests because of adverse weather conditions. For example, corn production fell from an average of 97 bushels per acre in 1972 to only 72 in 1974 (USDA 1975). Despite the 1976 drought in Europe, worldwide harvests have largely recovered from the disastrous period of a few years ago, and prices have fallen back from their peaks. While food prices in 1976 are higher than in 1970, there has been considerable inflation in farm input prices since then, of approximately the same amount. From December 1970 to December 1975, an index of farm input prices rose 70 percent (CRB 1976b). An index of prices received has risen only slightly more, 77 percent. By May 1976, production costs had risen so rapidly that the ratio of indices of farm input to output became the same as it was in the late 1960s (CRB 1976a).

Because agricultural commodity prices were mostly free from price supports in the mid-1970s and also had receded from the levels achieved during the period of temporary excess demand of the early 1970s, it appears fairly safe to view average 1975–1976 prices as a relatively good approximation to long-run average production costs for most commodities.

Organic markets. When we turn to organic farming, we find far fewer farmers. For most products, there is no reason to believe that cooperation in pricing would be effective, however. There are enough producers or potential producers in most markets to provide some competitive pressures. The major wholesalers buy from dozens of producers, some from hundreds, though individual products may be obtained from only one grower. One of the larger companies buys its grains and beans from between one and five farms, half of the commodities from only one, with an average of 1.8 growers per commodity. In some cases, there are only a few growers in the whole national or regional market. There is only a handful of commercial-scale organic apple producers for the fresh market in the eastern United States, and only a few producers easily fill the national demand for organic rice.

There is perhaps even more concentration on the buyer side of the organic food market. About half a dozen moderately large wholesalers (about $1 to $2 million annual sales) dominate the national grain and bean market. But these firms are comparatively new and independent. And there is no effective national organization of organic food wholesalers. Competition is enforced by the possibility of farmers selling their products on conventional markets. Organic meat and grain products generally meet or exceed quality standards of conventional markets. Quality standards of organic fresh produce, such as lettuce, may fall below conventional. A lettuce grower may find that he has no alternative but to sell to the organic wholesaler, and so may receive a lower price. Farmers can also sell directly to retail stores and many do.

Brand loyalty. A number of the organic food producers have attempted to develop brand loyalty based on their particular soil or climate, which they claim produces particularly valuable food (for example, Deaf Smith "highly mineralized soil," an Arrowhead Mills brand; and Ted Witmer's "rich Montana soil"); or on their good name and ethics or freshness (retired missionaries with many years of public, faithful service at Walnut Acres), or on more traditional lines of favorable associations with brand names (Better Foods, Mennonite Country, Balanced, Old Mill). This development has been more pronounced in the area of processed foods. Similar advantages in mass marketing are present in natural processing as in conventional food. In comparing farm production costs, the only concern would be the extent that brand loyalty extends to unprocessed commodities. It is, of course, much weaker there. There are many small local or regional distributors, often farmers that have vertically integrated. The assumption will be made that there are no excess profits arising from brand loyalty at the primary production stage of the industry. To the extent that this is not true, it would bias the estimates of organic food production costs upwards.

Excess demand. Sales of organic food have been on the increase in recent years, reflecting increased consumer demand (Chapter 8). Since it takes a few years to complete a changeover to organic farming, it is reasonable to ask whether there may be unsatisfied demand at long-run equilibrium prices, causing temporary excess profits for those fortunate enough to have converted earlier. Excess profits are probably less a factor at the farm level than at retail. Many farmers already use largely organic techniques, but sell their crops on conventional markets because they have no reasonably priced alternative. For example, an organic apple grower in Ontario sells 90 percent of his crop in conventional channels. According to buyers, there is still a reservoir of farmers ready to change over if the market were there. There has been much confusion over the definition of organic food, and much food has been sold as organic that was not in fact raised that way at all. In the absence of enforced standards in the industry, with consumers generally unable to tell the difference, fraud has been able to satisfy any temporary excess demand to a large extent. In any event, there does not appear to be any simple way to measure the effect of excess demand, so it will be neglected. As in the case of brand loyalty, neglect of excess demand will bias estimates of organic food production costs upwards.

Personal relationships and fair prices. There is some market power among buyers and sellers of organic food at the farm stage. Exercise of this power could distort prices from their long-run average cost or fair return to the farmer and his investment. However, certain features of the situation would appear to make large departures from fair returns unlikely.

Both sides of the market are highly concentrated, so a balance of power would result in bargaining. Generally, the outcome of bargaining is undetermined. In the case of organic food, bargaining is likely to reach a price that gives a fair return to all parties. This is because of the nature of the relationships between buyer and seller, and also because of the farmer's other options, that is, to sell direct or sell on conventional markets.

The main factor that would work to keep prices in line with costs is the personal relationship between the small businesspeople in the organic and natural food business. In some respects, we have an organic food community including growers, distributors, retailers, and consumers. In fact, many regional organizations include both growers and consumers. There is of course a financial conflict of interest between these member groups. But personal relationships require a sense of fairness to all parties. Trust is of the essence in organic food markets, for appearance tells little. Each member must feel he is being treated fairly.

Many of the individuals in the organic food movement reject what they perceive as the dominant business ethic of maximizing profits. Thus there is a great sensitivity to any appearance of excess profits. This social pressure puts downward pressure on prices. Since organic farmers are not in the business as much for the money as for other satisfaction, the probability that they would take advantage of temporary excess demand is minimized. (See Chapter 9.)

Wholesale market prices for fresh vegetables sometimes fluctuate more in commercial markets than in organic. Organic prices move more slowly in response to market forces, reflecting a personal relationship between buyer and seller. For example, organic lettuce prices remained constant during the first six months of 1976 in California, except for one month when prices were about 10 percent higher. Commercial prices fluctuated over a range of 20 percent from the average price during this period. (One standard deviation for the commercial prices, using first Wednesday of each month [FSMNS 1976], was 23 percent; for organic, 5 percent.)

In conclusion, while there would appear to be some possibility for excess profits at the farm stage of organic food production, there are enough factors working in the direction of a fair return that normal profits appear a reasonable assumption. To the extent that farmers receive some premium above cost because of their market power, this will bias estimates of the cost of raising organic food upward.

Organic food quality. Two products must be of comparable quality in order to make a comparison of quantity or price. Grains and beans are graded according to United States Department of Agriculture standards, and so are meats. These products can be compared on this basis. When organic markets require lower moisture content, adjustments can be made for that. Whether organic grain has some other quality dimensions has been explored in Part I, and will not be considered here.

Fruit and vegetables are more difficult to compare. Organically grown citrus fruit often has discolored skins and may be downright ugly. Inside, however, the quality is generally as good as that found in supermarket products. It seems only fair to make production cost comparisons on the basis of internal quality.

From my experience observing produce in supermarkets and in natural food stores over the last few years, my impression is that the overall quality is at least as good in natural food stores on the average as in supermarkets. Organic food is often fresher, but there are sometimes signs of insect infestation or decay. The insect damage is generally superficial on outer leaves that are discarded from supermarket produce. Decay from storage is more a result of lack of preservation than production method. Organic food is not waxed or chemically treated. Actually, organic food probably would keep better if treated in the same manner as conventionally raised food (Chapter 3).

Barriers to Enter Organic Farming

If we can take farm prices as fair measures of the average total cost of producing organic and conventional food, we can estimate the difference in production cost from a comparison of these prices. However, the measured difference must be adjusted for any barriers to entry.

While land resources can move freely from organic farming to conventional farming, they do not move freely in the reverse direction. In changing over to organic farming, an initial crop loss generally occurs, particularly if done quickly. Soil life needs to be built. Biological controls may have been weakened or destroyed by chemicals. It may take up to three or four years for residues to lose their effect (DeBach 1974). This loss decreases until, after a few years, production levels have reached their equilibrium levels under organic husbandry (which may be lower than under the chemical regime). For example, the Rodale experimental farm reported corn yields of only 60 bushels per acre after changeover from continuous corn, about half the previous year's yield, even with 15 tons per acre manure application. Second year yields were back to 85 bushels per acre, cutting the first year loss approximately in half (Cox undated).

Generally, after the initial drop in yield, the yield steadily rises. Sometimes, however, there is a smaller drop after a few years, say in the fourth. Allowing for this possibility would seem to add unnecessary complexity. We will therefore assume decreasing losses with time (*cf.*, Pfeiffer 1945; Balfour 1974). Interviews with individual farmers are also consistent with this assumption. Since maximum availability of nutrients from organic fertilizers does not occur until the second year following application, it is reasonable to expect fertility loss for at least two years (Thompson and Troeh 1973). This loss can be at least partially overcome by using compost.

Because an initial loss from going "cold turkey" can be high, some organic farming advocates recommend changing over only one field at a time, say, one quarter of the farm each year (Balfour 1974). Larry Eggen, manager of an organic grain company in Minnesota, recommends a three-year transition period, which avoids serious yield losses, but which involves some investment. Most damaging to soil life is the liquid ammonia fertilizer. This is replaced by urea for the three-year transition. A consultant is hired to make detailed analyses of soil conditions at a cost of $3 to $4 per acre. Mineral or other fertilizer is used to bring the soil into balance at a cost of from $15 to $600 per acre, but generally no more than $75 to $100. Then, by the third year, soil life has recovered to the point where organic production can be initiated with little or no temporary yield loss.

Whether done quickly or gradually, there is generally a cost of changing over from conventional to organic production. This cost must be paid for by consumers, and will make farm prices for organic food higher than long run production costs during a period of expanding or steady demand.

Even if higher prices are in the offing, farmers may not be able to finance the changeover, or may be fearful of entering a new market without government support. Chemical fertilizer programs have received federal support; organic farmers have not been so blessed. Price supports give no premium for organic food. Markets for organic food are poorly organized. Often promises of purchase are made by the easy-going folks in the city alternative-food cooperative, but then not followed through. Such uncertainty and risk raises additional barriers, and to the extent that they influence farmers' decisions on whether or not to enter the organic food market, estimates of production costs will be overstated.

If the farmer is planning on having his land certified residue-free, there may be a further wait before any premium for organically raised food is received.

If a farmer is considering a crop for which there is considerable ignorance regarding alternative growing techniques, additional barriers are raised. Many successful organic farmers today have spent years experimenting at their own expense. Often they have experienced low yields or crop failures, just as might happen at any state experiment station. These farmers may feel a fair price should help them recoup some of this investment. Thus, in small markets, as in the eastern states, prices are significantly above current average cost for some commodities.

Increased price of organic food due to barriers to entry. We will now derive some estimates of the price increases of organic food due to the cost of changing over from conventional production. If the demand for organic food were stable or falling, farm prices in competitive markets would reflect the value of the resources to society, that is, the long-run average total cost, which includes a fair return to all the factors of production including the farmer himself (normal profits). However, if the demand for organic food is increasing, as it presently is (Chapter 8), prices will not fall to long-run average cost. This is because prices must be high enough to attract new firms to enter, that is, to induce some farmers to go to the expense of changing over from conventional to organic production. The prices of organic food must be high enough not only to provide a fair return for the resources employed, but also to compensate the new (marginal) farmer for the cost of changing over.

Figure 11-1 illustrates graphically the increased price due to barriers to entry experienced by potential organic farmers. The long-run supply curve is shown by S_{LR}, which is horizontal, reflecting constant returns to scale

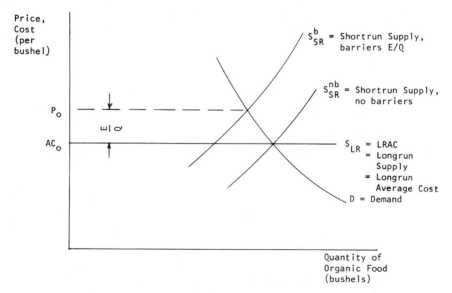

Figure 11-1. Equilibrium in Organic Food Markets with Barrier to Entry

(constant unit costs) as the industry expands. Thus S_{LR} is also the long-run average cost, LRAC. We are assuming constant costs for simplicity here; Chapter 13 will explore qualifications, which appear small. The organic farming markets are assumed to have effective competition or sufficient balance of power or moral suasion so that long-run equilibrium price would fall to LRAC, the average cost of producing organic food. The short-run supply would be S_{SR}^{nb} in that case of no barriers. However, we assume that there are barriers to enter of \$E per acre or E/Q per bushel (or other unit), with Q the yield in bushels per acre. Price is thus higher than long-run production costs by the amount E/Q, and the short-run supply curve is S_{SR}^{b}, which intersects the demand curve, D, at the observed farm price, P.

Let us now formalize the price differences of organic and conventional food in terms of production cost (average cost) differences. The observed price of organic food, p_o, is

$$P_o = AC_o + \frac{E_L}{Q} + \frac{E_I}{Q} + \pi_{BL} + \pi_{ex} + \pi_{MP} \qquad (11.1)$$

Here AC_o is the average (long-run) cost of production of organic food, Π_{BL} is any monopoly profit resulting from organic food brand loyalty at the farm stage; Π_{ex} is any excess profit in organic food due to lags between production and demand, in excess of changeover cost; Π_{MP} is any monopoly profit resulting from scarcity and a limited number of sellers; E_L/Q is the barrier due to yield loss in the first few years after changeover; and E_I/Q is the barrier due to an initial investment required to effect the changeover from conventional farming. All quantities are expressed in value (\$) per unit measure (*e.g.*, bushels), except the E's which are per acre, so that they must be divided by the yield, Q. We have assumed that the last three terms in Equation 11.1 are negligible, so we have

$$P_o = AC_o + \frac{E_L}{Q} + \frac{E_I}{Q} \qquad (11.2)$$

This form corresponds to Figure 11-1, with $E_L + E_I = E$. Since we assume long-run equilibrium in conventional food production at normal returns to the factors of production, the price of conventional food, p_c, is equal to its long-run average cost, AC_c:

$$P_c = AC_c \qquad (11.3)$$

Subtracting Equation 11.3 from Equation 11.2, we have

$$\Delta p = \Delta AC + \frac{E_L}{Q} + \frac{E_I}{Q} \qquad (11.4)$$

(where $\Delta p = P_o - P_c$ and $\Delta AC = AC_o - AC_c$)

In Appendix B, formulae are derived for the barriers, as functions of the interest rate, r, the percent loss in yield the first year of changeover, d, and the recovery ratio, a (the ratio of consecutive years' yield losses). Substituting Equations B.13 and B.15 into Equation 11.4, we have

$$\Delta p = \Delta AC + \frac{p_o dr}{1+r-a} \tag{11.5}$$

$$\Delta p = \Delta AC + \frac{C(1+r)^2 r}{Q_o} \tag{11.6}$$

Equation 11.5 is for a changeover in one year, and Equation 11.6 for an investment of $C per acre, an organic yield of Q_o bushels per acre, and full changeover in the third year. In practice a combination of both may occur. For typical values of the variables, the price increase is on the order of 5 to 10 percent. For example, suppose a=0.5, d=0.5, and r=0.1, that is, the farm experiences a 50 percent loss in the potential organic yield in the first year, and each succeeding year the preceding year's loss is cut in half. This is in accord with the experience at the Rodale experimental farm cited above. The interest rate is 10 percent. Then dr/(1+r−a)=0.0833. Thus, the price of organic food is about 8.3 percent above the real cost of production for the values of the parameters assumed. In Figure B-1 (see Appendix B) the required increase in organic food prices is graphed as a function of the first year loss for representative values r and a.

Similar conclusions with regard to increased price are obtained by substituting typical values of the variables into Equation 11.6. If an investment of $100 per acre is needed on land that produces 80 bushels per acre of corn with a value of $2.50 per bushel in conventional markets, the price increase for organic markets would have to be at least $C(1+r)^2 r/Q_o=$ $100(1.1)^2 \cdot 0.1/80 = $0.15 per bushel. This is about 6 percent of the price of conventional corn.

Survey of Organic and Conventional Food Prices

Prices of conventional food are available from United States Department of Agriculture publications. Prices of organically grown food were obtained from the major wholesalers and a midwest organic grain company. Two of the wholesalers also act as grain companies, marketing grain and beans to other wholesalers. Organic wholesalers are located mainly on the east coast and in California. Six were contacted by telephone and asked about their pricing methods. Detailed price information was obtained from four on the basis of personal interview or questionnaire. When possible, information on markups was obtained so that responses could be compared with wholesale prices adjusted back to the farm. These checks confirmed the farm price information received. Farmers and marketing agents also supplied some price information.

Grains and beans. Most of the farm prices of grains and beans are set in relation to the national or regional commodity markets for conventionally grown food (referred to as commercial food in this context). According to the major wholesaler in the area, peanut, grain, and bean prices in the Southwest average 10 to 15 percent higher for organically raised than for commercial commodities. In Table 11-1, wheat prices paid by a northeastern wholesaler are compared with commercial prices. The following steps are necessary to determine the premium that organic growers obtain, shown in the table. At the top of Table 11-1 is the organic FOB (Free On Board, not including freight) price at the point of purchase, the farm. Next, the cleaning and bagging charge is deducted. Average rates by state were obtained from the organic grain company. Rates vary from $1.00 to $2.00, although the farmer can generally do it more cheaply himself. Next, a premium for having a lower percent moisture than average commercial grain is deducted. The cost to dry down to the organic moisture content from the commercial level is used. This gives us an estimate of the price the farmer receives for his wheat. The commercial prices are taken for the

Table 11-1   Wheat Prices Paid by a Northeastern Wholesaler, 100 lb. Bags, Summer, 1976

	Hard Winter Wheat, #1, 13% Protein ($)	Soft Winter Wheat US #1 ($)	Hard Amber Durum ($)
Organic price, FOB	10.00 (Kansas)	9.00 (N.Y., Mich.)	11.60 (Montana)
Deduct:			
Cleaning and bagging	(1.50)	(1.50)	(1.50)
Grain company margin	(0.85)	(0.75)	(1.01)
Premium for 10.5 percent moisture rather than 13.0 (cost to dry)	(0.12)	(0.12)	(0.12)
Price to Farmer	7.53	6.63	8.97
Commercial price, June 1976	7.10 (Kansas City)	6.21 (Portland)	7.14 (Minneapolis)
Difference, organic less commercial	0.43	0.42	1.83
Percent increase, organic over commercial	6.1	6.8	25.6
Wheat variety percent U.S. production, 1974	77.6	18.0	4.4

Sources: ERS 1976c;   USDA 1975;   Survey by author.

nearest commodity market for which prices are quoted. Prices are 6 to 7 percent higher for the organic winter wheat, which makes up 77.6 percent of United States production. Prices for the organic durum were 25.6 percent higher than commercial, but durum makes up only 4.4 percent of the national market.

In the Northeast, organic grain can be purchased from old-order Amish farmers. There is presently a surplus supply. Farmers with consistently high-quality grain (high percent protein and low percent moisture and damaged kernels) are purchased from consistently. The wholesaler picks up the wheat at the farm and pays a premium of 15 percent over what the farmer would get at the local mill for ordinary wheat. Because of its high quality, the mill would pay a premium of about $0.25 per bushel or about 7.3 percent. The wholesaler is thus paying only a 7.3 percent premium. The main reason for the premium is not to compensate for the cost of organic production, however, but to maintain a stable relationship with the supplier, assuring that the grain does not end up at the mill. Since the farmer normally transports his own grain to the mill, some premium is paid because the wholesaler must transport the grain himself. The added inconvenience to the farmer of having to coordinate with a small business probably balances some of his saving in not transporting the grain.

The midwest organic grain company arranges sales of organic grains and beans from 14 states, mostly in the Midwest. These crops include corn, popcorn, soybeans, wheat (hard, soft, durum), buckwheat, oats, rye, edible beans and flaxseed. With the exception of rye, prices have generally been set in comparison to the quoted prices at the Minneapolis and Chicago grain markets. Average futures prices are marked up 20 to 22 percent, and $1.00 is added to this figure for cleaning and bagging, somewhat less than the present going rate, but more than it costs a farmer to do it himself once he sets up for it. The grain company takes a commission of 10 percent of the sales price, which leaves the farmer with a premium of 8 to 10 percent of the commercial price. The 10 percent premium, which has been standard for this company, apparently was derived from ideas of parity prices. When the grain company was set up in 1970, parity prices were an average of 10 percent above market prices. The company's idea was to offer parity prices for noncommercially grown commodities. The 10 percent premium stuck, and it does seem to be about standard across the country. Though farmers may wish they could obtain higher prices, they are evidently willing to continue to sell at the 10 percent premium.

Rye prices are set differently by the grain company. Commercial prices of rye have been far below parity for years, often more so than other crops. Prices of rye have been set some two-and-a-half times the commercial market price, at a price which is considered a fair or just price. The high price is also thought to be justified because of the difficulty of raising rye without ergot infestation. At any rate, rye is such a small percent of national grain sales that its price would have no impact on estimates of national production costs. But the pricing does illustrate the different approach taken by organic merchants.

The precipitous drop in commercial field crop prices during 1977 left organic farmers with a far larger premium. Dealers have not been able to maintain such a differential, however, and organic prices began easing downward in late 1977.

All the data collected from grain and bean buyers point to a 10 percent premium for organically raised field crops in normal times. If a 5 percent deduction is made for changeover cost, this leaves a premium of about 5 percent for these crops.

Rice. Premiums for organic rice are considerably higher than those for other grains. Table 11-2 compares rice prices paid by organic wholesalers in July 1976. The organic rice averaged 36 percent higher in price than commercial. Some of this higher price may represent marketing expense of the growers, or their small number. But the price increase also reflects some real increased production costs. Unlike the other grains, rice is grown in flooded conditions, making weed control more difficult for organic growers.

Table 11-2   Organic and Commercial Rice Prices, 100 lb. Bags, July 1976

		Mill Price, US#1, July 1976		
Rice Variety	State of Origin	Organic	Commercial	Percent Increase, Organic Over Commercial
Northeast Buyer:				
Short	Arkansas	24.00	15.15	37
Short	California	29.00	15.15	51
Medium	Louisiana	21.00	15.50	26
Long	Arkansas	24.50	17.00	31
Mid-Atlantic Buyer:				
Long	Texas	29.50	16.50	44
Long	Arkansas	26.80	17.00	37
Medium	Arkansas	21.30	15.50	27
Short	Arkansas	25.00	15.15	39
Average				36

Sources: FSMNS 1976c; survey by author.

Fruit and vegetables. The most highly developed markets for organic fruit and vegetables in this country are in California. Fresh organic produce is shipped from California on a year-round basis. There are only a few large organic wholesalers in California. Price information was requested from two of the largest, and also was obtained from a small dealer who ships out of state. Both large wholesalers generally pay prices that are closely tied to commercial wholesale prices, although sometimes a premium of 10 percent is paid for organic produce. The largest organic produce dealer in California made available his prices paid during the first week in August 1976, which were felt to be representative. (Organic prices are more stable than are commercial.) These prices are shown in Table 11-3, the second to the last column. These are "wholesale market prices," the prices the wholesaler pays farmers for produce delivered to the wholesale market.

Commercial vegetable and fruit prices are quoted on a daily basis by the Federal-State Market News Service in Los Angeles. The organic prices are for San Jose, somewhat farther north, but the prices should be roughly comparable. None of our contacts had reason to believe they would not be. The News Service regularly uses Wednesday prices in computing their averages; so did we. The average prices for the first two Wednesdays in August 1976 are shown in Table 11-3, the fourth column. Prices are quoted for good grade, sometimes also for a low grade, frequently much lower, and sometimes also a higher grade. All the organic prices were quoted for "U.S.#1." We took this to be equivalent to "good quality and condition" at the Los Angeles market. This would seem a reasonable assumption, in the light of the high standards of visual quality required by commercial channels, and the organic produce man who supplied the prices agreed. The average price of the good quality range for commercial produce is shown in the fifth column of Table 11-3.

Since some fruit and vegetables are not in season, and some prices vary considerably depending on the season, some adjustment had to be made to the commercial prices. Organic wholesalers who enjoy a personal relation with the farmers generally keep a much steadier price throughout the season. So, for example, when grapes are just coming into season, as they are in early August, the commercial prices are about $2.00 a lug (a wooden crate) higher than they will be a month later at peak season, according to average 1975 price variations (FSMNS 1976b). The organic price, on the other hand, will remain fairly constant throughout the season. If anything, the way we made this adjustment would tend to make the organic products appear more expensive than is actually the case. We used the low, in-season price as a reference for commercial prices, rather than the yearly average price. And organic prices will probably fall some also as the season progresses. When differences were less than $0.50 between early August prices and in-season (lowest) prices in 1975, no correction was made. There is a good bit of variability in fresh market prices, so some small price

Table 11.3 1976 California Fresh Fruit and Vegetable Wholesale Market Prices, Commercial and Organic

Crop	Variety	Pack	Commercial Price ($) Aug 4, 11 range	Average	Seasonal Adjustment	Commercial Price ($)	Organic Price[b] ($)	Percent Increase Organic to Comm.
Vegetables								
Cabbage	Cannonball	50#[a] carton	2.75-3.00	2.90	0.00	2.90	2.75	-5.2
Carrots	Emperauder	25# sack	1.75-2.25	2.00	0.00	2.00	2.10	5.0
Cucumbers	(regular)	30# lug	2.50-2.75	2.65	0.00	2.65	2.50	-5.7
Lettuce	Head, iceberg	2 doz, 40#	4.50-5.00	4.75	-0.50	4.20	4.50	7.1
Lettuce	Romaine	2 doz, 40#	4.00-4.50	4.25	-1.00	3.75	4.00	23.1
Lettuce	Red leaf	2 doz, 40#	4.50-5.50	5.00	-1.00	4.00	4.00	0.0
Lettuce	Butter	2 doz, 40#	4.00-4.50	4.25	-1.00	3.75	4.00	23.1
Onions	Yellow	50# sack	2.25-2.75	2.50	0.00	2.50	3.50	40.0
Potatoes	White rose	50# carton	3.50-4.00	3.75	0.00	3.75	3.50	-6.7
Potatoes	Russet, 8 - 10 oz	50# carton	4.50-5.00	4.75	0.00	4.75	4.50	-5.3
Tomatoes	Santa Clara	20# lug, 3x4 layers	2.75-3.50[c]	3.50[c]	0.00	3.50[c]	3.50	0.0
Vegetable average								6.9

Citrus Fruit								
Grapefruit	White	40# carton	3.25-4.00	3.65	-0.50	3.15	3.25	3.2
Grapefruit	Ruby	40# carton	3.25-4.00	3.65	0.00	3.65	3.50	-4.1
Oranges	Valencia	40# carton	3.75-4.25	4.00	0.00	4.00	4.00	0.0
Citrus average								-0.3
Non-citrus Fruit								
Plums	Santa Rosa	30# lug	3.50-5.50	4.50	0.00	4.50	4.50	0.0
Pears	Bartlett	24# lug	4.00-4.50	4.25	0.00	4.25	3.00	-29.4
Apples	Delicious	40# carton	11.00-13.00	12.00	-6.00	6.00	5.00	-8.3
Apples	Pippin	40# carton	6.00	6.00	-0.50	5.50	6.00	9.1
Grapes	Seedless	22# lub	7.50-8.50	8.00	-2.00	6.00	5.00	-16.7
Strawberries	Tufs	12 pint carton	4.75-5.75	5.25	0.00	5.25	4.50	-14.3

aPounds
bRepresentative prices, first 10 days of August.
cPacked 4 x 4, that is, smaller tomatoes.

Sources: FSMNS 1976a; 1976b; survey by author.

differences do not mean very much. The adjusted prices are in the seventh column of Table 11-3. The differences between organic and commercial prices were calculated, and the percent increase or decrease in organic prices is shown in the last column. While some seasonal and other variability is inherent in the data, taking an average over many crops should given an indication of real cost differences.

The differences between organic and commercial prices are small and often favor the organic. Average organic vegetable prices are about 7 percent higher than the commercial, mainly because of the 40 percent difference in onion prices, which may be an anomoly. The differences in citrus fruit also average out to about zero. Organic grapes and strawberries are cheaper, but this may mean a faulty correction for effects of the season. Organic deciduous fruit (apples, pears, plums) have markedly lower prices than their commercial counterparts. Again, this may reflect faulty seasonal adjustments or actual quality differences. Also, fruit prices are not as stable as vegetable prices. Some years there is a very large harvest, others bring a disaster. The former may lead to disastrous prices. Presently there is an overabundance of apples nationally, so that apple prices may not be a good indication of long-run production costs. It *is* possible that, because there are only a few organic buyers in California, produce prices are artificially low. This appears unlikely to any significant extent, as explained above.

The smaller organic dealers, in closer contact with growers, tend to quote higher premiums for organic produce. While organic produce can often be obtained at the same wholesale cost as commercial, such produce may be organic by default rather than by intention, such as obtained from neglected orchards. Thus, organic citrus and apples are often available at the same price as commercial. But for top-of-the-line organic produce, one small dealer estimated that he often pays 50 percent over commercial prices. This is really luxury production, for which nothing is too good, no corners are cut. All weeding would be by hand, much attention would be placed on soil building and balance, and picking is to order at peak quality. But part of this premium also reflects the small scale of the organic growers supplying these small dealers. For one dealer, his largest grower has less than 60 acres (Southern California irrigated land, known as "desert"). Small organic orange growers may get 50 to 100 percent more in organic channels than they would get from regular commercial buyers. That difference, however, reflects the buying power of the major commercial buyer, as much as the increased cost of organic food production.

In eastern organic produce markets, premiums are higher than in California for regular organic production. In 1977, the premium (markup) for carrots was about 35 percent, and that for onions and potatoes, about 60 percent. These premiums do not appear to be a reflection of production cost (see next chapter), but rather are largely due to proximity to the eastern market where there may be temporary excess demand. Established growers also must recoup their research investment.

In Table 11-4, we compare price differences between conventional and organic crops in Europe and America. The price differences in this country are consistently lower than those in Europe. Beans are about the same, but cereal and grain prices run about 10 percent higher in Europe than in this country for organically raised compared to commercial. This may reflect better natural soil fertility in this country, or a climate which may be more conducive to organic production. More likely, the differences between Europe and America reflect the more intensive cultivation and higher yields in Europe. Average wheat yields in Europe were almost twice the American in the early 1970s (USDA 1975). It may be more difficult for organic farmers to match costs and yields at high fertilization levels.

Table 11-4   Price Differences Between Conventional and Organic Production in the United States and Europe

| Crop | Percent Increase in Cost of Organic Food Compared to Conventional | | |
	United States	France (biological)	West Germany (bio-dynamic)
Field crops			
Cereals and grains	10	20[d]	20 to 25
Beans	10	-[d]	0
Vegetables			
Potatoes	5 (?)	5 to 20[c]	20 to 40
Other	5		0
Fruit			
Deciduous	15	10 to 50[b]	50 to 100[b]
Citrus	0	-	
Milk, butter, cheese	-	10 to 30	-
Meat	-	5 to 10[a]	-

[a]Compared with "prime" meat raised in the traditional manner.
[b]There is overproduction of apples in Europe, therefore conventional prices are below cost.
[c]All vegetables including potatoes.
[d]Not available.

Sources: France, Aubert 1972; West Germany FFBDW 1972; U.S., estimates by author, from this chapter and chapter 12.

Germans believe that the difficulty they have in matching commercial prices has to do with a conscious effort of the European governments to keep food prices low (Heinze 1976).

Except for potatoes, vegetable prices in Germany are about the same for organically raised as commercially raised, similar to the California data of Table 11-3. French vegetable prices appear relatively higher, but the French estimates do not separate potatoes from the other vegetables. In Germany and France, organic apple prices are much higher than commercial because of a state of overproduction of commercial apples. Apparently biological and bio-dynamic apple prices have been supported at what is considered to be a fair price.

In conclusion, organic grains and beans can be produced in this country for about 5 to 10 percent more than conventional products. For most vegetables, premiums of from 0 to 50 percent are paid for organic produce. Although no price difference was observed in California, production experience in the eastern United States indicates a substantial yield loss for some organic production (Chapter 12), which would be more in line with the European situation. Citrus fruit costs about the same whether grown organically or conventionally. While non-citrus fruit appears to cost about the same or less in this country, that may reflect overproduction. Estimates are given in the following chapter for apple price differences, derived from production cost considerations. From those calculations, we would expect that the real cost of producing deciduous fruit organically is probably about 15 percent higher than conventional, perhaps more in the future as machine harvest becomes prevalent.

12 Input Requirements for Organic Farming

A survey of organic farm production costs in the eastern and midwestern United States was carried out. In addition, six California organic growers were interviewed. This survey was supplemented by a review of published comparisons of organic and commercial inputs and yields in this country. The main study is by Lockeretz *et al.* (1975, 1976; also Klepper *et al.* 1977), of organic and conventional Corn Belt farms. Some information is also available on costs and yields in France (EPAB 1974). Our discussion will focus on differences in two key areas: yield, that is, land requirements, and labor costs. For the most part, other differences balance out or are negligible. Organic farmers cultivate more, but spray less. Fertilizer costs in vegetable crops are similar. The data are admittedly sparse, but some indications of relative yields and labor requirements can be obtained. As new data become available, the estimates can be refined.

The main crops of interest are those which provide the largest proportion of our food resources, and also, from an environmental point of view, those which require the most agricultural chemicals. From both points of view, corn is of prime importance. Our most valuable crops in terms of farm prices are shown in Table 12-1. Corn heads the list.

Corn also requires 41 percent of herbicides and 17 percent of insecticides used (Table 4-2) and is a heavy feeder on nitrogen fertilizers. Grapes, oranges, and apples are the three largest fruit crops. Two of them, apples and oranges, are the largest users of pesticides among fruit and vegetable crops. Among vegetables, potatoes and tomatoes are the most valuable crops.

First, the survey will be explained, and then the rest of the chapter will examine the available evidence on production cost and yield comparisons between organic and conventional production. This chapter considers

Table 12-1 Major United States Crops and Farm Value, 1974

Crop		Value (millions of $)	Percent Total
Grains	Corn	13,717	27.5
	Wheat	7,242	14.4
	Sorghum	1,751	3.4
	Rice	1,195	2.3
	Oats	928	1.8
	Barley	822	1.6
	Flaxseed	126	.2
	Rye	47	.1
Hay		5,770	11.5
Beans and nuts	Soybeans	8,246	16.4
	Peanuts	658	1.2
	Edible beans	420	.8
	Almonds	171	.3
	Other nuts	138	.3
Sugar	Cane	1,205	2.3
	Beets	1,036	1.9
Vegetables and Melons	Potatoes	1,461	2.8
	Tomatoes	793	1.5
	Lettuce	353	.7
	Snap beans	168	.3
	Onions	158	.3
	Sweet corn	125	.2
	Carrots	124	.2
	Cucumbers	124	.2
	Peas	112	.2
	Sweet Potatoes	107	.2
	Cantalopes	94	.2
	Cabbage	92	.2
	Celery	92	.2
	Other	513	1.0
Fruit	Grapes	610	1.2
	Oranges	601	1.2
	Apples	546	1.1
	Peaches	259	.5
	Strawberries	153	.3
	Grapefruit	153	.3
	Pears	125	.2
	Cherries	114	.2
	Other non-citrus	308	.6
	Other citrus	117	.2
Total Value of Major Crops		49,679	100.0

Sources: USDA 1975; CRB 1975a, 1975b.

current cost of production only; no consideration is given to availability of input requirements. The latter question, whether there might be increasing costs or resource constraints as organic food production expands, will be examined in the following chapter. Then Chapter 14 will put the information together for some estimates of the implications of a full changeover to organic production in the United States.

The focus here is on feed grains, because of their large percent of crop value. We will also analyze production of one vegetable, tomatoes, and one fruit, apples, in some detail, and also report data on some other vegetables.

The Farm Survey

Names of organic farmers were obtained from regional organic farming organizations, Rodale's listing of organic producers, organic food wholesalers, and an extension agent. I asked the presidents of some of the main farmers' organizations to supply me with names of farmers they believed would desire to cooperate. The list was limited for the most part to farmers who raised primarily crops for sale rather than for feeding to their own cattle. Livestock farms have been studied by Lockeretz *et al.* (1975, 1976) and I made use of their data for this type of farm. The livestock farms have manure available for fertilization. I wanted to see if other farms could do as well without a ready source of nitrogen fertilizer.

Sixty organic farmers were contacted by phone and/or by letter. Generally a telephone conversation established initial personal contact if the farmer lived out of the Maryland-Virginia-Pennsylvania area. If the farmer offered cooperation, after the purpose of the project was explained, he was sent an explanatory letter and data forms, one for each crop. A sample form is in Appendix C. The form is intentionally brief to encourage useful responses and avoid burdening the farmers. In addition to the questions on the form, orchardists were also asked about spacing and variety of trees. If farmers indicated wide yield variability, information on that was also solicited.

Ideally, a study of this nature would be carried out during the entire year, working with the farmers to collect data as it accumulated. This was not possible due to the limited nature of this preliminary survey. We relied instead on farmers' recall of average costs and yields. While this method is less than ideal, most farmers have a good idea of what they spend and what their yields are. Some actually keep detailed records. Farmers who expressed uncertainty in this regard were dropped from the survey. Also farmers who had been farming organically for less than four years were not included.

Data collection and farmer recall were made easier because this study is only interested in *comparisons* between organic and conventional farmers, not absolute costs. I took the average state costs of raising the particular crops and made adjustments based on organic farmer responses to estimate organic farm costs. Organic farmers were asked to respond only with the costs of production which *differed* significantly from their neighbors. In particular, they were queried about their costs of fertilizer and pest control, especially weed control. It was assumed that organic farmers had about the same investment and upkeep expenses on farm equipment and buildings. This was the conclusion of the Lockeretz *et al.* (1976) study, and also was the opinion of the farmers I interviewed. One farmer, however, a large New York State grain grower, did complain of higher maintenance costs on the cultivating machinery, compared to what is required to keep up spray equipment.

Since farmers' responses were relied upon for cost and yield data, the question arises as to whether there might be some systematic error introduced. Since we are only interested in differences, and since we believe that we have isolated the major differences, there should not be any large systematic errors introduced. Because of the fact that organic farmers are people who generally have a set of values that mean more to them than money and the opinion of neighbors and experts, it is more likely than not that they would respond honestly. The incentives present to shade figures appear to balance each other out. On the one hand, organic farmers would like to give the impression that they are successful, and so might tend to overstate yield and understate cost. But balancing this is the desire to justify the higher price that they usually are able to obtain in organic channels. A higher price can only be justified if costs are higher and/or yields lower. Taking this into consideration, most of the responses are probably the best estimate that the farmer can make.

Results. Of the 60 farmers contacted, responses were received from 34. Of these, 22 gave information on the costs of raising specific crops and the resulting yields. These crops and the states represented are listed in Table 12-2. Most of the respondents are from New York and Pennsylvania, but data were also received from Kansas, Michigan, Minnesota, Montana, Ohio, Virginia, California, and Ontario, Canada. Most of the responses were for the major field crops and the important vegetables and fruit, potatoes, tomatoes, and apples.

Field Crops and Hay

Field crops include corn, wheat, oats, barley, sorghum, and soybeans, and are the most important crops in both volume and value (Table 12-1). Producers of organic food consistently report "comparable" or slightly lower yields for field crops. Corn in particular generally suffers in yield when raised organically because it responds so well to nitrogen fertilizer. These impressions are confirmed by the only controlled study of organic farms in this country, by Lockeretz *et al.* (1976, 1977), and also by our survey. First we will review the results of the Lockeretz study.

Table 12-2 Farmers' Responses to Survey

Crop	Number of Farmers	States Represented
Grains and beans		
Corn (field)	4	Michigan, Minnesota, Pennsylvania (2)
Wheat	5	Kansas, Michigan, Montana, New York, Pennsylvania
Sorghum	1	Kansas
Oats	4	Michigan, Minnesota, New York, Pennsylvania
Rye	1	New York
Soybeans	3	Michigan, Minnesota, Pennsylvania
Hay (alfalfa)	2	Kansas, Michigan
Vegetables		
Potatoes	4	New York, Pennsylvania (2), Ohio
Tomatoes	3	New York, Pennsylvania, Virginia
Snap beans	1	Pennsylvania
Onions	2	New York, Ohio
Sweet corn	2	Pennsylvania, Ohio
Carrots	3	Pennsylvania (2), Ohio
Peas	1	Pennsylvania
Fruit		
Apples	3	Ontario, New York, California
Oranges	1	California
Grapes	2	California

Lockeretz matched 16 pairs of comparable farms in the Corn Belt, all of which raised animals as a major output. Thus, the farms had manure available, which was spread on the fields. Farms were closely matched in land value, geography, and size. Table 12.3 shows yields for the pairs of farms which raised the same crops for the first two years of the study, 1974 and 1975. Better weather in 1975 contributed to better yields on both kinds of farm, but the conventional yields increased far more than the organic. This is what we should expect from the discussion of the causes of yield increases in Chapter 10. Successful use of chemical fertilizer requires good weather, that is, plenty of moisture. In 1974, yields of the two groups were not statistically different. But in 1975 the conventional farmers did much better, particularly with corn for which the organic yield was only 79 percent of the conventional, or about 20 percent less. Wheat yields were

Table 12-3   Average Yields of Field Crops and Hay on Corn Belt
             Livestock Farms

| Crop | Yield Per Acre | | | | Average Difference Conv.- Organic | Percent Organic Less Than Conventional |
| | Organic | | Conventional | | | |
	1975	1974	1975	1974		
Corn (bu)	74	74	94	76	11	13
Soybeans (bu)	35	32	38	29	0	0
Wheat (bu)	28	28	38	29	5.5	16
Oats (bu)	58	56	60	60	3	5
Hay (tons)	4.5	5.0	3.9	3.4	-1.1	-30

Source: Lockeretz et al., 1976.

down 26 percent. Soybean and oat yield differences are probably not statistically significant. The organic farmers made up some of the differances by better hay yields, 30 percent higher on the average over the two years.

Results from our survey of non-livestock farms confirm the low corn yields and the more comparable yields of the other field crops. Three farmers reported raising corn with lower yields, two in Pennsylvania and one in Michigan. Our Minnesota and Ohio farmers reported yields comparable to the state average. Yields, state averages, and percent differences are shown in Table 12-4. In two cases, farmers reported differences between their yields and those of neighboring conventional farmers, and in those cases, these differences were used in computing the average percent that organic yield falls below conventional. This is really a better estimate of the yield loss, since land values and yields vary widely within states. Yields were adjusted for proportional time land rested. Actually more of this proportion should probably go to the corn in the rotation, since corn is the heavy feeder which requires the rest year. The average decline in yield is 15 percent, 2 percent more than that found in the Lockeretz *et al.* (1976) study of livestock farms.

Farmers frequently report that yields are better for other grain than for corn. Of the four wheat farmers interviewed, one reported 10 percent above the state average (Pennsylvania), and two others 10 percent below. But a large wheat farmer in Montana reported 25 percent lower yields than neighbors. A study of wheat production on organic farms in New York State (Berardi 1976) found yields of the organic farms to be an average of five bushels per acre below the area county average reported by extension agents (39 bushels per acre average for the counties in which the farms were located compared with 34 for the organic farms). This amounts to a 12.8 percent lower yield. A loss on the order of 10 to 15 percent appears average nationwide, considering all the available data.

Yields of other small grains are commonly reported by farmers as 10 to 15 percent below neighbors, as with wheat. Our Kansas farm reported 1.25 tons per acre (dry) sorghum yield compared to a state average of 1.48 tons per acre, 15.5 percent less. (The organic grain was raised on poor land, however.) Some organic farmers do much better with small grains than with other crops. Farmers in Minnesota and New York reported better than the state average for rye and oats, in contrast to corn and wheat. For oats, the differences are quite large in favor of the organic farmers. The Minnesota farmer who gets about average corn yields obtains oat yields some 80 percent above the state average. Presumably this reflects some very good land or better treatment. The comparison also indicates that one of the changes in crop mix that would take place in a changeover to organic production would be a replacement of some corn production by small grains like oats. Present market prices and yield-cost ratios favor corn production, which is 14 times greater than oat production. A large New York farmer also reported oat yields above state averages by 32 percent for his organic production. That farmer also raised organic rye and obtained average yields of 34 bushels per acre compared to 30 for the New York state

Table 12-4   Corn Yields on Organic Non-livestock Farms Responding to Survey

State		Yield (bu/acre)	1972-1974 State Average (bu/acre)	Percent Organic Less than Conventional
Pennsylvania				
Farm 1	1975	100	77	-30[a]
Farm 2	1975	64	77	-17[b]
Michigan	1975	(67% of neighbors)	74	-33[a]
Minnesota	1975	65	61	+ 7[b]
	1974	100	93	
Ohio	1977	120 to 160		0[a]
Average				-15

[a]Based on farmer estimate.
[b]Based on state yield average.

Source: Survey by author.

average in 1972 to 1975. These data indicate that it would be fair to assume at least comparable yields for small grain production under organic farming, somewhat better than the average 5 percent lower oat yield for Corn Belt organic farmers (Table 12-3).

Three farms in our survey reported raising soybeans. One in Pennsylvania had yields 15 percent above the state average, while another in Michigan reported yields 22 to 27 percent below neighboring farms if allowance is made for leaving the land to rest once every seven years. (Yields were estimated by the farmer as 10 to 15 percent lower.) The Minnesota farmer who did well with corn and oats also did well with soybeans: 34 bushels per acre compared with a state average of 26 in 1972 to 1974, 33 percent higher. Again the soybeans do comparatively better than corn.

The farmers in the Lockeretz (1976) sample did best with hay. We had one farmer in Kansas report alfalfa hay production, and his yield was 6.6 tons per acre, about two times the state average of 3.2 tons per acre. Though he did worse than the state average with wheat and sorghum, he did better with alfalfa. This is consistent with the 30 percent higher organic alfalfa production of Table 12-3.

In conclusion, our limited survey confirms the Lockeretz *et al.* (1976) findings (Table 12-3), indicating that similar comparative yields appear to apply to non-livestock farms as well as livestock farms. Corn yield loss may be somewhat greater than their results, perhaps 15 to 20 percent nationally; small grains probably less, perhaps no different from conventional yields.

One grain does require more effort to grow than the others mentioned so far. That is rice. The main problem here is weeds, like other organic grain crops. But since rice is grown in flooded land, weeds cannot be controlled by cultivation. Water level control must be precise, deep at first to kill grasses; then later the field is drained to control water weevils. After the ground is dry, the land must be reflooded. Some weeds must be handpulled. These increased costs and lower yield are reflected in the significantly higher organic rice prices (Chapter 11) (Garrich undated).

Profitability. Lockeretz *et al.* (1976) compared the profitability of the organic farms in their sample with the matched conventional farms, assuming that the crops had been sold at market prices instead of fed to cattle on the farm. The organic farms had lower operating costs, particularly in expenditures for pesticides and fertilizers. Table 12-5 shows the breakdown of costs for the two classes of farms. Organic farmers had higher costs for the field operations and manure spreading. The former reflects more cultivation to control weeds; the latter, presumably a more careful husbanding of manure resources (hauling to the corn fields, rather than simply disposing of the manure on fields close to the barn or allowing

Table 12-5   Field Crop Operating Costs for Conventional and Organic
              Corn Belt Livestock Farms

	Ferti-lizers[a]	Field Opera-tions	Manuring	Pesti-cides	Other[b]	Total
Organic						
Cost ($/a)	6.17	11.92	1.37	0.36	11.16	30.95
Percent value of production		7	1	0.2	7	19
Conventional						
Cost ($/a)	17.33	11.09	0.90	5.23	13.77	47.32
Percent value of production	10	6	1	3	8	27

[a] Includes trace minerals, organic fertilizers and soil amendments.
[b] Includes hauling, crop drying and seeds.

Source: Lockeretz et al. 1975.

it to stand and lose nutrients). These higher costs are far more than compensated by the increased expenses of conventional farmers for chemical fertilizers and pesticides, producing a net saving of about $16.50 per acre for the organic farmer in purchased inputs. The lower operating costs per acre of the organic farmers were roughly compensated by their lower yields, so that the two classes of farms had approximately the same net income per acre; in fact, the two-year average returns per acre were identical for the two groups at $133 per acre.

Labor. Average labor requirements for the main crops are compared in Table 12-6 for the Lockeretz (1977) Corn Belt farms. Except for soybeans, the organic farms require only slightly more labor per acre. When calculated on a *per bushel* basis, however, organic farms require about 20 percent more labor on corn and soybeans and 5 percent more on the small grains.

Financial viability of organic farms and recent economic conditions. The Lockeretz study has been attacked on two fronts, mainly because of its finding that organic farms were equally profitable with conventional farms. First it was argued that the comparable profits are a result of high fertilizer prices in 1974 (Aldrich 1975). And second, the study admittedly makes no allowance for differences in managerial quality.

As for managerial quality, there is no simple way to take it into

Table 12-6   Crop Production Labor Requirements on Conventional and
Organic Corn Belt Livestock Farms, 1975

	Labor (hours per acre)		Labor (hours per bushel)		
Crop	Organic	Conventional	Organic	Conventional	Percent Increase Organic Over Conventional
Corn	3.9	3.8	0.0534	0.0448	19.2
Small grains	1.9	1.9	0.0333	0.0317	5.1
Soybeans	3.1	2.6	0.0925	0.0775	20.0

Source: Lockeretz et al. 1976.

consideration. There is no relationship between another year in college and yield per acre. Furthermore, the large army of public and private advisors available to conventional growers should outweigh possible higher levels of private human capital on organic farms.

It is true that fertilizer prices were high in 1974 compared to previous years. In fact, nitrogen cost more than twice what it cost in 1973. Prices increased even further in 1975. Table 12-7 shows fertilizer prices and use together with corn yields and prices for 1973 through 1977. Prices have dropped from their 1975 peaks, but are still higher than they were in 1974.

If 1973 fertilizer prices had continued to prevail, conventional farmers would have spent about half as much for fertilizer for the same level of application (Table 12-7). This would have increased their profits per acre by about $8.50, or to about 6 percent above their organic counterparts. However, in 1974–1975, the increased prices of fertilizer were almost wholly compensated by increases in the price of corn. Thus, in 1973, conventional farmers paid less for fertilizer, but they also received less for their corn. Thus the Lockeretz profit comparisons appear sound. In fact, with 1977 corn prices only a little over $2 a bushel, the relative position of the organic farmer has improved.

In 1975, corn prices were $2.46 per bushel and the additional fertilizer required to achieve the last or incremental (marginal) bushel at typical application and yield levels was $1.32.* But 1976 found corn selling for

$$((\$265/\text{Ton} \times 7\ \text{lbs N}/1\ \text{bu corn})/2000\ \text{lbs/Ton}) \times (1 + 265 \times 108/(265 \times 105 + 118 \times 58 + 102 \times 67))$$

$2.20 per bushel and fertilizer cost per marginal bushel only $1.49, so that it was still profitable to use chemical fertilizer.

Vegetables

Potatoes. Four farmers in our survey reported raising potatoes, two in Pennsylvania and one each in New York and Ohio. State average data for 1972 to 1974 was 390 bushels per acre for upstate New York and 280 bu/acre for Ohio. (No data were reported separately for Pennsylvania.) (USDA 1975). The four organic farms reported yields of 250, 220, 300, and 400 bushels per acre, an average of 290 bu/acre. This is 26 percent below

---

Table 12-7 Fertilizer Use, Corn Yields and April 15 Prices

	1972	1973	1974	1975	1976	1977[d]
April 15 Price per Ton ($)						
Anhydrous Ammonia (N)		83	183	265	191	188
Superphosphate						
(20% P_2O_5)		54	91	118	95	103
Potash (60% K_2O)		62	81	102	96	97
Rate applied on corn receiving fertilizer (lb/acre), average						
N		114	103	105	127	128
P_2O_5		64	62	58	67	68
K_2O		71	73	67	78	82
Yield (bu/acre), corn (U.S. average)	97.1	91.2	71.4	86.2	87.4	90.8
Price per bushel[a] ($)	1.57	2.55	3.03	2.54	2.20	2.10[c]
Marginal cost of NPK fertilizer per bushel of corn ($)[b]		0.51	0.98	1.32	1.49	1.51

[a]Average from October of given year to September of following year.
[b]Calculated from Ibach and Adams 1968. At average yield levels, and 100 lb N, 7 additional pounds of nitrogen produce 1 bushel of corn, assuming proportionate increases in potassium and phosphate. Includes cost of purchasing such proportionate amounts of phosphate and potassium. Cost of spreading is assumed fixed for small changes in rate. At 120 lb N rate, it takes 10 lb N to get 1 more bushel.
[c]ERS estimate.
[d]Prices for May 15.

Source: ERS 1977b; USDA 1975, 1977a, 1977b.

---

the New York state average, though slightly higher than the Ohio average. The Ohio farmer, who got 400 bu/acre, indicated that these yields were still about 20 percent below those of his neighbors in his naturally fertile area. This was the only crop that this farmer found to have substantially lower yields than with conventional methods. The New York farmer estimated his yield as 50 percent below that of his neighbors. These low potato yields are similar to those observed in Europe in plot studies (Chapter 10). A 20 percent fall in yield means a 25 percent increase in land requirements for the same gross yield $(0.80 \times 1.25 = 1.00)$.

Tomatoes. Table 12-8 shows the cost structure of an organic tomato grower serving the fresh market in the Washington, D.C., area. The yield, 12 tons per acre average, is comparable to that attained by conventional growers for the processing market, but far higher than average fresh market yields. Average tomato yields for the processing market in 1974 were 9 tons per acre and 5.5 tons per acre in Maryland and Virginia, respectively. A farmer in New York reported 2.6 tons per acre for the fresh market, and lost money on the operation (Snyder 1975).

One special feature of the organic production shown in Table 12-8 is the very large expenditure on straw for mulching. The straw is raised on the farm as a cover crop after the corn; the figure shown for its cost is its market value. Labor costs were 70 percent of the organic costs. The cost of the straw mulch—which provides some fertilization, protection against drought, and weed control—was almost $500 per acre. And cultivation and hand weeding were still necessary.

At an average sales prices of 12 cents per pound, a profit to the entrepreneur of about $1000 per acre was realized. While this is his most intensive crop, which covers about 5.5 acres, this farmer also raises 150 acres of sweet corn (conventionally) and 50 acres of other vegetables with various degrees of purity. Overall, he estimates his return for labor to be about $3 to $4 per hour. The senior partner, a former government statistician, is making only a fraction of what his education would allow, even though the operation is vertically integrated into marketing and diversified at the retail level into fertilizers and other food products. While he is not maximizing his income, he *is* maximizing his satisfaction, that is, his own personal well-being, from the reward mix of personal, natural farming and marketing (cf. Chapter 9). One important reason that the operation is profitable is the availability of cheap labor. If this grower had to pay $3 per hour instead of $2, the profit would be cut by about two-thirds.

Tomato yield for the processing market in Pennsylvania appears only slightly less than the state average of 12.5 tons per acre, when raised organically. The major organic tomato grower in the state averages 15 tons per acre, but rests his land one year in five, so the real yield is only fourfifths of this, or 12.0 tons per acre. (Yields in the major tomato-

Table 12-8 Cost Structure for Organic Tomato Production for the Fresh Market, Virginia, 1975, 12 tons per acre

Operation	Times	Non-Labor Direct Cost ($ per Acre)	Labor (hrs)
Growing			
Plowing	1	4.00	1
Disking	3	3.00	3
Planting	1	1.00	10
Cultivating, tractor	1	2.00	1
Weeding, hand	3		6
Manure: haul & spread	2	6.00	5
Straw: haul & spread	1	60.00	75
Raise plants		2.00	10
Lime		2.00	1
Place hot caps			40
Total growing		80.00	152
Harvesting			
Picking			350
Grading		5.00	120
Total harvesting		5.00	470
Seed, fertilizer, etc.			
Straw		360.00	
Seed		30.00	
Lime		5.00	
Hot caps		30.00	
Basket replacements		25.00	
Total seed, fertilizer, etc.		450.00	
Other costs			
Land (agricultural rental value)		50.00	
Labor: 622 hours x $2.00		1244.00	
Total costs per acre		1829.00	
Cost per pound		7.6¢	
Average sales price per pound		12.0¢	
Profit per acre		1056.00	

Source: Survey by author; field operation costs from Stevens 1970.

growing states of Ohio and California run about 20 tons per acre.) It is probably unfair to dock the tomato yield for this share of the land rest, however. The crop that benefits is the corn which is grown following the rest in the rotation. So yields are probably as good or better than the state average.

A large-scale tomato grower in central California has used strictly biological control for 17 years, with only a couple of exceptions. Yields are comparable to those with chemical control. With no pest damage, pest control costs are down 75 percent. He would use organic fertilizer if he were convinced it made a difference and if the market were there. Processed tomato products in health food stores are only differentiated by their lack of additives, so there is presently little market for strictly organic production.

Other vegetables. Data on other vegetables were obtained from farmers in Ohio, Pennsylvania, and New York State. Yields for carrots, snap beans, onions, peas, and sweet corn are shown in Table 12-9. The most striking feature of these data is the large differences between the Ohio and Pennsylvania yields. These differences reflect soil conditions and management practices, which do vary greatly between growers. One of the larger organic producers in the East, our Ohio grower generally achieved yields comparable to those of commercial growers. He makes liberal use of seaweed for fertilization and pest control, and fertilizes with a blend of compost, seaweed, bacteria, and rock phosphate. The Pennsylvania and New York farmers, with a more traditional organic approach and poorer soil, did not do as well. Nevertheless, if we changed to a locally grown food system, some parts of the country would experience yield losses of the magnitude shown. Table 12-9 shows organic vegetable yield down 0 to 55 percent compared with neighbors or state averages.

Labor. Labor required to produce 15 tons per acre of tomatoes for the processing market comes to 150 manhours per acre (Snyder 1975): 128 hours to pick (OSU 1976) leaves 22 for growing. The labor required for raising processing tomatoes is virtually identical for organic and conventional. Similar operations are carried out with these exceptions:

1) Organic production requires more cultivation, five times instead of three. This means about 2.8 more manhours per acre.

2) Organic production requires less spraying, three as against ten, a saving of perhaps one to two manhours per acre.

3) Organic production requires the spreading of manure, about three tons per acre, for an additional 2.0 manhours per acre.

The net of about three to four manhours per acre is only about 2 percent of total labor required, which is mainly for harvest. If a comparison were made for machine harvest, however, the percent would be larger.

Table 12-9   Organic Vegetable Yields, New York, Pennsylvania, and Ohio

Crop and State	Organic Yield (per acre) 1974	State Average (per acre) 1972 - 1974	Organic Percent Loss Compared with State Average
Carrots, Ohio (bu)	500	665(N.Y.)	0[b]
Carrots, Pa. (bu)	460		31
Onions, N.Y. (bu)	250	410	39
Onions, Ohio (bu)	300	510	0[b] to 41
Snap beans, Pa. (lb)	3000	5360	44
		3533 (U.S.)	10
Peas, Pa. (tons)	1.5	1.31 (Md)	-15
Sweet corn, Pa. (lb)	2400[a]	5350	55
Sweet corn, Ohio (1977)	6000	6000	0

[a]Yield was 3000 lb/acre, but one year in five is in grass.
[b]Farmer estimate compared with neighbors.

Source: Survey by author;   USDA 1975

Reported conventional labor requirements for fresh market tomatoes in Ohio were 316 hours for 2.6 tons per acre (OSU 1976). This is substantially less than the yield obtained using organic methods (Table 12-8). The organic production per labor hour is 12 tons/699 hours = 34.4 pounds of tomatoes per manhour. The conventional producer in the Ohio survey averaged only 8.2 pounds per manhour. Evidently this kind of intensive organic tomato production is not as labor-intensive as some extensive production, probably because of the many trips to the field required when producing for the fresh market.

Organic sweet corn labor requirements depend greatly on the farmer. Average labor required to grow and harvest one acre of sweet corn in New York State in 1975 was three manhours per acre for a yield of 6600 pounds (Snyder 1976). Organic production in Pennsylvania required nine manhours for less than half the yield. The main factors are five hours per acre of cultivation and two hours per acre for spreading manure at three tons per acre. Per pound of production, this is an increased labor requirement of some six times. While our Ohio farmer also needs more field operations, he gets higher yields. Labor increases are less than half as much.

The labor requirements for pea production appear comparable for organic and conventional production, both requiring about five manhours per acre (Snyder 1975).

Commercial carrot production requires about 17 manhours per acre (Snyder 1975). Organic labor requirements depend on the level of purity desired. We may distinguish three levels. The cheapest would use the approved oil herbicide for weed control and have roughly the same labor requirements as the commercial. A small addition of two hours for manure or compost handling would increase labor requirements about 12 percent. Our Ohio organic farmer uses a highly volatile version of the herbicide only early in the season, the most difficult time for carrot growers. Fields must then be weeded twice by hand at an additional labor cost of about 50 manhours per acre, making labor requirements about three times or 200 percent over commercial. With labor costing $2.30 per hour, the cost of carrots is up $115 per acre or about 0.5 cents per pound (5 to 6 percent). If no herbicides were used, this farmer estimated that weeding costs might triple to about $350 per acre, a 15 to 20 percent increase in carrot cost. This figure is comparable to the increased cost experienced at a large Pennsylvania farm where no herbicides are used at all. One hand weeding of about 100 hours costs $250. But five cultivations are necessary, perhaps two more times through the field than for commercial production. Pure organic production requires about six times the labor of conventional production. A new mulching machine developed in Germany could help cut this spread (Vogtmann 1977).

In conclusion, labor differences between organic and conventional producers vary widely for the cases examined. This variability reflects the small number of farmers interviewed, and the experimental nature of much organic production. Except for intensive tomato cultivation for the fresh market, organic production does require more labor.

Fruit

It is difficult to relate fruit prices in any meaningful way to production costs. Most fruit production requires a large investment, which only pays off over a number of years. When there is excess supply, as presently is the case with citrus and apples, prices may easily fall far below average costs. It is also unrealistic to estimate real cost differences from the average costs of present orchards. Tree fruit production technology is rapidly changing, becoming far more mechanized. Because establishment of an orchard is a long-term investment, adoption of mechanization by conventional growers is only in its infancy. For these reasons, we felt it good to take a different tack in assessing organic and commercial production cost differences. We will take the cost structure of the modern commercial apple orchard, and obtain estimates of increased organic production costs by imposing the organic constraints. Organic yield and nonchemical cost estimates are taken from our grower survey.

Apples. In terms of value of production, apples are only slightly behind the top fruit, grapes and oranges (Table 12-1). There are many varieties of apples, differing markedly in disease resistance, productivity, and quality characteristics of the fruit. Of course, the other deciduous fruit differ even more. Nevertheless, similarities in production and harvest make it reasonable to treat them together in seeking an estimate of organic food production requirements and yields. Most apple data are for Delicious and McIntosh, the top varieties. The main source for information on conventional growers and hand versus machine harvest in the following discussion is Childers (1975).

We received useful responses from two organic apple orchards in New

Table 12-10 Organic and Conventional Apple Production, Northeast, Early 1970s, 800 bushels per Acre Yield

Operation	Production Cost ($/bu)			Labor Cost ($/bu)		
	Conventional	Organic	Org. % Increase	Conventional	Organic	Org. % Increase
Growing[a]	1.00	1.06	6	0.11	0.26	136
Hand harvest	0.55	0.55	0	0.55	0.55	0
Total hand harvest	1.55	1.61	3	0.66	0.81	23
Machine harvest[b]	0.21	0.55[b]	260	0.06	0.55	820
Labor -0.49						
Orchard						
Life 0.09						
Machine 0.05						
Land 0.01						
Net saved -0.34						
Total machine harvest	1.21	1.61	33	0.17	0.81	376
Increase organic 11 percent[c]						
Hand harvest	1.55	1.72	11	0.66	0.83	26
Machine harvest	1.21	1.72	42	0.17	0.83	390

[a]Assumes pest control costs for organic are $50 less than conventional (one-half); and thinning cost increases from $36 to $130 for a net increase of $44 or $0.06 per bushel at 800 bu/a yield for the organic. This is added to the average conventional cost of $1.00/bu. See text.
[b] Organic still hand harvests.
[c]Organic suffers 10 percent yield loss, so growing costs are 11 percent higher. See text.

Source: adapted from Childers 1975; also Stevens 1970; survey by author.

York and Ontario. Data on a third was obtained from a published report (Rodale 1961), which was checked with the grower against current practice. These orchardists have been in the business for over 30 years each, and have orchards of mixed apple varieties covering 40 acres each. They have experimented with fertilization and weed and pest control, and have developed systems which produce high-quality apples without the use of conventional agricultural chemicals. An occasional pesticide may be used in desperate situations, for which no other means of control has been discovered. The main differences between their systems and those of conventional growers are increased site-preparation cost, machine-mowing instead of herbicides, biological control of insects, and hand thinning.

Site preparation takes one to three years when an organic orchard is planned. Cover crops are grown and plowed under, compost and rock fertilizers are used at high rates. For example, one grower used 15 tons per acre of compost balanced with about 7 tons per acre of limestone, in addition to the phosphate rock which might be applied by any orchardist. Five hundred pounds of crushed limestone rock were also applied in a six-foot area around each trunk to discourage mice, form a mulch, and provide nourishment (Rodale 1961). This extra investment comes to about $230 per acre (Table 12-11, p. 213) for one year spent on site preparation, perhaps twice that for three years. In conversion from a conventional orchard there may be two to three years without a marketable crop (Rose 1974).

Besides attempting to have the healthiest trees possible and using generally accepted cultural controls and dormant oil sprays, organic growers have a long list of biological methods of keeping pests in check (which may also be used by conventional growers), including some of quite recent origin. These include electric insect traps, sex attractants, and an insect disease. Seaweed sprays provide some pest protection, foliar fertilization with trace minerals, and also certain hormones that may encourage blossoming. (Conventional growers use a variety of chemical sprays for this purpose.) Mice are poisoned by strychnine (a highly poisonous "natural" extract) in artificial tunnels. Perhaps 25 to 50 percent of conventional growers' cost is pest control, on the order of $100 per acre. Organic growers spray less often with less costly materials, for perhaps half that cost or less (Table 12-10).

Conventional orchards are moving toward hedgerow plantings, rather than the traditional equal spacing of trees. Weed control under young trees in hedgerows almost dictates herbicides. Hedgerows are more efficient for machine operations, commonly used for chemical application and harvesting. Since organic growers make less use of machines, they are not excessively inconvenienced by avoidance of herbicides. Also apples do well when surrounded by a mulch of hay or other organic material, which decreases the need for other weed control.

The major operating cost differences between conventional and organic growers come from hand thinning and harvest instead of chemical thinning and mechanical harvest. For chemical thinning (required to produce fewer, larger fruit of higher quality), labor costs per acre are cut by 25 to 90 percent or more. Hand thinning of heavily loaded trees can cost as much as $400 per acre; so savings from chemical treatment can be substantial. We have assumed a cost for the organic grower of $130 per acre in Table 12-10, based on a yield of about one-third the maximum of 3000 bushels per acre.

Hand harvest of fruit trees is still common for apples, but machine harvesting is already satisfactory for the processing market and it is only a matter of time before it is used for the fresh market. For other fruit, machine harvesting is already common practice, including some fresh fruit, such as cherries. Organic growers are generally restricted from using machine harvest because they must avoid the chemical sprays required to loosen the grip of the stems on the branches. Mechanical harvesting of apples uses from one-eighth to one-tenth the labor of hand harvesting, a saving of almost 50 cents a bushel in labor costs in the early 1970s. Based on experience with cherries, hand harvested trees do have about twice the useful life of machine harvested trees. The difference in an initial investment of $2500 per acre to bring an acre of trees to bearing age paid off over 30 years instead of 15 years at 9 percent interest is $70 per acre or about nine cents a bushel with an 800 bushel per acre yield ($307 per year payment compared with $237 per year). Also, assuming trees are replaced on a rotation basis, about 80 percent of a machine harvested orchard will be productive at any one time compared with closer to 90 percent for a handharvested orchard. This raises effective land investment per bushel about 10 percent for the machine harvest. Machines cost about $20,000 or about 5 cents per bushel for a 40-acre orchard yielding 1000 bushels per acre. All these results are summarized in Table 12-10.

Yields for organic orchards, in the range of 600 to 800 bushels for semidwarf, are comparable to those found in typical low-density commercial orchards, from 500 to 1000 bushels per acre. Quality is also comparable by United States grade standards. (Organic growers, of course, reject these standards.) Our Ontario grower averages 80 percent fancy grade, the northeast United States average (Podany *et al.* 1973). His culls (fruit of quality so low that packing is not justified) run only about 2 percent, however, well below the average of 7 percent. Chemical sprays can lower loss from pre-harvest fruit-drop from perhaps 20 percent to only 5 percent of the crop. This would imply about a 16 percent lower organic yield, other things being equal. However, with perhaps 5 percent greater saleable yield, the net loss may be closer to 10 percent (so that the net organic yield would be 10 percent less or 720 bu/a). The last lines of Table 12-10 make this adjustment.

As shown in Table 12-10, under the current conditions of hand harvest, organic production has about 11 percent higher production costs because it needs about 26 percent greater labor, primarily in hand thinning. If there is a general shift to machine harvest which cannot be followed by organic growers, 42 percent higher costs will be incurred, again, due to higher labor requirements, this time some five times greater than the (projected) conventional requirements. (Actually the increase would be somewhat less because of higher land values for the level land required for machine harvest. The modern intensive cultivation makes this a small factor, however.) The cost difference calculated for machine harvest is probably close to the difference in production costs between organic and conventional cherry orchards, where machine harvest is already widely adopted. Harvesting labor costs have been running about 20 cents per bushel in the Northwest, about 40 percent less than in the Northeast (Podany and Fuchs 1974). This may help explain the low apple prices in California (Chapter 11). The high organic production cost estimates derived here are consistent with a survey of French biological farms (Bates 1976). That survey found comparable yields and profits for most crops except for orchard.

Successful organic apple production depends greatly on climate and choice of variety. Integrated pest management, using small amounts of the less toxic chemicals, can often achieve the same or greater yield as conventional programs. But a widespread changeover to fully organic production could cut marketable yields by 50 percent. Production would shift to cooler, drier locations. A return to more resistant varieties would also be encouraged (Aubert 1978).

Entry barriers in apple production. Because of the large initial investment in preparing land for an organic orchard, and because changing over existing orchards may result in large yield losses for a few years, organic apple prices must rise above long-run production costs to induce new entry, in times of expanding demand (Chapter 11). Table 12-11 shows costs of preparing an orchard site for one-year and three-year preparation programs.

Site preparation costs more than twice as much for the three-year program than the one-year, $566 versus $230. Since an approximately eight-year waiting period must be interspersed between setting out trees and the time when the orchard reaches its maximum potential (somewhat shorter for dwarf trees, longer for full size), the investment builds over this time according to the interest rate. At 10 percent, the $230 becomes $485 and a 10 percent return on this investment would be $48.50 or $0.06 per bushel for an 800-bushel-per-acre yield. This would only add 3 percent to the cost of organic apples. This is rather unrealistic, however, since producing for the organic market is a high-risk business, and eight or ten years is a long time to have your money tied up if you are unsure of the results and may have to sell your apples on the conventional market. Including a risk premium of 5 percent per year to the interest rate raises

Table 12-11 Barriers to Entry in Apple Growing

Operation	Labor, gas.50¢/ gal ($)	$3/hr. ($)	Machinery, $2/hr ($)	Materials ($)	Percent In- crease	Total ($)
A. One year program, site preparation						
Haul, compost & spread manure etc. 15T/a	2.50	10.50	7.00	0.00		
Lime, 7T/a	0.40	1.70	1.10	17.50		
Crushed limestone rock 500 lbs/tree	3.00	12.00	9.00	30.00		
Cover crops: alfalfa 2x, custom rate			30.00	40.00		
Totals	5.90	34.20	47.10	87.50		174.70

Other costs: cost to hold land for one year
$500/a at 10% = $50.00
Taxes at 1%   =   5.00

	55.00
Total investment per acre	229.70
Total investment per acre after 8 years at 10%	485.00
Barrier = 10% return on investment, per acre	48.50
Barrier per bushel with 800 bu/a yield	0.06
Percent increase in cost 3.5	

B. Three year program, site preparation

One year investment after two years, at 10%	211.50
Repeat one year investment under A	174.70
Interest on land for 3 years at 10%, $500/acre	165.00
Real estate tax, 1% per year, $500/a	15.00
Total investment per acre	566.20
Total investment per acre after 8 years at 10%	1198.00
Barrier per bushel, 10% return, 800 bu/a yield	0.15
Percent increase in cost 8.5	

C. Convert existing orchard, lose two years' production

Percent increase in cost, with interest, 10%	21.0	
Barrier per bushel		0.37

Source: Estimates by author based on grower requirements; data taken
from Childers 1975; Stevens 1970.

the entry barrier to 5 percent of the price; if a risk premium of 10 percent is required, the entry barrier is 7 percent. A three-year preparation program means an entry barrier somewhat more than twice the preceding figures. The inclusion of risk explains why some orchardists prefer to convert existing orchards rather than prepare new ones. Also there is presently an excess supply of orchards in this country. If two years' production is lost during changeover, the organic apple price must be 21 percent above production costs (10 percent for each year plus 10 percent interest on the first 10 percent). Together with the production cost data of Table 12-10, these calculations imply an organic apple price of about 30 to 35 percent higher than the price of conventional apples, under the present system of hand harvest.

13 Expanding Organic Farming: Resource Constraints

When an industry expands, unit production costs generally do not remain constant. Sometimes they fall, for example, because of economies of scale in a supplier industry. More often they increase because the expanding industry must entice resources away from another sector of the economy or because inputs are scarce. For example, since more labor is needed in organic farming, expansion could push labor costs up. Sometimes certain raw materials may be relatively important for an industry. In organic farming, humates, crushed rock and kelp are widely used. While these materials may appear to be in abundance when an industry is small, a large expansion may result in resource scarcity, depletion, and higher prices, and in fact may place an absolute limitation on industry expansion. Also, a particular quality attribute of a resource may be in short supply, even if the resource is not. In the case of organic farming, certain climates and regions are more congenial to organic farming than others for particular crops. There also may be a limit to the number of people willing to become farmers dedicated to a personal relationship with the earth.

Studies of geographic changes and pesticide use were reviewed in Chapter 10. There appears to be quite some potential for rearranging crop production in a manner that reduces pest damage. Apparently more than half of pesticide use could be eliminated without raising costs. Eventually costs would have to rise, however, for some crops more than others. Some shifts in production between crops would be necessary. However, the extent of increasing cost depends on technological progress in natural pest control methods. There is quite a potential here, largely undeveloped (see Chapter 4).

Four other possible limits on expansion of organic production have yet to be discussed: labor, nitrogen, soil amendments, and seaweed. There does not appear to be any serious limitation on soil amendments and seaweed. Unskilled labor costs would rise to organic farmers if organic production expanded greatly. And chemical nitrogen production is already nearing the potential organic nitrogen supply. These factors, together with climate, may increase production costs if organic farming expands to a national scale.

Labor

Two general classes of workers are of interest in organic farming: entrepreneurs, that is, farmers, and laborers.

Organic farming requires more labor than conventional farming. Would this labor be available? An examination of recent unemployment rates would seem to produce an affirmative answer. The unemployment rate has been above 5 percent almost continuously since 1970, indicating over four million workers unemployed. The rate has been over 8 percent since early 1975 (8.0, June 1976 [BLS]). In 1975 there were 4.35 million farm workers, made up of 3.0 million family workers and 1.3 million hired (CEA 1976). With the number of farm workers on the order of the number of unemployed, there does not appear to be any large barrier in making farm production somewhat more labor-intensive. In fact, this could even be seen as a boon by those who believe that we are entering a period of chronic unemployment.

When we come to qualitative characteristics of farm workers, however, serious questions arise regarding the possibility of large-scale expansion of organic agriculture. Organic farming requires a much more personal relation with the soil and a commitment of availability for timely cultivation and other farm operations, which must be better coordinated with the weather and pest status than under conventional management. While there are many farmers who are still willing to make this commitment, could enough be found to make large-scale organic production practicable without forcing economic returns higher? The same questions must be raised with regard to hired labor. Today organic farmers often turn volunteer labor away. The conventional farmer has difficulty finding and keeping workers. But the organic farmer can choose among college students, dropouts, and others who want to go "back to the land" and learn how to farm in harmony with nature. This kind of information is presently not available at universities. Life on an organic farm also provides the natural food and country living these people seek. The organic farmer is often in the position of paying a wage not because it is demanded by the worker, but because he feels a minimum wage is only fair, or because such is required by law.

If organic farming became widely adopted, this cheap labor would have plenty of opportunity to enter farming, and would thus be lost to the labor supply. And those who were left would now be spread over a much larger number of farms. It seems certain that organic farm labor costs would have to rise, presumably at least to the level of agriculture as a whole. And the latter wage level appears to be on the increase as a result of successful unionization and the first legislation recognizing organizing and bargaining rights of farm unions.

For the farm entrepreneur himself, we may draw upon the farmer attitude surveys cited in Chapter 8 to reach somewhat different conclusions. Most farmers are quite attached to the land and have a strong belief in environmental quality. We can only conclude that, if guaranteed a reasonable income, the average farmer would not be averse to using more ecologically sound techniques. To be widely accepted, however, biological techniques must be perfected to the point where they are not so greatly different from chemical methods in convenience. Can the average farmer learn the complexity of biological-control decisionmaking? The main barrier here is not the farmer, but the agricultural research and extension complex which serves him. While the research is complex, farm application of organic techniques is often little different than similar time honored cultural methods followed by uneducated farmers for generations. The phenomenon of the highly educated organic farmer is more a result of the requirement of doing his own research than actually carrying it into practice. The decisions regarding timing and appropriate response to pest population changes are highly complex, however. Only highly trained entomologists can make sound recommendations based on ecological principles, available techniques, and field conditions. Presently there is a scarcity of such personnel, but supply is expanding. Integrated pest management services, which recommend pesticides on an as-needed basis, comprise only about 1 percent of total management and application services (DeBach 1974).

Nitrogen Fertilizer

The organic farmer relies substantially upon wastes of the food system for fertilizer: manure, food processing wastes and, probably to an increasing degree, sewage sludge and garbage. From a materials balance point of view, there would be no need to import any other materials once a fertile soil had been established. Thus, a long-run equilibrium can be established with nutrient input equaling nutrient output. Such a cycle has been in operation in China and other Far East nations where soil fertility has been maintained by recycling for thousands of years (King 1911). Such a system is theoretically possible for this nation as well. If every bit of material that is removed in crops eventually finds its way back to the land, together with all soil lost by erosion, the land will maintain its production potential. No inputs of fertilizers will be necessary from outside the system.

As a practical matter, nutrients can in fact be lost to the system, particularly in our dispersed civilization. Minerals can be leached from land or waste and escape the system into the ocean. And nitrogen can escape back into the atmosphere. These are not irretrievable losses. Ocean minerals can be returned through the use of seaweed. And nitrogen can be fixed from the air through use of appropriate crops, sufficient soil organic matter, and a healthy soil life (cf. Chapter 3). Soil innoculation with blue-green algae looks highly promising. Preliminary tests indicate equal or higher yields and quality when "algae" (a form of bacteria) are used in place of chemical fertilizer. Bumper crops, however, have generally depended on some imported nitrogen fertilizer. So it is of interest to examine the limits of organic sources, including manure, sludge, and food and other plant processing wastes. Organic fertilizers also supply abundant amounts of humus. But often it is useful to add naturally occurring humic materials (see next section).

Organic wastes: problems in use. Our nation's feedlots, factories, and cities are vast generators of organic waste materials. Disposal has been a serious problem, but they are potentially highly valuable as fertilizers. Farmers have used manure as a fertilizer for ages. Regional specialization has brought a separation of crop production from animal feeding. The same is true for human populations. We are crowded into cities, so human wastes are also concentrated in places which have been far removed from food production. Thus, in the past, the application of wastes to land has been thought of as a way to dispose of waste material rather than a way to nourish soil and crops. The capacity of land to absorb organic wastes depends on soil and weather conditions. But for any soil, a point is reached where land disposal causes toxic buildups of minerals or salts, pollution of ground or surface water, and crop production which is lowered in yield and perhaps even toxic to consumers. When wastes are used for fertilizers, the application rate is much lower, and most of these difficulties are unlikely to appear. There are still problems, however. The main ones are a buildup of some naturally rare metals, odor, weather conditions, and spread of disease (Walker 1975).

Odor can be objectionable when there are residential neighbors near the farm using waste for fertilizer. This is not a serious drawback, however, since odor can be virtually eliminated by plowing the wastes under soon after application or, more completely, by composting. Composting produces a material that is odorless and largely free of disease organisms. The experience of communities that have been using land disposal of sewage sludge is encouraging. A survey of Ohio communities did not find complaints by neighbors (Manson and Merritt 1975).

Disease organisms are a more serious problem, and have been a concern of public health officials. This problem also can apparently be resolved satisfactorily. As mentioned, composting of sludge and manure destroys most of the bacteria. Those remaining generally do not last long in the soil. If wastes are sprayed on fields, animals need only avoid grazing for a few days. Normally ten hours of bright sun will destroy bacteria on the forage (Bell 1976). If sewage sludge is used to raise human food, a year is recommended between application of wastes and resumption of food production for the fresh market (Walker 1975). This delay is apparently a large margin of safety since no human illness from eating such food has been documented. But since most diseases do not affect both man and animals, no such wait need apply to land used for animal feed. Some organic (specifically, bio-dynamic) farmers would not use sewage on human food anyway.

Weather is a limiting factor in colder climates. Sewage slurry may freeze in pipes or trucks. This problem can be handled by providing sufficient storage capacity to weather the cold, or by using a processing method, such as composting, which is not greatly hindered by weather (Walker 1975).

Sewage may contain substances that are toxic to plants or which may make the plant toxic to consumers, human or animal. Most organic wastes are degradable in the soil, but heavy metals (metals with high atomic weights), especially cadmium, lead, zinc, and copper, can build up in the soil and in plants and, perhaps, be concentrated as they move up the food chain. These heavy metals are most likely to occur in sewage which includes industrial wastes. One straightforward method of dealing with such contamination is to stop it at the source: place effluent limits on industrial users of the waste disposal system. This is precisely what is done in West Hertfordshire, England, which uses its sewage for crop production. Factories are regularly monitored and stiff fines are levied for exceeding heavy metal effluent limits (Walker 1975). Unfortunately, metals also pass into the water system from domestic pipelines, and thus residential wastes may have undesirably high levels of copper and zinc. The only way to eliminate these elements at the source would be to change over from flush to compost toilets. It is possible also to extract these metals from the sludge (Ember 1975).

Application rates must be regulated to avoid heavy metal buildup. Nevertheless, heavy metal toxicity is less of a problem when sludge is viewed as a fertilizer rather than as a waste. At application rates comparable to current chemical fertilization levels, heavy metal buildup in soils should be within safe tolerances. Current recommendations place limits of 1500 and 750 parts per million of dry matter for zinc and copper, respectively. A sampling of sludge from six municipal treatment plants in Pennsylvania found levels of between 1053 and 6540 parts per million for zinc, and between 872 and 1718 for copper. Application rates of 10 tons per acre dry weight for three years are considered safe, with testing at that point before further application. The nitrogen content of sludge varies from about one to 8 percent of the dry matter, with an average value of perhaps 4 to 5 (Shipp and Baker 1975; Larson *et al.* 1975). Four percent of 10 tons is 800 pounds of nitrogen, about half of which would be available in the first crop year. One quarter of this rate should suffice for organic farmers, probably less. They not only would need less fertilizer, but they grow crops in rotation. So they would need to fertilize the same land only once every three to five years. If we assume a heavy metal content twice the permissible level, application rates would have to be cut at least in half, which would be no problem for organic production. An application rate of 5 tons per acre would provide on the order of 400 pounds of nitrogen (200 the first year) and could be safely continued for 12 years under present guidelines. Possibly such a rate could be continued indefinitely, possibly not. Heavy metal limits depend on the soil type and crop grown. The action of heavy metals in the soil and effects on the crop and on human health are still not completely understood. Clearly some caution is indicated. It would be ironic to add more potential toxins to the food supply in the name of organic farming.

When considering the use of sludge and other wastes in agriculture, production cost of these materials is not really an issue. It is environmental constraints which force a municipality, feed lot, or factory to dispose of its wastes on land in a manner which will harm neither land, crop, nor environment. Under these conditions, the supply price of waste products is simply their value in agriculture. Presently, the perceived value is rather low. Sludge has often been given away, with the farmer merely providing some transportation; often not even that. The same was true of manure. As chemical fertilizer prices rise, or if chemical use were restricted, the value of manure in agriculture would rise. Today many farms that used to give away their manure keep it to spread on their own fields.

Sewage sludge is presently being used to grow crops by a number of municipalities in Europe, Australia, and America (Walker 1977). Baltimore, Maryland, currently gives away its sewage sludge in dried form to gardeners and farmers, or uses it on city lands (Kuchta 1975). Denver, Colorado uses all its sludge for agriculture, and is planning an expansion via a 22-mile pipeline (Wolf 1975).

Availability of organic nitrogenous fertilizers. Table 13-1 lists the major sources of nitrogen in United States waste material and compares these with nitrogen commonly available from soil, rainfall, and chemical fertilizer. The potential from human waste is small compared to that from livestock manure because of less nutrients and the heavy metals problems. The livestock manure nitrogen is approximately the amount presently used in chemical fertilizers. Much manure is already being spread on the land, so the potential for further replacement of chemical fertilizer is that

Table 13-1   Nitrogen Fertilizer Available to American Farms

Source	Nitrogen Content (million tons)
Release from soil organic matter	20
Livestock manure	10
Fixed by soil organisms[a] (20 pounds per acre)	10[a]
Added in rainfall (5 pounds per acre; varies greatly)	3
Chemical fertilizer (1975)	9
Human waste (0.048 pounds per person per day)	2

[a]This would be higher under organic farming.   Innoculation can generate sufficient nitrogen to match average chemical fertilizer treatment.

Source: Aldrich 1972 in Singh 1975;   chemical fertilizer from USDA 1975.

much less. However, much of the chemical fertilizer is lost before it is used by the plants: about half on the average. And much of the manure that is used is not used efficiently since the goal has often been waste disposal rather than fertilization.

Nitrogen is the critical fertilizer element. Organic farmers can make use of phosphate rock, and potassium is usually adequately supplied in animal wastes. From Table 13-1, it appears that we have nitrogen fertilizer resources of a magnitude comparable to the amount of chemical fertilizer presently used on crops. As environmental controls tighten, the cost of waste materials to farmers will decline. To what extent an increased cost is involved to society depends on progress in waste processing technology and in the development of nitrogen fixation by non-legumes and soil bacteria. Recall that neglect of nitrogen fixation was one of the key neglected areas cited by National Academy of Sciences advisory groups (Chapter 1).

Soil Amendments

Organic and other farmers use a variety of mined materials to improve the quality of the soil, primarily humates and zeolites. Both increase the cation exchange capacity and water-holding capacity of soils. Zeolites hold nitrogen fertilizer, chemical or organic. Humates also increase crop yield and quality in many cases (Senn and Kingman 1973). While all organic fertilizers eventually decompose into humus, humus can be provided quickly by processed mineral deposits containing humates. The main sources of humates are leonardite, shale, and deposits precipitated from solution along coastlines (Shacklette and Severson 1975).

Leonardite is generally found in conjunction with deposits of lignite, a soft coal. The leonardite is an oxidized lignite, and thus occurs in the surface layers of the lignite deposit. So leonardite reserves must be only a small fraction of lignite reserves. Total United States known reserves of lignite are about 478 billion tons, mostly strippable in shallow beds. This is about 28 percent of total coal reserves of 1.7 trillion tons (USGS 1975). Geologists estimate that there are about one billion tons of agriculturally useful humate shale deposits in New Mexico, currently the major source of mined agricultural humates in that region (Cohea 1975). One humate firm recommends a 400-pound-per-acre application (Taylor 1976). At this rate, the one-billion-ton New Mexico deposit would be sufficient for a single treatment on about five billion acres of farmland, or about 15 treatments on each of the nation's 330 million acres of cropland. Since some soil types inactivate the humates, there is really more than this available for appropriate conditions.

Zeolites are common silicate sedimentary rocks (Sheppard 1973). They are much more commonly used in Japanese agriculture than in the United States. Some ten trillion tons of zeolites may be located in the continental United States. Although quality and type vary, this quantity is far more than would ever be recommended for agricultural use for generations (Shacklette and Severson 1975).

Since these mineral deposits must be strip-mined for the most part, there is an environmental cost to their production. Reclamation can be a costly process, especially in the drier parts of New Mexico, the location of many deposits currently being exploited. Cost per acre may exceed $4000 for full reclamation (Kottlowski 1976). Thus, as environmental regulations tighten, the cost of mineral soil amendments is bound to rise.

Seaweed

Seaweeds are giant marine algae. They serve a variety of functions in organic (and other) farming, including supplying trace minerals and plant hormones, increasing yield and quality (for example, sugar content), and protecting against some pest attacks (Stephenson 1974). The main use of seaweed in this country is as a source of chemicals for food processing (FWS 1962).

Major world seaweed resources are estimated at somewhere from 100 million (Chapman 1970) to several billion wet tons (Plimpton 1976). Seaweed grows very rapidly, and it is possible that the whole crop could be harvested annually. But probably a more reasonable estimate of the maximum sustainable annual harvest is half the total mass. Since, to some extent, seaweed can be planted and raised for harvest, world potential production is probably closer to the high side of the current resource estimates. This would mean a maximum yearly production of about one billion wet tons, or about 100 million tons dry weight. Such a harvest would have to include remote areas and less commercially desirable species, however.

Current world production is only about 3.5 million tons wet weight, over two-thirds in Asia. Production has varied from year to year, but no strong upward trend in production was evident during the 1960s (Hunter 1975).

A pilot project is underway at the Naval Undersea Center, San Diego, California, to set up a 100,000-acre demonstration seaweed farm in the Pacific Ocean. Project leaders predict a 300 to 500 wet tons per acre harvest, or about 40 million tons per year from just this one farm (Wilcox 1975). If these trials are successful, world seaweed production could be far larger than the potential harvest of natural beds.

In trials with a variety of vegetables at Clemson University, increased yields for most crops were obtained for application rates of 250 pounds of seaweed meal per acre, but applications of 500 pounds per acre generally produced lowered yields (Stephenson 1974). These results would imply an optimal application rate in the 200 to 300 pounds per acre range (dry weight). This is the range typically recommended commercially (Maxicrop). Seaweed is also commonly used as a spray on plants. Typical recommendations are one gallon total per acre per year of seaweed solution. One wet ton produces about 60 gallons of solution or enough for about 60 acres.

If we match the above typical application rates to the maximum annual harvest, we find that the potential harvest of 100 million dry tons could fertilize some one billion acres at 200 pounds per acre application rate. At the rate of one gallon of solution per acre, 60 billion acres could be sprayed. World cropland totals a little over five billion acres, and United States' around 300 million acres. It thus appears that, even if all land were to receive annual applications of seaweed, the amount available would probably be sufficient to meet foreseeable demand.

Seaweed is also useful as an animal feed. Seaweed has about the same percent protein as good quality hay. The protein is of a high quality, close to that of eggs (Beleau *et al.* 1974). And of course seaweed is a good source of minerals. Seaweed has been fed to livestock in quantities of up to 30 percent of the total diet, but 5 to 10 percent is generally recommended (Stephenson 1974). American livestock, including chickens, consumed 453 million tons of feed in 1973 (including grazing) (USDA 1975). Five percent of this is about 22 million tons, which is only two percent of the possible world harvest from naturally occurring beds.

The environmental impact of large-scale seaweed harvesting would have to be evaluated. Some increased labor costs would appear inevitable. Most seaweed used in America is imported from Scandinavia and Ireland, because of lower wage rates, particularly in Ireland. Production methods presently require much hand labor. If the industry were to expand significantly, labor costs would rise. On the other hand, mechanization would probably be developed, which would moderate the cost increase. In any event, seaweed is a small cost of organic farming. One seaweed formulation, sold under the trade name Maxicrop, costs about $4.50 for enough to make one gallon of concentrate when purchased in bulk (Zook and Ranck, Gap, Pennsylvania, March 1976 price). This is a small percent of the value of production for most crops. In 1974 the average acre of tomatoes grossed $3100; corn, $2100; and apples, from $3000 to $15,000. Since there are presently only about five firms marketing seaweed in a small market characterized by considerable brand loyalty, prices are as likely to fall as rise, with economies of large-scale marketing and more effective competition.

14 Conclusions and Recommendations

Organic farming is rare mainly because of market failures, not inherent higher production costs. These large market failures may be affecting human health and future well-being. Risk has been introduced into the food system, especially through widespread agricultural chemical use. Although organic yields per acre are far higher than those in earlier eras and the price differences between organic food and conventional food are far smaller at the farm than at retail, still it does cost more to produce organic food. The market failures and the potential social benefits from more widespread adoption of organic methods argue for a federal role in promoting research into, and adoption of, organic farming.

The Quality Dimensions of Food

Food production and consumption directly and indirectly affect both consumer and environment. Conventional agricultural production has led to widespread use of chemical fertilizers and pesticides, both of which have large negative impacts on the environment and human health. Chemical pesticide residues and also physiological effects of pesticides on food crops increase the probability of cancer, birth defects, or genetic damage in consumers. Reliance on fertilization by chemicals rather than nourishing a rich soil life which feeds plants in a more balanced or life-giving manner, may result in a long-term decline in consumer vitality, perhaps not noticeable for a number of generations. Organic farming provides an alternative which avoids dangerous chemicals and nourishes plants and animals in a balanced fashion, using organic wastes and nutrients produced by, and made available by, microbial activity in the soil.

Conventional agriculture has had a large negative impact on the quality of life of soil organisms, plants, animals, and farm workers. These living beings, together with the land itself, are viewed by conventional agriculture as merely inputs into a technological system seeking to maximize gross production and minimize factor costs. Plants and animals are viewed as having no inherent value. Farming has become mechanized to a degree that animals often appear to be appendages of the machines, such as a chicken in an egg factory. While many farmers have embraced the new technology, others have felt a loss of independence and self-worth, as they became managers of a business involved in exploiting natural resources and dependent on the industrial sector for supplies. The traditional farmer was more of an independent husbandman working with nature.

Farmers and consumers have chosen organic food for many similar reasons: avoidance of potentially toxic chemicals and a desire for a more natural, less mechanized, lifestyle being among the most important. These people have been comparatively few in number, however. The small number of organic farmers is mainly a result of market failures. The same can be said to some extent of the low level of consumer demand.

Government and private research and advisory services have emphasized the development and use of chemical fertilizers and chemical pest control. Alternatives, such as compost and manure for fertilizer, biological nitrogen fixation, and biological controls of pests, have suffered from comparative neglect. The main reasons for this neglect are the comparative lack of private sales potential for natural methods, and various institutional factors and prejudices that have discouraged their use. Chemical pesticides are patentable and usually are effective against a broad spectrum of pests. But biological controls are generally neither. Most farmers are uninformed regarding alternatives to agricultural chemicals. And the alternatives are often more complex to use and have large benefits to others besides the farmer using the method (large positive externalities). Government neglect appears to be a result of a combination of special interest pressure, research difficulties, and the common tendency to underinvest in public goods.

Research into the effects of chemicals gives quick results. Biological systems are complex, and research into biological controls or fertilization methods may require many years and extreme care. Furthermore, research into organic farming methods may have to take into consideration the personal relationship between farmer or researcher and the animals (and possibly even the plants) under study. Some of the experience and beliefs of organic farmers contradict conventional scientific thinking, making an unbiased investigation rather unlikely.

Consumers neglect organic food partly because they generally put a low value on avoiding ill effects which will not occur until some years in the future. Consumers are uninformed as to the facts of nutrition, and the effects of eating habits on health are often far removed in time, so that associations between cause and effect are hard to establish. And retail prices are comparatively high.

Market failures within the food system also discourage organic farming. The trend toward product differentiation through processing and food additives leads to a view of farm production as a raw material for the manufacturing sector. Food processors prefer standardized products and may require a pesticide spray schedule to provide freedom from imperfections. Mass marketing has tended to eliminate the high range of quality, where the organic farmer may have an advantage. The increasing distance from farmer to consumer in the food chain leads to each disregarding the effects of his decisions on the welfare of the persons at the other end of the chain.

Conventional agriculture relies heavily on fossil fuels, when compared to primitive, traditional, and organic agricultures. This comparative energy-intensiveness allows modern farmers to raise more food on less land with less labor. American farmers also raise more vegetables, fruit, and animal products than farmers in other countries, and these commodities are more energy-intensive than grains and beans. Organic farming in general uses less energy than conventional American farming, but some particular operations require more energy. Energy used in field operations can be cut significantly if herbicides are used for weed control instead of, or in addition to, cultivation.

Systems of Organic Farming

Organic farming provides an alternative to the conventional agricultural system. Organic farming, also known as biological, ecological, or natural farming, comprises a group of systems of agriculture which avoids chemical pesticides and fertilizers, and seeks to increase soil fertility through feeding soil microlife with residues from life, such as composted (decomposed) garbage and sewage, manure, plant residues, food processing wastes, and kelp. In its developed forms, organic farming is not a throwback to previous eras, but an alternative modern system of production, which seeks to rely solely on biological processes, to obtain high quality and yields which are often as good as those achieved using conventional techniques. Organic farming may make use of certain methods which are not appreciated by conventional agriculture, such as a personal relation between man and land, using seaweed to control pests, or planting by the phases of the moon. Conventional and organic farming are to a large extent distinct production systems, composed of interlocking, complementary elements. Agricultural chemicals, machinery, and the new varieties of plants developed to fit the new conditions all work well together. Life in the soil and natural insect controls may be harmed by chemicals and heavy machinery, and may take a number of years to be rebuilt if a changeover from conventional to organic practices is attempted. Thus, simple modifications to one system, such as withdrawal of pesticides from the conventional system, cannot give a valid picture of what can be achieved with another system.

Increased Costs of Organic Production

While organic food production solves most of the environmental and health problems which are of concern today, it does so at a price. However, the price increase would be modest.

Retail prices of organic food are often much higher than those for conventionally raised food. One survey found that prices in health food stores averaged twice those in supermarkets. This price difference has led to a widespread belief that it costs far more to raise food organically than conventionally. However, the high price of organic food arises primarily from the higher transportation, processing, and selling costs of handling small quantities of organic food. Mistaken ideas about the costs of raising organic food also arise from making comparisons with production in previous eras and relying on studies made by university experiment stations. Agricultural productivity has increased greatly since the 1930s. But many of the benefits apply to organic farmers as well as conventional farmers. Resistant strains and modern field machinery are used by organic farmers. Since the 1930s there has also been much progress in techniques specifically applicable to organic farming, particularly in the biological control of plant pests. Experiment station studies are also unreliable indicators of production potential under organic farming. These studies are often biased in design; for example, "organic" plots are sometimes not weeded. And they are usually one-year studies, even though it takes at least three years to establish the biological balance in the soil and insect ecology to permit successful organic farming.

Production cost differences can be estimated from farm price differences. A survey of farm prices of organic food found little difference between organic and conventional vegetable and fruit prices in California. Nationally, the major field crops cost, on the average, 10 percent more when raised organically. The largest impact of a large-scale changeover to organic production in this country would be through the main field crops—corn, soybeans, and wheat. These effects would be offset to some extent by increased hay production. Land allocated to vegetable production would have to be increased, or else a more intensive cultivation would be required.

In Table 14-1 we estimate production cost increases of the major crop classes, using estimates from Chapters 11 and 12. We use figures in the high range of those estimates we have developed. If readers still feel that

Table 14-1 Increased Costs and Land Requirements of Organic Crop
Production Compared to Conventional

Crop	Value, 1974 (bil. $)	Organic Added Cost (%)	Added Cost, Organic Prod.[a] (bil. $)	Land, 1974 (1000a)	Organic Added Land (%)	Added Land, Organic Prod.[a] (1000a)
Corn, grain	13,717	15	1,958	65,194	20	13,039
Wheat	7,242	10	724	65,459	15	9,819
Other feed grains[b]	3,501	0	0	32,729	0	0
Rice	1,195	40	478	2,569		
Hay	5,770	0	0	60,564	-10	-6,055
Soybeans	8,246	5	412	52,460	0	0
Peanuts	658	10	66	1,472		
Potatoes	1,461	20	292	1,380		
Sugar crops	2,231			1,964		
Citrus	881	20	18			
Deciduous fruit	1,202	30	360			
Tomatoes	798	0	0	465		
Lettuce	353	10	35	226		
Sweet corn	212	20	42	628		
Other vegetables	1,221	10	120	1,708		
Total	48,086	9.2	4,505		9.5[c]	16,803[c]

[a]Production
[b]Oats, barley, sorghum
[c]Major field crops only

Sources: USDA 1975; Chapters 11, 12 of this study.

the estimated increased costs are too low, they may substitute their own figures. Even doubling the figures used in Table 14-1 would not have a disastrous effect on the national food supply.

Two crops cause the bulk of the increased production cost and increased land use in domestic crop production. These are corn and wheat, both because they are two of the largest crops and because they suffer as much or more than most other crops under organic production. Rice, potatoes, soybeans, and deciduous fruit also contribute significantly to increased production cost. Total increased cost to the farm sector from conversion to organic farming comes to about $4.5 billion or about 9.2 percent of total crop value. If changeover cost were included, this figure might be one and a half times or even twice as high. Retail food costs would not rise this much, however. On the average, farm prices of food make up about 38 percent of the retail value. So if the farm prices rose 9.2 percent, retail prices would only rise on the average about 3.5 percent.

Only estimates for increased land requirements of the major grain crops are given in Table 14-1. A total of about 17 million acres more land would be needed to raise the crops that were grown in 1974. This is about 5 percent of present cropland in the United States. A shift of production to small grains would moderate this increase.

Table 14-2 shows the labor presently used to raise our major crops, and some estimates of increased labor requirements under organic production. About half of this increase comes from fruit and nut production. Total increased labor may be on the order of 500 million hours, about 16 percent more labor than is presently used in crop production. This increased labor requirement represents about 3 percent of the number of people who were unemployed in America in 1977. (One man-year is about 2000 man-hours.) The estimates are subject to a considerable amount of uncertainty. However, even if effects of a changeover to organic production are 100 percent more than the estimates in Tables 14-1 and 14-2, this would still mean only approximately a 6 percent increase in food prices instead of a 3

Table 14-2　Farm Labor Used in Crop Production in 1974 and Increases Required by Organic Farming

| | Labor (1000 manyears) | Organic Added Labor | |
Crop		Percent	(1000 manyears)
Feed grains (corn, oats barley, sorghum)	440	16	71
Hay and forage	327	0	0
Food grains	223	5	11
Vegetables	364	30	109
Fruit and nuts	468	50[a]	234[a]
Sugar crops	67		
Cotton	287		
Tobacco	261		
Oil crops (soybeans, peanuts, and others)	254	20	51
Other	230		
Total	2,921	16	476

[a]Most fruit is still harvested by hand, so increase over present labor usage is moderate. See Chapter 12.

Sources:　ERS 1975;　Chapter 12.

percent increase. Smaller yields *would* force a more than proportional upward movement in farm prices. As a practical matter, however, eating higher quality food causes a decline in craving for food, so that gross consumption could well decline.

While the cost and factor requirements may or may not be understated by our estimates, there *is* reason to believe that they may be *over*stated, particularly in the long run. Lower yield is partially compensated by higher nutritive content. And technological change could lower organic production costs. The estimates assume that there are no significant increased costs due to input scarcities as organic production expands. The main conclusion of Chapter 13 was that this is a fairly good assumption. These estimates also assume that no shifts among products would take place as a result of a large-scale changeover to organic farming. Shifts would in fact occur, moderating to some degree the impact of a changeover.

Recommendations

Some selected recommendations follow:

1) Because of the positive externalities and public nature of non-chemical pest control, public research programs should be strengthened greatly. The private sector could be encouraged to develop natural controls if a firm were allowed to obtain temporary exclusive marketing rights to any product that it had proved efficacious. These temporary marketing rights would fulfill the role of patents with man-made products. A great deal more investment in biological control methods would be worthwhile. Small investments would pay large dividends in crop production and human health. And such research could significantly lessen organic food production costs.

2) Because of the potential health and environmental benefits that would arise from more widespread adoption of organic farming, it would be appropriate for some federal subsidy to be offered toward changeover costs from conventional to organic farming. Since actual production cost differences are modest, it makes sense to give serious consideration to a policy favoring organic farming. Taxes on chemical use are an appropriate tool to assist internalization of costs. A proportional tax on pesticides would help to compensate for the damage produced. For fertilizers, a tax which rises steeply after a certain minimum use would match the damages caused by nitrogen runoff.

3) Detailed studies of organic farming in different parts of the country are needed in order to obtain better estimates of the impact of widespread organic crop production on the economy. Initially, the focus should be on corn and wheat, because of their economic importance.

4) Probably the most important research that needs to be done in order

to evaluate organic farming relates to effects on long-run health. We need to know the tradeoffs between health costs and food costs. Controlled long-term studies of the effects of diets on test animals over many generations should be carried out to compare organic and conventional food. Both kinds of food should be raised in as ideal circumstances as possible. The comparisons must be made between the best conventional practice and the best organic practice, for unbalanced fertilization of either kind can have deleterious effects on consumers. Program managers must be sympathetic to the kind of crop and animal production they are studying. It would also be worthwhile to carry out epidemiological studies comparing segments of the population which eat food raised in differing manners.

APPENDIX A

The Growth in Demand
For Organic Food

We will derive a formula which relates the growth in demand for organic food to the rate at which consumers discount future discomfort.

Let P_t be the probability of contracting cancer t years in the future. We will assume that the larger the probability, the smaller the current satisfaction or utility. And we assume that the further off into the future the possibility is, the less the effect on current satisfaction. In other words, the consumer discounts the future at some rate, for example 10 percent, each year. The contribution to current disutility, D_t, would be

$$D_t = \frac{P_t}{(1+r)^t} \tag{A.1}$$

where r is equal to the discount rate. The total current disutility, TD_p, would be the sum of the future stream of disutilities, all discounted back to the present:

$$TD_p = \sum_t D_t \tag{A.2}$$

$$= \sum_t \frac{P_t}{(1 + r)^t} \tag{A.3}$$

The summation is over the individual's expected lifetime.

The probability of contracting the disease is assumed to be proportional to the total lifetime residue burden and any significant interactions between residues, provided that a latent period, T, has elapsed:

$$P_t = \sum_{\tau=0}^{t} \left(\sum_i a_i R_{i\tau} + \sum_i \sum_j a_{ij} R_{i\tau} R_{j\tau} \right) \qquad t > T \tag{A.4}$$

That is, the probability of contracting the disease is the sum of all the actions of the residues when more than time T has elapsed since first

233

ingestion. If time T has not elapsed,

$$P_t = 0 \qquad\qquad t < T \qquad (A.5)$$

Here $R_{i\tau}$ is the level of residue i consumed in year τ; a_i is the activity strength of residue i, that is, its effectiveness in inducing cancer; a_{ij} is the activity of interaction between residue i and j; and T is the minimum time required for effects to appear, on the order of perhaps twenty years.

For simplicity we will carry the analysis through for only one residue, and write

$$P_t = \begin{cases} 0 & t < T \qquad (A.6) \\[2ex] a\displaystyle\sum_{\tau=0}^{t} R\tau & t > T \qquad (A.7) \end{cases}$$

The total disutility from this future stream of adverse probabilities is found by substituting Equations A.6 and A.7 into Equation A.3:

$$TD_p = \sum_t \frac{\alpha \displaystyle\sum_{\tau=0}^{t} R_\tau}{(1 + r)^t} \qquad (A.8)$$

The consumer is faced with the decision of whether or not to ingest additional residues in the present time, P. The effect of such additional ingestion on his well-being is the marginal damage in time P, the derivative Equation A.8 with respect to the currently ingested residue, R_P.

$$MD_p = \frac{\partial TD_p}{\partial R_p} \qquad\qquad (A.9)$$

$$= a\sum_t \frac{1}{(1+r)^t} \qquad\qquad (A.10)$$

This means that the marginal disutility of consuming residue R_P is the sum of its effects over all future time periods. The sum extends to the end of the individual's life, which is assumed far enough away that the sum may be considered to infinity. Because of discounting, effects far in the future will have negligible impact on the summation.

Equation A.10 must be evaluated separately for time periods prior to T and following T, since prior to T, residue consumption has no effect until T has been reached. When $t > T$, we have simply,

$$MD_p = a \sum_{t=0}^{\infty} \frac{1}{(1+r)^t} \qquad (A.11)$$

$$= \frac{a}{1 - \frac{1}{1+r}} \qquad \text{(A.12)}$$

$$= \frac{a(1+r)}{r} \qquad \qquad P > T \quad \text{(A.13)}$$

When $P<T$, MD_P has a value of zero for all values of $t<T$. Let T_1 be the number of years between the present and T, that is, $T_1 = T - P$. Then

$$MD_P = a \sum_{t=T_1}^{\infty} \frac{1}{(1+r)^t} \qquad \text{(A.14)}$$

$$= a \left[\sum_{t=0}^{\infty} \frac{1}{(1+r)^t} - \sum_{t=0}^{T_1} \frac{1}{(1+r)^t} \right] \qquad \text{(A.15)}$$

$$= a \left[\frac{1}{1 - \frac{1}{1+r}} - \frac{1 - \left(\frac{1}{1+r}\right)^{T_1}}{1 - \frac{1}{1+r}} \right] \qquad \text{(A.16)}$$

$$= a \left(\frac{1+r}{r}\right) \left(\frac{1}{1+r}\right)^{T_1} \qquad P < T \quad \text{(A.17)}$$

Equations A.13 and A.17 relate the disutility of consuming residues in the present time period to the activity strength of the residues, a, and the rate at which the future is discounted, r. The quantity $1/(1+r)$ in Equation A.17 is less than one, since $r>0$. Thus, as the exponent T_1 shrinks, that is, as the critical year of enlightenment, T, approaches, the quantity, $(1/(1+r))^{T_1}$, increases, and does so at the rate r. Thus the marginal damage also increases at the rate r when we have not yet reached critical time T. This implies that the demand for organic food, the way a consumer can avoid the residues, should increase also, other things (like prices and income) being equal, at approximately rate r.

Once time T has been reached, however, the marginal damage remains constant (Equation A.13). Thus no further increase in demand for organic food is expected once the critical time has arrived and the effects of residues are known.

APPENDIX B

Entry Barriers
To Organic Farming

There are two kinds of costs associated with changing over from conventional farming to organic farming. These are an initial but declining yield loss upon changeover, and an initial investment in special fertilizer and consultant services. These investments are short-term losses which must be compensated by higher incomes in the future, that is, by the expectation of a higher price. The initial losses may be considered to be borrowed at prevailing interest rates. Then the higher income in the future must compensate not only for the investment, but also for interest costs. One way to take this into consideration is to discount all payments and incomes back to the present, so that income in the distant future has less weight than that in the near term. We will look at the two cases separately, since they are two different ways to change over from conventional to organic farming.

Changeover in one year. If changeover takes place without any preparation, a yield loss will be suffered in the first year. The Rodale experience and that of others cited in Chapter 11 indicates that this loss declines each year at a roughly constant rate. Let the loss in the first year be a certain fraction, d, of the long-run equilibrium yield, Q. The income in the first year will be

$$y = p_o \ (1-d) \ Q \qquad\qquad (B.1)$$

where p_o is the price for the organic production in dollars per bushel, and the units of y and Q are dollars per acre and bushels per acre, respectively, or some similar set of units. The net gain to the farmer from the first year's crop is $y - \bar{y}$, where $\bar{y}$ is equal to AC_oQ, that is, $\bar{y}$ is the income a farmer would need to cover his long-run average costs, AC_o. Since this is current year income, no adjustment need be made to obtain the present value of the gain, PV_1:

$$PV_1 = y - \overline{y} \qquad\qquad (B.2)$$

$$= y_o\,(1-d) - \overline{y} \qquad\qquad (B.3)$$

where we have replaced p_oQ_o by y_o, the income from organic production after the full yield has been achieved. In the second year, the loss will be reduced by some amount, and the gain will have to be adjusted for the interest rate to obtain the present value of the second year's gain (or loss). Let the ratio of yield losses in succeeding years be a. Then

$$PV_2 = \frac{y_o(1-ad) - \overline{y}}{(1+r)} \qquad\qquad (B.4)$$

The present value of the gain in the nth year is

$$PV_n = \frac{y_o(1-a^nd) - \overline{y}}{(1+r)^n} \qquad\qquad (B.5)$$

The present value of this set of gains (and losses) must be at least zero for new farmers to change over to organic farming. That is, no farmer is going to change over unless he expects to achieve normal returns in the long run. Thus we will find the minimum price, y_o, which will induce new entry, if we sum up all the present values of the gains and losses and set this sum equal to zero:

$$0 = \sum_{n=0}^{\infty} PV_n \qquad\qquad (B.6)$$

$$= \sum_{n=0}^{\infty} \frac{y_o(1-a^nd) - \overline{y}}{(1+r)^n} \qquad\qquad (B.7)$$

Rearranging terms, we obtain

$$0 = (y_o-\overline{y}) \sum_{n=0}^{\infty} \frac{1}{(1+r)^n} - dy_o \sum_{n=0}^{\infty} \left(\frac{a}{1+r}\right)^n \qquad\qquad (B.8)$$

Making use of the formula, $\displaystyle\sum_{n=c}^{\infty} x^n = 1/(1-x)$ for $x^2 < 1$, we obtain

$$0 = (y_o - \bar{y}) \ \frac{1}{1 - \frac{1}{1+r}} - dy_o \ \frac{1}{1 - \frac{a}{1+r}} \tag{B.9}$$

Solving this equation for $y_o / \bar{y}$, we obtain the relation

$$\frac{y_o}{\bar{y}} = \frac{1}{1 - \frac{d \ r}{1+r-a}} \tag{B.10}$$

Since $y_o = P_o Q_o$ and $\bar{y} = AC_o Q_o$, then

$$\frac{y_o}{\bar{y}} = \frac{P_o Q_o}{AC_o Q_o}$$

$$= \frac{P_o}{AC_o}$$

Therefore

$$\frac{P_o}{AC_o} = \frac{1}{1 - \frac{d \ r}{1+r-a}} \tag{B.11}$$

This is the desired relationship, showing the price increase required to induce changeover to organic production in terms of the interest rate and the crop loss parameters.

Equation B.11 is graphed in Figure B-1 for representative values of the parameters. For typical values of $a = 0.5$, $d = 0.5$ and $r = 0.1$, $P_o / AC_o = 1.0833$ or an increase in price over average long-run cost of about 8.3 percent.

Equation B.11 can be solved for the value of the entry barrier, E_L / Q_o (Chapter 11) where E_L is the investment per acre:

$$\frac{E_L}{Q_o} = P_o - AC_o \tag{B.12}$$

$$= \frac{P_o \ d r}{1 + r - a} \tag{B.13}$$

Three-year adjustment period with investment in first year. It is somewhat easier to specify the required price increase to compensate a farmer for an

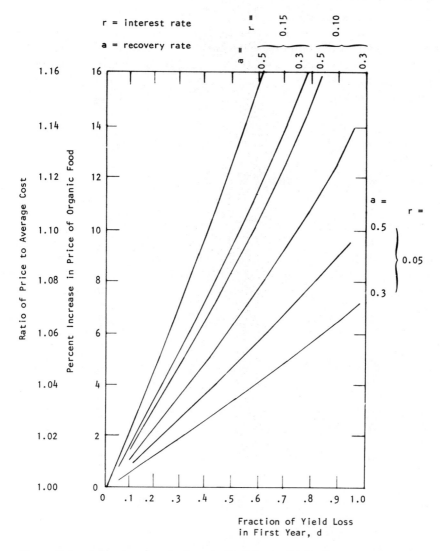

Figure B-1. Price Increase in Organic Food Due to Yield Loss on Changeover as a Function of Initial Loss, Recovery Rate, and Interest Rate

initial investment and a waiting period before he receives a return on that investment. Let the initial investment be C ($ per acre). In the third year the investment will amount to $C(1+r)^2$, since interest must be paid. At this point, a higher income will be received from the sale of the organic crop, and this increased income must at least cover the interest on the loan. Thus we set

$$C(1 + r)^2 r = (p_o - AC_o)Q \qquad\qquad (B.14)$$

The entry barrier, E_I/Q (Chapter 11), is, again, $p_o - AC_o$, or

$$\frac{E_I}{Q} = \frac{C(1+r)^2 r}{Q} \qquad\qquad (B.15)$$

For example, if an investment of $100 per acre is needed on land that produces 80 bushels per acre of organic corn with a value of $2.50 per bushel in conventional markets, the price of organic corn must be $p_o = \$2.50 + \$100\,(1.1)^2 \cdot 0.1/80 = \$2.65$, or about 6 percent higher.

APPENDIX C

SAMPLE DATA SHEET

Farm _____   Land_____ acres _____ cropable
_____ grazing

Purchases		
Seed cost ____ /acre		
Fertilizer	Rate/a	Cost
Phosphate		
Potash		
Other		
Lime		
Insecticides		
Other		

Soil type _____

Approx. land value $ _____ /acre

Value of farm buildings $ _____

Rotation	Crop	2nd Crop	Cover/green manure fertilizer
1			
2			
3			
4			

Operation:	# Times	# Workers	Hours/acre
Growing:			
Chopping			
Disking			
Plowing			
Harrowing			
Planting			
Hoeing			
Cultivating			
Spraying			
P&K Bulk Spreading			
Other Ferti- lizer, etc.			
Compost/Manure			
Wagons, etc.			
Other			
Harvest & Storage			
Harvest			
Hauling			
Drying			
Storage			
Other			

Farm labor
_____ Full time
_____ part time for
_____ weeks/year
_____ part time for
_____ weeks/year

References

Chapter 1

Ball, A. Gordon, and Earl O. Heady. 1972. "Trends in Farm and Enterprise Size and Scale," in A. Gordon Ball and Earl O. Heady, ed., *Size, Structure and Future of Farms.* Ames, Iowa: Iowa State University Press.

Butz, Earl. 1971. "Meet the Press," television and radio interview, NBC, December 12; quoted in *Yearbook of Spoken Opinion: What They Said in 1971*; and in William Lockeretz *et al., A Comparison of the Production, Economic Returns, and Energy Intensiveness of Corn Belt Farms That Do and Do Not Use Inorganic Fertilizers and Pesticides,* Report No. CBNS-AE-4, St. Louis, Mo.: Center for the Biology of Natural Systems, Washington University.

Childers, Norman F. 1975. *Modern Fruit Science*, 6th ed. New Brunswick, N.J.: Horticultural Publications, Rutgers University.

CRA. 1973. *Report of the Committee on Research Advisory to the USDA.* Springfield, Va.: National Technical Information Service.

FPD. 1975. "Egg Replacer Provides Caloric Reduction, Total Functionality and Convenience," *Food Product Development* 9 (June), 12–13.

Hall, Ross H. 1974. *Food for Naught.* New York: Harper & Row.

Kendrick, J. B., Jr. 1976. "What is Agricultural Research?" *Science* 191 (27 February), 813.

Koepf, Herbert H. 1976. "What is Bio-dynamic Agriculture?" *Bio-Dynamics* 117 (Winter), 15–43.

Mishan, E. J. 1971. "On Making the Future Safe for Mankind," *The Public Interest* 34 (Summer), 33–61.

NAS. 1975. *Enhancement of Food Production for the United States.* Washington, D.C.: National Academy of Sciences.

Samuelson, Robert J. 1976. "Scrambling Back: The Battered Egg," *Washington Post* (1 August), C3.

Singer, Peter. 1975. *Animal Liberation.* New York: Random House.

USDA. 1945. *Agricultural Statistics.* Washington, D.C.: U.S. Dept. of Agriculture, G.P.O.

———. 1975. *Agricultural Statistics.* Washington, D.C.: U.S. Dept. of Agriculture, G.P.O.

Wade, Nicholas. 1973a. "Agriculture: NAS Panel Charges Inept Management, Poor Research," *Science* 179 (5 January), 45–47.

———. 1973b. "Agriculture: Critics Find Basic Research Stunted and Wilting," *Science* 180 (27 April), 390–94.

———. 1975. "Agriculture: Academy Group Suggests Major Shake-Up to President Ford," *Science* 190 (5 December), 959.

Wilson, Wilbur O. 1966. "Poultry Production," *Scientific American* (July).

Chapter 2

Baker, Kenneth F., and R. James Cook. 1974. *Biological Control of Plant Pathogens.* San Francisco: W. H. Freeman.

Ball, A. G., and E. O. Heady, eds. 1972. *Size, Structure and Future of Farms.* Ames, Iowa: Iowa State University Press.

Bellerby, J. R., ed. 1970. *Factory Farming.* Oxford, England: Alden and Mobry.

Berry, John H. 1971. "Effect of Restricting the Use of Pesticides on Corn-Soybean Farms," in *Economic Research on Pesticides for Policy Decisionmaking.* Washington, D.C.: Economic Research Service, U.S. Dept. of Agriculture, 137–49.

Berry, Wendell. 1974. "The Culture of Agriculture," speech to the Agriculture on a Small Planet Symposium, Spokane, Washington. Printed in *Tilth Newsletter*, Olympia, Wash. 10 (March), 12–14.

———. 1977. *The Unsettling of America.* San Francisco: Sierra Club Books.

Breimeyer, Harold F. 1973. "Man, Physical Resources, and Economic Organization," *American Journal of Agricultural Economics* 55 (February), 1–9.

———. 1975. Letter to author.

Breimeyer, Harold F., and Wallace Barr. 1972. "Issues in Concentration Versus Dispersion," in *Who Will Control U.S. Agriculture?* Special Publication 27. College of Agriculture, Cooperative Extension Service, Urbana, Ill.: University of Illinois.

Brett, Abigail Trafford. 1975. "Molds in the Corn," *Washington Post* (15 June), C2.

CRA. 1973. *Report of the Committee on Research Advisory to the USDA.* Springfield, Va.: National Technical Information Service.

Crossland, Janice. 1975. "Power to Resist," *Environment* 17 (March), 6–11.

Cunha, T. J. 1972. "The Value of Hormones and Feed Additives for Animals," *Feedstuffs* 44 (15 May), 42–43.

Darrow, Norbert A. 1972. "Policies Affecting Capital Accumulation and Organizational Structure," in *Who Will Control U.S. Agriculture?* Special Publication 27. College of Agriculture, Cooperative Extension Service, Urbana, Ill.: University of Illinois.

DeBach, Paul. 1974. *Biological Control by Natural Enemies.* London: Cambridge University Press.

EPA. 1974. *Farmer's Pesticide Use Decisions and Attitudes on Alternative Crop Protection Methods.* EPA-540/1-74-002. Washington, D.C.: U.S. Environmental Protection Agency, G.P.O.

ERS. 1968. *Farmers' Pesticide Expenditures for Crops, Livestock and Other Selected Uses in 1964.* Agricultural Economic Report No. 145. Washington, D.C.: Economic Research Service, U.S. Dept. of Agriculture, Washington, D.C.: G.P.O.

———. 1969. *Changes in Farm Production and Efficiency.* Statistical Bull. No. 233. Washington, D.C.: Economic Research Service, U.S. Dept. of Agriculture.

———. 1973. *Changes in Farm Production and Efficiency.* Statistical Bull. No. 233. Washington, D.C.: Economic Research Service, Dept. of Agriculture.

———. 1974. *Farm Income Situation (July)*. Washington. D.C.: Economic Research Service, U.S. Dept. of Agriculture.

FDA. Undated. "Antibiotics and the Foods You Eat." Consumer Memo. DHEW Publication No. (FDA) 73-6001. Washington, D.C.: U.S. Dept. of Health, Education and Welfare.

Fox, Austin, Theodore Eichers, and Paul Andrilenas. 1968. *Extent of Farm Pesticide Use on Crops in 1966*. Agricultural Economics Report No. 147. Washington, D.C.: Economic Research Service, U.S. Dept. of Agriculture.

Gavett, Earle E. Undated ca. 1974. "Agriculture: Energy Use and Conservation." Washington, D.C.: Economic Research Service, U.S. Dept. of Agriculture.

Hall, Ross H. 1974. *Food for Naught*. New York: Harper & Row.

Heady, Earl O. 1975. "The Basic Equity Problem," in Earl O. Heady and Larry R. Whiting, eds., *Externalities in the Transformation of Agriculture*. Ames, Iowa: Iowa State University Press, 3–21.

Hightower, Jim. 1973. *Hard Tomatoes, Hard Times*. Cambridge, Mass.: Schenkman.

Kiesner, Jack. 1971. "Natural Estrogens Found in Some Food, but DES Ban Likely if Residues Persist," *Feedstuffs* 43 (18 December), 4.

———. 1972. "No Immediate Impact of FDA's Antibiotics Report Expected," *Feedstuffs* 44 (7 February), 1.

Krause, K. R., and L. R. Kyle. 1970. "Economic Factors Underlying the Incidence of Large Farming Units: The Current Situation and Probable Trends," *American Journal of Agricultural Economics* 52 (December), 748–61.

———. 1971. "Midwestern Corn Farms: Economic Status and the Potential for Large and Family-Sized Units." Agricultural Economic Report No. 216. Washington, D.C.: Economic Research Service, U.S. Dept. of Agriculture.

Krutilla, J. V. 1967. "Conservation Reconsidered," *American Economic Review* 57 (September), 777–86.

Kyle, Leonard R., W. B. Sundquist, and Harold D. Guither. 1972. "Who Controls Agriculture Now?— The Trends Underway," in *Who Will Control U.S. Agriculture?* Special Publication 27. College of Agriculture, Cooperative Extension Service, Urbana, Ill.: University of Illinois.

MacKenzie, Mary Ann. 1975. Community Services Administration. Personal communication.

McNew, George L. 1966. "Progress in the Battle Against Plant Disease," in *Scientific Aspects of Pest Control*. Washington, D.C.: National Academy of Sciences–National Research Council.

Madden, J. Patrick. 1967. *Economies of Size in Farming*. Washington, D.C.: Economic Research Service, U.S. Dept. of Agriculture.

Mayer, Leo V. 1970. Untitled. In *Benefits and Burdens of Rural Development*. Ames, Iowa: Iowa State University Press.

Miller, Judith. 1973. "Genetic Erosion: Crop Plants Threatened by Government Neglect," *Science* 182 (21 December), 1231–33.

NRC. 1972. *Genetic Vulnerability of Major Crops*. Washington, D.C.: National Academy of Sciences–National Research Council.

P&E. 1976. "Pioneering Appropriate Technology," *People and Energy* 2 (March), 1–2.

Quance, Leroy, and Luther G. Tweeten. 1972. "Policies, 1930–1970," in A. Gordon Ball and Earl O. Heady, eds., *Size, Structure and Future of Farms*. Ames Iowa: Iowa State University Press.

Raup, Philip M. 1972. "Societal Goals in Farm Size," in A. Gordon Ball and Earl O. Heady, eds., *Size, Structure, and Future of Farms*. Ames, Iowa: Iowa State University Press.

Schmitz, Andrew, and David Seckler. 1970. "Mechanized Agriculture and Social Welfare: The Case of the Tomato Harvester," *American Journal of Agricultural Economics* 52 (November), 569–77.

Schumacher, E. F. 1973. *Small Is Beautiful*. New York: Harper & Row.

USDA. 1975. *Agricultural Statistics*. Washington, D.C.: U.S. Dept. of Agriculture, G.P.O.

Wade, Nicholas. 1973. "Agriculture: Social Sciences Oppressed and Poverty Stricken," *Science* 180 (18 May), 719.

Weiss, Kay. 1973. "Afterthoughts on the Morning-After Pill." *Ms* 2 (November), 22–26.

Wirth, M. E., and L. F. Robers. 1970. "The Changing Nature and Environment of United States Farm Firms," in *A New Look at Agricultural Finance Research*. Agricultural Finance Program Report 1. Urbana, Ill.: Dept. of Agricultural Economics, University of Illinois. C. 2, 12–27.

Chapter 3

Aenelt, E., and J. Hahn. 1978. "Animal Fertility: A Possibility for Biological Quality-Assay of Fodder and Feeds?" *Bio-Dynamics* 125 (Winter), 36–46.

Albrecht, William A. 1975. *The Albrecht Papers*. Charles Walters, Jr., ed. Raytown, Mo.: Acres, U.S.A.

Allaway, W. H. 1975. *The Effect of Soils and Fertilizers on Human and Animal Nutrition*. Agriculture Information Bull. No. 378. Washington, D.C.: G.P.O.

Allison, F. E. 1973. *Soil Organic Matter and its Role in Crop Production*. New York: Elsevier Scientific Pub. Co.

Balfour, E. B. 1975. *The Living Soil and the Haughley Experiment*. London: Faber & Faber.

Bear, Firman E. 1953. *Soils and Fertilizers*. New York: John Wiley.

Beeson, Kenneth C. 1972. "What About the 'Organic' Way?" *New York Times* (16 April), Section II, 33.

Commoner, Barry. 1971. *The Closing Circle*. New York: Alfred A. Knopf.

DeHart, P. H., and R. M. DeHart. 1962. "Health and Vigor Depend on the Soil," in J. I. Rodale, ed., *The Complete Book of Food and Nutrition*. Emmaus, Pa.: Rodale Books, 774–84.

Dhar, N. R. 1961. "Nitrogen Problem." Presidential Address, 48th Indian Science Congress, Roorkee. Calcutta: Indian Science Congress Association.

Dlouhy, J. 1977. *Vaxtprodukters Kvalitet vid Konventionell och Biodynamisk Odling*. Reports of the Agricultural College of Sweden, Series A, Nr 272. Uppsala, Sweden.

Dubos, Rene. 1965. *Man Adapting*. New Haven, Conn.: Yale University Press.

ERS. 1976. *Fertilizer Situation (June)*. Supplement No. 1 to FSS. Washington, D.C.: Economic Research Service, U.S. Dept. of Agriculture.

FDA. 1973. "Vitamins, Minerals and the FDA." *FDA Consumer* (September) DHEW Publ No. (FDA) 73-7018. Washington, D.C.: Food and Drug Administration, U.S. Dept. of Health, Education and Welfare.

Fogg, G. E., W. D. P. Stewart, P. Fay, and A. E. Walsby. 1973. *The Blue-Green Algae*. New York: Academic Press.

Frank, Allan. 1976. "Tide of Doom May be Sweeping Long Island Beaches," *Washington Star* (26 July), A1.

Fryer, Lee, and Dick Simmons. 1976. *Food Power from the Sea*. New York: Mason/Charter.

Hall, Ross H. 1974. *Food for Naught*. New York: Harper & Row.

Harnish, Stuart. 1976. "Redefining Organic: Two Views. The Mineral," *The Natural Farmer.* Newsletter of the Natural Organic Farmers Association, Plainfield, Vt. (April), 1–17.

Hay, Christian. 1977. "Preliminary Reports on the Effects of Various 'Biological' Treatments on Crop Yield." MacDonald College. Mimeographed.

Hinnen, Dean. 1975. "Taylor Returns to the Soil Wars," *The Hutchinson News* (March).

Kavanagh, L. R. 1957. *The Story of Hybrid Maize.* Division of Plant Industry, New South Wales Dept. of Agriculture.

Kehr, August E. 1974. "Genetic Engineering to Remove Undesirable Compounds and Unattractive Characteristics," in Philip L. White and Nancy Selvey, eds., *Nutritional Qualities of Fresh Fruits and Vegetables.* Mount Kisco, N.Y.: Futura.

Kinsey, Neal. 1976. (Dept. of Agricultural Research, Ambassador College). Letter to Ken Farmer, President, Genesis II, Athens, Texas.

Koepf, H. H. 1976. "Biological Agriculture Work Study." Lecture to 2nd Annual Biological Agriculture Workshop. Boys Town, Neb. Condensed summary report.

Koepf, H. H., B. D. Pettersson, and W. Schaumann. 1974. *Biologische Landwirtschaft.* Stuttgart, Germany: Verlag Eugen Ulmer. Translated, 1976, as *Bio-Dynamic Agriculture.* Spring Valley, N.Y.: Anthroposophic Press.

Krasil'nikov, N. A. 1958. *Soil Microorganisms and Higher Plants.* Translated by Y. Halperin. Jerusalem: S. Monson. Available from Office of Technical Services, U.S. Dept. of Commerce, Washington, D.C.

Linder, M. C. 1973. "A Review of the Evidence for Food Quality Differences in Relation to Fertilization of the Soil with Organic and Mineral Fertilizers," *Bio-Dynamics* 107 (Summer), 1–11.

Love, Thomas. 1976. "Florida Phosphate Mining: Uranium, Water Factors," *Washington Star* (31 May), A1.

McAllister, Bill. 1976. "Methane: Richmond's Peril," *Washington Post* (4 April), A1.

Manson, R. J., and Clifford A. Merritt. 1975. "Farming and Municipal Sludge: They're Compatible," *Compost Science* 16 (July–August), 16–19.

Martin, W. P., W. E. Fenster, and L. D. Hanson. 1970. "Fertilizer Management for Pollution Control," c. 9, 142–58 in Ted L. Willrich and George E. Smith, eds., *Agricultural Practices and Water Quality.* U. S. Dept. of the Interior, Federal Water Pollution Control Administration, PB199828. Springfield, Va.: National Technical Information Service.

Miller, Judith. 1974. "Agriculture: FDA Seeks to Regulate Genetic Manipulation of Food Crops," *Science* 185 (19 July), 240–42.

Mintz, Morton. 1976. "EPA Aides Fault Pesticide Studies," *Washington Post* (10 April), A1.

Mitchel, H. H., T. S. Hamilton, and Jessie R. Beadles. 1952. "The Relationship Between the Protein Content of Corn and the Nutritional Value of the Protein," *Journal of Nutrition* 48 (December), 461–76.

Nelson, E. M. 1959. *Yearbook.* Washington, D.C.: U.S. Dept. of Agriculture, G.P.O.

NRC. 1975. *World Food and Nutrition Study. Enhancement of Food Production for the U.S.* Washington, D.C.: National Academy of Sciences–National Research Council.

Patton, Stuart. 1969. "Milk." *Scientific American* (July).

Perelman, Michael. 1972. "Farming with Petroleum," *Environment* 14 (October), 8–13.

Pettersson, B. D. 1976. *Vaxtprodukters Kvalitet vid Vanlig och vid Biodynamisk Odling.* Jarna, Sweden: Nordisk Forskningring.

Pfeiffer, Ehrenfried. 1938. *Bio-Dynamic Farming and Gardening.* New York: Anthroposophic Press.

Robertson, J. M., C. R. Toussain, and M. A. Jorque. 1974. *Organic Compounds Entering Ground Water from a Landfill.* EPA-660/2-74-077. Washington, D.C.: U.S. Environmental Protection Agency.

Russell, E. Walter. 1961. *Soil Conditions and Plant Growth.* London: Longmans.

Sauberlich, H. E., Wan Yuin Chang, and W. D. Salman. 1953. "The Comparative Nutritive Value of Corn of High and Low Protein Content for Growth in the Rat and Chick," *Journal of Nutrition* 51 (December), 623-35.

Schuphan, W. 1970. "Die Problematik dungungsbedingter Hochstertrage aus phytochemischer und ernahrungsphysiologischer Sicht," *Qual. Plant. Mater. Veg.* 20 (1-2), 35-68.

———. 1972. "Effects of the Application of Inorganic and Organic Manures on the Market Quality and on the Biological Value of Agricultural Products," *Qual. Plant. Mater. Veg.* 21 (4), 381-98.

———. 1973. "Food Plants—Fresh, Prepared, Processed—in Relation to Standards of Living and Potential Diseases of Civilization," *Qual. Plant—Pl. Fds. Hum. Nutr.* 23 (1/3), 33-74.

———. 1974. "Nutritional Value of Crops as Influenced by Organic and Inorganic Fertilizer Treatments," *Qual. Plant—Pl. Fds. Hum. Nutr.* 23 (4), 333-58.

Senn, T. L., and Alta R. Kingman. 1973. *A Review of Humus and Humic Acids.* Research Series No. 145. Clemson, S.C.: Clemson University Horticulture Dept.

Shapley, Deborah. 1976. "Nitrosamines: Scientists on the Trail of Prime Suspect in Urban Cancer," *Science* 191 (23 January), 268-70.

———. 1977. "Will Fertilizers Harm Ozone as much as SST's?" *Science* 195 (18 February), 658.

Stare, F. J. 1961. "Are There Poisons in Your Food?" *Farm Journal* 85 (February), 42A.

Taylor, Leland B. 1975. *"Organic" Liar Detection.* Albuquerque, N.M.: Farm Guard Press.

———. 1976. (President, Farm Guard Products, Albuquerque, N.M.) Letter to author.

Teuscher, H., and R. Adler. 1960. *The Soil and its Fertility.* New York: Reinhold.

Thompson, Louis M., and Frederick R. Troeh. 1973. *Soils and Soil Fertility.* New York: McGraw-Hill.

Viets, Frank G., Jr., and Richard H. Hageman. 1971. *Factors Affecting the Accumulation of Nitrate in Soil, Water, and Plants.* Agriculture Handbook No. 413. Washington, D.C.: Agricultural Research Service, U.S. Dept. of Agriculture, G.P.O.

Wolff, I. A., and A. E. Wasserman. 1972. "Nitrates, Nitrites, and Nitrosamines," *Science* 177 (7 July), 15-19.

Zillinsky, F. J. 1975. "Improving Nutritional Quality in Cereals at CIMMYT," in *Proceedings of the 20th Annual Meeting of the Canadian Society of Agronomy,* 51-56.

Chapter 4

Adkisson, P. L. 1971. "Objective Uses of Insecticides in Agriculture," in *Agricultural Chemicals—Harmony or Discord.* J. E. Swift, ed. University of California, Division of Agricultural Sciences.

Allaway, W. H. 1975. *The Effect of Soils and Fertilizers on Human and Animal Nutrition.* Agriculture Information Bull. No. 378. Washington, D.C.: G.P.O.

Allison, F. E. 1973. *Soil Organic Matter and its Role in Crop Production.* New York: Elsevier Scientific Pub. Co.

Anderson, T. W., B. W. Reid, and G. H. Beaton. 1972. "Vitamin C and the Common Cold, a Double-Blind Trial," *Canadian Medical Association Journal* (September 23).

Andrilenas, Paul A. 1971. "Evaluating the Economic Consequences of Banning or Restricting the Use of Pesticides in Crop Production," 49-62 in *Economic Research on Pesticides for Policy Decisionmaking.* Washington, D.C.: Economic Research Service, U.S. Dept. of Agriculture.

ASCS. 1974. *The Pesticide Review*. Agriculture Stabilization and Conservation Service. Washington, D.C.: U.S. Dept. of Agriculture.

Baker, Kenneth F., and R. James Cook. 1974. *Biological Control of Plant Pathogens*. San Francisco: W. H. Freeman.

Beal, G. M., J. M. Bohlen, and H. G. Lingren. 1966. *Behavior Studies Related to Pesticides: Agricultural Chemicals and Iowa Farmers*. Ames, Iowa: Iowa State University, Agricultural and Home Economics Experiment Station. Special Report No. 49.

Bevenue, A., and Y. Kawano. 1971. "Pesticides, Pesticide Residues, Tolerances and the Law," *Residue Review* 35, 103–49.

BW. 1975. "Farm Turmoil from a Model Law," *Business Week* (13 October), 88.

CA. 1976. "Agriculture and Related Agencies. Appropriations for 1977." Hearings before a Subcommittee of the Committee on Appropriations, H.R., 94th Cong., 2nd Sess. Part 1. Agricultural Programs. Washington, D.C.: G.P.O.

Carper, Jean. 1970. "Danger of Cancer in Food," *Saturday Review* (5 September), 47–57.

Carriere, D. C. 1976. "Rx for Erodible Southern Soils," *Agricultural Research* 24 (June), 5.

Carson, Rachel. 1962. *Silent Spring*. Boston: Houghton-Mifflin.

Carter, Luther J. 1976a. "Pest Control: NAS Panel Warns of Possible Technological Breakdown," *Science* 191 (27 February), 836–37.

———. 1976b. "Pesticides: Three EPA Attorneys Quit and Hoist a Warning Flag," *Science* 191 (19 March), 1155–58.

Cole, LaMont C. 1966. "The Complexity of Pest Control in the Environment," in *Scientific Aspects of Pest Control*. Washington, D.C.: National Academy of Sciences–National Research Council, 13–25.

CRB. 1975. *Agricultural Prices. Annual Summary*. Crop Reporting Board, Statistical Reporting Service. U.S. Dept. of Agriculture.

Culliton, Barbara J. 1974. "The Destroying Angel: A Story of a Search for an Antidote," *Science* 185 (16 August), 600–601.

Davidson, A., and R. B. Norgaard. 1973. "Economic Aspects of Pest Control." OEPP/EPPO Bull. 3 (3), 63–75.

Davis, Donald E. 1974. "The 2,4,5-T Story—Is This the End?" *Weeds Today* 5 (Spring), 12.

Davis, Velmar W., Austin S. Fox, Robert P. Jenkins, and Paul A. Andrilenas. 1970. *Economic Consequences of Restricting the Use of Organochlorine Insecticides on Cotton, Corn, Peanuts, and Tobacco*. Agricultural Economics Report No. 178. Washington, D.C.: Economic Research Service, U.S. Dept. of Agriculture, G.P.O.

Day, Boysie E. 1966. "The Scientific Basis of Weed Control," in *Scientific Aspects of Pest Control*. Washington, D.C.: National Academy of Sciences–National Research Council, 102–14.

DeBach, Paul. 1974. *Biological Control by Natural Enemies*. Cambridge, England: Cambridge University Press.

Delvo, Herman W. 1974. *Economic Impact of Discontinuing Aldrin Use in Corn Production*. ERS-557. Washington, D.C.: Economic Research Service, U.S. Dept. of Agriculture.

Delvo, Herman W., Austin S. Fox, and Robert P. Jenkins. 1973. *Economic Impact of Discontinuing Farm Uses of Heptachlor*. ERS-509. Economic Research Service, U.S. Dept. of Agriculture.

Dixon, Orani, Peter Dixon, and John Miranowski. 1973. "Insecticide Requirements in an Efficient Agricultural Sector," *Review of Economics and Statistics* 55 (November), 423–32.

Djerassi, Carl. 1974. "Insect Control of the Future: Operational and Policy Aspects," *Science* 186 (15 November), 596–607.

Edwards, William F. 1969. *Economic Externalities in the Agricultural Use of Pesticides and an Evaluation of Alternative Policies.* Ph.D. dissertation, University of Florida.

Eichers, T., P. Andrilenas, H. Blake, R. Jenkins, and A. Fox. 1970. *Quantities of Pesticides Used by Farmers in 1966.* Agricultural Economic Report No. 179. Washington, D.C.: Economic Research Service, U.S. Dept. of Agriculture, G.P.O.

EPA. 1975. *Production, Distribution, Use and Environmental Impact Potential of Selected Pesticides.* EPA 540/1-74-001. Washington, D.C.: U.S. Environmental Protection Agency.

Epstein, Samuel S. 1970. "A Family Likeness," *Environment* 12 (July–August), 16–25.

——, and Marvin S. Legator. 1971. *The Mutagenicity of Pesticides.* Cambridge, Mass.: MIT Press.

ERS. 1977. *Agricultural Outlook* (November) AO-27. Washington, D.C.: Economic Research Service, U.S. Dept. of Agriculture.

Feinberg, Lawrence. 1976. "Weevils Run Rampant in Maryland, Threaten to Destroy Alfalfa Fields," *Washington Post* (24 April), B1.

Ford, Frank. 1975. (President, Arrowhead Mills, Hereford, Texas.) Personal communication.

Fournier, E. 1971. "Toxicologie Humaine des Pesticides," *Qual. Plant. Mɐier. Veg.* 20: 69–99.

Galston, Arthur W. 1976. "How Safe Should Safe Be?" *Natural History* 85 (April), 32–35.

Gerlow, Arthur R. 1973. *The Economic Impact of Cancelling the Use of 2,4,5-T in Rice Production.* ERS-510. Washington, D.C.: Economic Research Service, U.S. Dept. of Agriculture.

Giese, Ronald L., Robert M. Peart, and Roger T. Huber. 1975. "Pest Management," *Science* 187 (21 March) 1045–52.

Graham, Frank, Jr. 1970. *Since Silent Spring.* Boston: Houghton-Mifflin.

Hall, E. R. 1972. "Down on the Farm," *Natural History* (March), 8–12.

Headley, J. C., and J. N. Lewis. 1968. *The Pesticide Problem: An Economic Approach to Public Policy.* Washington, D.C.: Resources for the Future.

Heady, E. O., and R. F. Brokken. 1968. *Interregional Adjustments in Crop and Livestock Production, a Linear Programming Analysis.* Technical Bull. No. 1396. Washington, D.C.: Economic Research Service, U.S. Dept. of Agriculture.

HEW. 1969. *Report of the Secretary's Commission on Pesticides and Their Relationship to Environmental Health.* Parts I and II. Washington, D.C.: U.S. Dept. of Health, Education and Welfare, G.P.O.

Hillebrandt, P. M. 1960. "The Economic Theory of the Use of Pesticides, Part I," *Journal of Agricultural Economics* 13 (January), 464–72.

Hoffmann, C. H. 1971. "Restricting the Use of Insecticides—What are the Alternatives?" in *Economic Research on Pesticides for Policy Decisionmaking.* Washington, D.C.: Economic Research Service, U.S. Dept. of Agriculture, 21–30.

Huffaker, C. B., ed. 1971. *Biological Control.* New York: Plenum.

Hunt, Eldridge G. 1966. "Biological Magnification of Pesticides," in *Scientific Aspects of Pest Control.* Washington, D.C.: National Academy of Sciences–National Research Council, 251–62.

IRRI. 1975. *Annual Report for 1974.* Los Banos, Philippines: International Rice Research Institute.

Jefferies, D. J. 1975. "The Role of the Thyroid in the Production of Sublethal Effects by Organochlorine Insecticides and Polychlorinated Biphenyls," in F. Moriarty, ed., *Organochlorine Insecticides: Persistent Organic Pollutants.* New York: Academic Press, 132–230.

Johnson, Julius E., and Etcyl H. Blair. 1972. "Cost, Time and Pesticide Safety," *Chemical Technology* 2 (November), 666–69.

Kolata, Gina Bari. 1976. "Chemical Carcinogens: Industry Adopts Controversial 'Quick' Tests," *Science* 192 (18 June), 1215-17.

Lederberg, Joshua. 1971. "Foreword," in Samuel S. Epstein and Marvin S. Legator, *The Mutagenicity of Pesticides.* Cambridge, Mass.: MIT Press.

Lichtenstein, E. P. 1966. "Persistence and Degradation of Pesticides in the Environment," in *Scientific Aspects of Pest Control.* Washington, D.C.: National Academy of Sciences–National Research Council, 221-29.

———. 1973. "Environmental Factors Affecting Penetration and Translocation of Insecticides from Soils into Crops," *Qual. Plant—Pl. Fds. Hum. Nutr.* 23: 113-18.

Luckmann, William H., and Robert L. Metcalf. 1975. "The Pest Management Concept," in Robert L. Metcalf and William H. Luckmann, eds., *Introduction to Insect Pest Management.* New York: John Wiley. C. 1, 3-35.

Luginbill, P. 1969. *Developing Resistant Plants—the Ideal Method of Controlling Insects.* Production Research Report III. Washington, D.C.: Agricultural Research Service, U.S. Dept. of Agriculture.

McCullough, M. L. 1975. "Biological Aids for Livestock Show Promise," *Hoard's Dairyman* (25 October), 1179.

McNew, George L. 1966. "Progress in the Battle Against Plant Disease," in *Scientific Aspects of Pest Control.* Washington, D.C.: National Academy of Sciences–National Research Council, 73-101.

Marx, Jean L. 1976. "Briefing: Clearinghouse for Chemical Carcinogens," *Science* 192 (16 April), 242.

Measday, Walter S. "The Pharmaceutical Industry," in Walter Adams, ed., *The Structure of American Industry,* 4th ed. New York: Macmillan.

Mintz, Morton. 1976. "EPA Aides Fault Pesticide Studies," *Washington Post* (10 April), A1.

NACA. 1976. *1975 Industry Profile Study.* Washington, D.C.: National Agricultural Chemicals Association.

NRC. 1968a. *Plant-Disease Development and Control.* Washington, D.C.: National Academy of Sciences–National Research Council.

———. 1968b. *Control of Plant-Parasitic Nematodes.* Washington, D.C.: National Academy of Sciences–National Research Council.

———. 1968c. *Effects of Pesticides on Fruit and Vegetable Physiology.* Washington, D.C.: National Academy of Sciences–National Research Council.

———. 1969. *Insect-Pest Management and Control.* Publication 1695. Washington, D.C.: National Academy of Sciences–National Research Council.

———. 1975. *Pest Control: An Assessment of Present and Alternative Technologies.* Washington, D.C.: National Academy of Sciences–National Research Council.

NS. 1976. "Sudden Rise in U.S. Cancer Deaths," *New Scientist,* 69 (1 January), 5.

Perelman, Michael, and Kevin P. Shea. 1972. "The Big Farm," *Environment* 14 (December), 10-15.

Perry, H. B. 1972. "Corn Insect Pest Management," in *Implementing Practical Pest Management Strategies.* Proceedings of a National Extension Pest Management Workshop. Lafayette, Ind.: Purdue University, 107-15.

Pimentel, David. 1973. "Realities of a Pesticide Ban," *Environment* 15 (March), 18-30.

Pimentel, David, Donald Chang, Arthur Kelman, Robert L. Metcalf, L. D. Newsom, and Carroll Smith. 1965. "Improved Pest Control Practices," Appendix Y11 in *Restoring the Quality of our Environment.* Report of the Environmental Pollution Panel, President's Science Advisory Committee. Washington, D.C.: G.P.O., 230-91.

PMA. 1974. *Annual Survey Report 1973-74*. Washington, D.C.: Pharmaceutical Manufacturers' Association.

Reuben, David. 1975. *The Save Your Life Diet*. New York: Random House.

Rudd, Robert L. 1964. *Pesticides and the Living Landscape*. Madison, Wis.: University of Wisconsin Press.

Salomon, Milton. 1974. "Influence of Agronomic Practices on Nutritional Values," in Philip L. White and Nancy Selvey, eds., *Nutritional Qualities of Fresh Fruits and Vegetables*. Mount Kisco, N.Y.: Futura.

Schuphan, Werner. 1972. "Effects of the Application of Inorganic and Organic Manures on the Market Quality and on the Biological Value of Agricultural Products," *Qual. Plant. Mater. Veg.* 21 (4), 381-98.

Schwecker, Edward L. 1975. (Cooperative Extension Service, University of Maryland, College Park, Md.) Personal communication.

Smith, E. H. 1966. "Advances, Problems, and the Future of Insect Control," in *Scientific Aspects of Pest Control*. Washington, D.C.: National Academy of Sciences–National Research Council, 41- 72.

Smith, J. Y. 1976. "Kepone Indictments Cite 1096 Violations. Contamination Problems Still Plague Va. Area," *Washington Post* (8 May), A1.

Swift, John E. 1969. "Unexpected Effects of Substitute Pest Control Methods," in James W. Gillett, ed., *The Biological Impact of Pesticides in the Environment*. Proceedings of the Symposium, August 1969. Corvallis, Ore. Environmental Health Sciences Center, Oregon State University, 156-60.

USDA. 1965. "Basic Documents Submitted by the Department of Agriculture Relating to the Use of Pesticides," in *Interagency Coordination in Environmental Hazards (Pesticides)*. Hearings Before the Subcommittee on Reorganization and International Organizations of the Committee on Government Operations, U.S. Senate, 88th Congress, 2nd Sess., Appendix I to Part 1. Washington, D.C.: G.P.O.

———. 1975. *Agricultural Statistics*. Washington, D.C.: U.S. Dept. of Agriculture, G.P.O.

van den Bosch, Robert. 1970. "Pesticides: Prescribing for the Ecosystem." *Environment* 12 (April), 20-25.

van Doren, D. M., Jr., and G. J. Ryder. 1962. "Factors Affecting Use of Minimum Tillage for Corn." *Agronomy Journal* (Sept-Oct), 447-50.

Victor, P. A., and W. M. Mansell. 1975. "Persistent Pesticides: An Economic and Legal Analysis," in F. Moriarty, ed., *Organochlorine Insecticides: Persistent Organic Pollutants*. New York: Academic Press, 249-95.

Whorton, James. 1974. *Before Silent Spring*. Princeton, N.J.: Princeton University Press.

Wilson, Wilbur O. 1966. "Poultry Production," *Scientic American* (July).

Wittmuss, Howard, Larry Olson, and Delbert Lane. 1975. "Energy Requirements for Conventional Versus Minimum Tillage," *Journal of Soil and Water Conservation* 30 (March-April), 72-75.

Zweig, Gunter. 1973. "Review. Pesticide Residues in Food," *Qual. Plant.—Pl. Fds. Hum. Nutr.* 23: 77-113.

Chapter 5

Bralove, Mary. 1974. "Most People Have No Taste; It's Been Lost in the Process," *Wall Street Journal* (30 April), 1.

Brecher, Edward M. 1972. *Licit and Illicit Drugs*. Boston: Little, Brown.

Burros, Marian. 1976. "Peanut Butter: Is Nothing Sacred?" *Washington Post* (15 July), E1.

BW. 1976. "Survey of Corporate Performance," *Business Week* (22 March), 70-89; also 24 March 1975, 58-77; 9 March 1974, 81-100; 10 March 1973, 82-101.

FTC. 1974. "Federal Trade Commission. Food Advertising. Proposed Trade Regulation Rule and Staff Statement," *Federal Register* 39 (11 November, No. 218), 39842–62.

Gussow, Joan. 1973. "'It Makes Even Milk a Dessert': A Report on the Counternutritional Messages of Children's Television Advertising," *Clinical Pediatrics* 12 (February), 68–71.

Hall, Ross H. 1974. *Food for Naught.* Hagerstown, Md.: Harper & Row.

Mishan, E. J. 1971. "On Making the Future Safe for Mankind," *The Public Interest* 34 (Summer), 33–61.

NCFM. 1966a. *Food From Farmer to Consumer. Report of the National Commission on Food Marketing.* Washington, D.C.: G.P.O.

———. 1966b. *The Structure of Food Manufacturing.* Technical Study No. 8, National Commission on Food Marketing. Washington, D.C.: G.P.O.

Root, Waverley. 1975. "Taste is Falling! Taste is Falling!" *New York Times Magazine* (February 16), 18–51.

Shapley, Deborah. 1975. "Health Planning: New Program Gives Consumers, Uncle Sam a Voice," *Science* 187 (17 January), 152–53.

Sullivan, Donald. 1976. "Economic, Personal Values, Demographic Shifts Will Limit Number of Successful New Products," *Food Product Development* 10 (March), 36.

USDA. 1972. *Market Structure of the Food Industries.* Marketing Research Report No. 971. Washington, D.C.: Economic Research Service, U.S. Dept. of Agriculture, G.P.O.

Vanderwicken, P. 1975. "New Way of Life?" *Wall Street Journal* (29 May), 1.

Whelan, Elizabeth M. 1975. "Healthier Than Life Itself," *The New York Times* (23 July), 35.

Williams, Roger J. 1971. *Nutrition Against Disease.* New York: Pitman.

Chapter 6

Adelman, M. A. 1970. *The World Petroleum Market.* Baltimore, Md.: Johns Hopkins Press for Resources for the Future.

Barnett, Harold J., and Chandler Morse. 1963. *Scarcity and Growth.* Baltimore, Md.: Johns Hopkins Press for Resources for the Future.

Beckerman, Wilfred. 1972. "Economists, Scientists, and Environmental Catastrophe," *Oxford Economic Papers* 24 (November), 327–44.

Boulding, Kenneth E. 1966. "Economics of the Coming Spaceship Earth," in Henry Jarrett, ed., *Environmental Quality in a Growing Economy.* Baltimore, Md.: Johns Hopkins Press for Resources for the Future. Pp. 3–14.

Boyd, Robert. 1972. "World Dynamics: A Note," *Science* 177 (11 August), 516–19.

Brubaker, Sterling. 1975. *In Command of Tomorrow.* Baltimore, Md.: Johns Hopkins Press for Resources for the Future.

BW. 1974a. "Boom in Agrichemicals," *Business Week* (8 June), 53–62.

———. 1974b. "The New Math for Figuring Energy Costs," *Business Week* (8 June), 88–89.

———. 1975. "Why Atomic Power Dims Today," *Business Week* (17 November), 98–106.

———. 1976. "A Threat to OPEC's Unity," *Business Week* (26 January), 91.

Carter, Harold O., and James G. Youde. 1974. "Some Impacts of the Changing Energy Situation on U.S. Agriculture," *American Journal of Agricultural Economics* 56 (December), 878–88.

CEA. 1975. *Economic Report of the President.* Washington, D.C.: Council of Economic Advisers, G.P.O.

Chancellor, W. J., and J. R. Goss. 1976. "Balancing Energy and Food Production, 1975-2000," *Science* 192 (16 April), 213-18.

Connor, Larry J. 1976. "Agricultural Policy Implications of Changing Energy Prices and Supplies." Dept. of Agricultural Economics, Michigan State University. Paper presented to the Conference on Energy and Agriculture, Center for the Biology of Natural Systems, St. Louis, Mo., June 16-19.

Cumberland, John. 1975. (Dept. of Economics, University of Maryland, College Park, Md.) Personal communication.

Daly, Herman E. 1972. "In Defense of a Steady-State Economy," *American Journal of Agricultural Economics* 54 (December), 945-54.

Davis, Charles H., and Glenn M. Blouin. 1976. "Energy Consumption in the U.S. Chemical Fertilizer System from the Ground to the Ground." (Tennessee Valley Authority, Muscle Shoals, Ala.) Paper presented to the Conference on Energy and Agriculture, at the Center for the Biology of Natural Systems, Washington University, St. Louis, Mo.

deWit, C. T. 1967. "Photosynthetic Limits on Crop Yields," in Anthony San Pietro, Francis A. Greer, and Thomas J. Army, eds., *Harvesting the Sun*. New York: Academic Press, 315-20.

Douglas, William O. 1972. "Dissent" in *Sierra Club* v. *Morton*. Reprinted in *The Living Wilderness* (Summer 1972), 19-29, also see Stone 1972.

Dubos, Rene. 1976. "Symbiosis Between the Earth and Humankind," *Science* (6 August), 479-62.

Dvoskin, Dan, and Earl O. Heady. 1976. *U.S. Agricultural Production under Limited Energy Supplies, High Energy Prices and Expanding Agricultural Exports*. CARD Report 69. Ames, Iowa: Center for Agricultural and Rural Development, Iowa State University.

EPP. 1974. *A Time to Choose. America's Energy Future*. Energy Policy Project of the Ford Foundation. Cambridge, Mass.: Ballinger.

Fisher, Anthony C., and Frederick M. Peterson. 1976. "The Environment in Economics: A Survey," *Journal of Economic Literature* 14 (March), 1-33.

Fritsch, Albert J., Linda W. Dujack, and Douglas A. Jimerson. 1975. *Energy and Food*. Washington, D.C.: Center for Science in the Public Interest.

Gandhi, Indira. 1972. "The Unfinished Revolution," *Bulletin of the Atomic Scientists* 28 (September), 35-38.

Georgescu-Roegen, Nicholas. 1971. *The Entropy Law and the Economic Process*. Cambridge, Mass.: Harvard University Press.

Hardin, Garrett. 1972. "Limits to Growth—Two Views," *Bulletin of the Atomic Scientists* 28 (November), 23-25.

Heichel, G. H. 1973. *Comparative Efficiency of Energy Use in Crop Production*. Connecticut Agricultural Experiment Station Bull. 739. New Haven, Conn.

———. 1976. "Agricultural Production and Energy Resources," *American Scientist* 64 (January–February), 64-72.

Hirst, Eric. 1973. *Energy Use for Food in the United States*. ORNL-NSF-EP-56. Oak Ridge, Tenn.: Oak Ridge National Laboratory.

———. 1974. "Food-Related Energy Requirements," *Science* 184 (12 April), 134-38.

Holdren, John P., and Paul R. Ehrlich. 1974. "Human Population and the Global Environment," *American Scientist* 62 (May-June), 282-92.

Huettner, David A. 1976. "Net Energy Analysis: An Economic Assessment," *Science* 192 (9 April), 101-4.

Johnson, D. Gale. 1974. "Are High Farm Prices Here to Stay?" *The Morgan Guaranty Survey* (August), 9-14.

Kneese, Allen V. 1973. "What Will Nuclear Power Really Cost?" *Not Man Apart* 3 (May), 16-17. Also in *Resources* 44 (September 1973), published by Resources for the Future, Washington, D.C.

Koopmann, T. C. 1977. "Concepts of Optimality and their Uses," *American Economic Review* 67 (June), 261-74.

Krutilla, J. V. 1967. "Conservation Reconsidered," *American Economic Review* 57 (September), 777-86.

Leach, Gerald. 1975. *Energy and Food Production*. Washington, D.C.: International Institute for Environment and Development.

Loomis, R. S., W. A. Williams, and A. E. Hall. 1971. "Agricultural Productivity," *Annual Review of Plant Physiology* 22, 431-68.

McHarg, Ian L. 1969. *Design with Nature*. New York: Doubleday.

Martin, Lee R. 1974. (Department of Agricultural and Applied Economics, University of Minnesota, St. Paul, Minnesota.) "Agriculture as a Growth Sector—1985 and Beyond." Staff Paper P74-4. Energy Policy Project of the Ford Foundation.

Meadows, Donella H., Dennis L. Meadows, Jorgen Randers, and William W. Behrens III. 1974. *The Limits to Growth*. 2nd ed. New York: Universe Books.

Moncrief, Lewis W. 1970. "The Cultural Basis for Our Environmental Crisis," *Science* 170 (30 October), 508-12.

Musgrave, Richard A. 1959. *The Theory of Public Finance*. New York: McGraw-Hill.

Nagel, Thomas. 1972. "Reason and National Goals," *Science* 177 (1 September), 766-70.

Nordhaus, W. D. 1973. "The Allocation of Energy Resources," *Brookings Papers on Economic Activity* (No. 3).

Nossiter, Bernard D. 1975. "Britain, Oil Firms Play Game of Bluff," *Washington Post* (22 August), D7.

NRC. 1975. *Enhancement of Food Production for the U.S.* National Research Council World Food and Nutrition Study. Washington, D.C.: National Academy of Sciences.

Odum, Howard T. 1971. *Environment, Power, and Society*. New York: John Wiley.

OEP. 1972. "The Potential for Energy Conservation." Executive Office of the President, Office of Emergency Preparedness. Washington, D.C.: G.P.O.

Osborn, Fairfield. 1948. *Our Plundered Planet*. Boston: Little, Brown.

Passmore, John. 1974. *Man's Responsibility for Nature. Ecological Problems and Western Traditions*. New York: Charles Scribner's Sons.

Pimentel, David, L. E. Hurd, A. C. Bellotti, M. J. Forster, I. N. Oka, O. D. Sholes, and R. J. Whitman. 1973. "Food Production and the Energy Crisis," *Science* 182 (2 November), 443-49.

Rawls, John. 1971. *A Theory of Justice*. Cambridge, Mass.: Belknap.

Ridker, Ronald G. 1973. "To Grow or Not to Grow: That's Not the Relevant Question," *Science* 182 (28 December), 1315-18.

Rowe, James L., Jr. 1976. "Natural Gas Price Rise Voted," *Washington Post* (28 July), A1.

Seuss, Dr. (Theodore Seuss Geisel). 1971. *The Lorax*. New York: Random House.

Singer, Peter. 1975. *Animal Liberation*. New York: Random House.

Smith, Adam. 1776. *The Wealth of Nations*. 1937 ed., Modern Library. New York: Random House.

Snyder, Gary. 1974. "On Wilderness," *The Living Wilderness* (Winter 1974-1975).

Starr, Chauncy. 1971. "Energy and Power," *Scientific American* 225 (September), 37-49.

Steinhart, John S., and Carol E. Steinhart. 1974. "Energy Use in the U.S. Food System," *Science* 184 (19 April), 307–16.

Stone, Christopher D. 1972. "Should Trees Have Standing? Toward Legal Rights for Natural Objects," *Southern California Law Review* 45, 450. Reprinted in *Should Trees Have Standing? Toward Legal Rights for Natural Objects*. Christopher D. Stone. Los Altro, California: William Kaufmann.

von Jeetze, Harmut. 1975. "Bio-Dynamic Relations Between Man and the Land." *Bio-Dynamics* 116 (Fall), 1–6.

Wallace, Henry A. 1938. "Foreword," in *Soils and Men. Yearbook of Agriculture.* Washington, D.C.: G.P.O.

Westman, Walter E. 1977. "How Much are Nature's Services Worth?" *Science* 197 (2 September) 960–64.

Chapter 7

Abele, Ulf. 1973. *Vergleichende Untersuchungen zum konventionellen und biologisch-dynamischen Pflanzenbau unter besonderer Berucksichtigung von Saatzeit un Entitaten.* Ph.D. dissertation, Justus-Liebig-Universitat, Giessen, Germany.

Albrecht, William A. 1975. *The Albrecht Papers.* Charles Walters, Jr., ed. Raytown, Mo.: Acres, U.S.A.

Aubert, Claude. 1972a. *Basic Techniques of Biological Agriculture and its Application in France.* AS/Agr (24) 7 Or. Fr. Strasbourg, France: Council of Europe.

———. 1972b. *L'Agriculture Biologique.* 2d ed. Paris: Le Courrier du Livre.

Balfour, E. B. 1975. *The Living Soil and the Haughley Experiment.* London: Faber & Faber.

Bizet, Mr. 1974. "Explanatory Memorandum," 2–15 of Part II of *Report on Methods and Trends of Organic Farming in Europe.* Strasbourg, France: Council of Europe.

Cadiou, Pierre, Francoise Mathieu-Gaudrot, Andre Lefebre, Yves LePape, Stephane Oriol. 1975. *L'Agriculture Biologique en France.* Grenoble: Presses Universitaires de Grenoble, France.

Carlson, Gerald A. 1971. "The Microeconomics of Crop Losses," in *Economic Research on Pesticides for Policy Decisionmaking.* Washington, D.C.: Economic Research Service, U.S. Dept. of Agriculture, 89–101.

COBL. 1977. *Alternative Landbouwmethoden.* Commissie Onderzoek Biologische Landbouwmethoden. Wageningen, Holland: Centrum voor Landbouwpublikaties en Landbouwdocumentatie.

Coleman, Eliot. 1975. *Biological Agriculture in Europe.* Harborside, Me.: Small Farm Research Association.

Coomaraswamy, Ananda K. Undated. *Art and Swadeshi.* Madras: Ganesh. Referenced in Schumacher, 1973.

Daly, Herman E. 1972. "In Defense of a Steady-State Economy," *American Journal of Agricultural Economics* 54 (December), 945–54.

Davis, Velmar W., Austin S. Fox, Robert P. Jenkins, and Paul A. Andrilenas. 1970. *Economic Consequences of Restricting the Use of Organochlorine Insecticides on Cotton, Corn, Peanuts and Tobacco.* Agricultural Economic Report No. 178. Washington, D.C.: Economic Research Service, U.S. Dept. of Agriculture, G.P.O.

EPAB. 1974. *Encyclopedie Permanente d'Agriculture Biologique.* Paris: Editions Debard.

Grotzke, Heintz. 1976. "Bio-Dynamic Methods for Growing Quality Herbs, Vegetables and Flowers." Lecture given in Washington, D.C., 10 January by proprietor of Meadowbrook Herb Garden, Wyoming, R.I.

Harnish, Stuart C. 1976. "Redefining Organic: Two Views. The Mineral." *The Natural Farmer* (April), 1–17. Newsletter of the Natural Organic Farmers Association, Plainfield, Vt.

Howard, Albert. 1940. *An Agricultural Testament.* London: Oxford University Press.

———. 1945. *Farming and Gardening for Health or Disease.* London: Faber & Faber.

IFOAM. 1977. "IFOAM Research Group Announces Details of First International Conference." IFOAM Bull. No. 22 (3rd Quarter). Oberwil, Switzerland: International Federation of Organic Agriculture Movements.

Jeavons, John C. 1972. *The Life-giving Biodynamic/French Intensive Method.* Preliminary Research Report. Palo Alto, Ca.: Ecology Action of the Midpeninsula.

———. 1974. *How to Grow More Vegetables.* Palo Alto, Ca.: Ecology Action of the Midpeninsula.

———. 1976. *Resource-Conserving Agricultural Method Promises High Yields.* 1972–1975 Research Report Summary. Palo Alto, Ca.: Ecology Action of the Midpeninsula.

Johnson, Ogden C. 1974. "The Food Fad Boom." *FDA Consumer* (December 1973–January 1974) DHEW Publication No. (FDA) 74-2019. Washington, D.C.: U.S. Dept. of Health, Education and Welfare, G.P.O.

King, Lawrence J. 1966. *Weeds of the World. Biology and Control.* New York: Interscience.

Koepf, Herbert H., Bo D. Pettersson, and Wolfgang Schaumann. 1974. *Biologische Landwirtschaft.* Stuttgart: Verlag Eugen Ulmer. Translation, J. Collis, *Bio-dynamic Agriculture.* Spring Valley, N.Y.: Anthroposophic Press.

Koepf, Herbert H. 1976. "What is Bio-dynamic Agriculture?" *Bio-Dynamics* 117 (Winter), 15–43.

Leverton, Ruth M. 1974. "Organic, Inorganic: What They Mean," Shopper's Guide. *1974 Yearbook of Agriculture.* Washington, D.C.: U.S. Dept. of Agriculture, G.P.O. Pp. 70–73.

Linder, Maria. 1975. "Compost as Fertilizer." Paper presented to the 1975 Bio-dynamic Farm and Garden Conference, Spring Valley, N.Y.

McCarthy, Coleman. 1973. "Farmers Rooted to the Soil," *Washington Post* (1 September), A14.

Martin, Hubert, ed. 1968. *Pesticide Manual.* British Crop Protection Council.

Mellanby, Kenneth. 1976. "Food and Nutrition," *Soil Association (England) Quarterly Review* 2 (June), 9.

NLR. 1975. "Results of Survey Show: Neb. Farmers Successfully Kick Chemical Habit," *New Land Review* 1 (Winter), 3.

OGF. 1975. "Organic Producer Listing," *Organic Gardening and Farming* (22 September). Emmaus, Pa.

———. Undated. "Regional Organic Farming Groups," *Organic Gardening and Farming.* Emmaus, Pa.

OSDA. 1974. "Standards, Labeling, and Other Requirements Relating to Organic Foods." CH. 603, Oregon Administrative Rules Compilation. Salem, Ore.: State Dept. of Agriculture.

Pank, C. J. 1976. *Dirt Farmer's Dialogue: Twelve Discussions about Bio-dynamic Farming.* Sprakers, N.Y.: B-D Press.

Pfeiffer, Ehrenfried E. 1938. *Biodynamic Farming and Gardening.* Spring Valley, N.Y.: Anthroposophic Press.

———. 1947. *The Earth's Face and Human Destiny.* Emmaus, Pa: Rodale.

———. 1962. *Bio-Dynamic Farming. Articles 1942–1962.* Spring Valley, N.Y.: Bio-Dynamic Farming and Gardening Association.

Philbrick, Helen, and Richard Gregg. 1970. *Companion Plants and How to Use Them.* Old Greenwich, Conn.: Devin-Adair.

Philbrick, John, and Helen Philbrick. 1963. *'The Bug Book': Harmless Insect Controls.* Wilkinsonville, Mass.: John and Helen Philbrick.

Rodale, J. I., ed. 1961. *How to Grow Vegetables and Fruits by the Organic Method.* Emmaus, Pa.: Rodale.

Saddam, Alma. Undated. "Foods in a Changing Society," in *Let's Take a Look at Organic Gardening.* Bull. 555. Columbus, O.: Cooperative Extension Service, Ohio State University, 16–18.

Schumacher, E. F. 1973. *Small is Beautiful.* New York: Harper & Row.

Schwecker, Edward L. 1975. (Cooperative Extension Service, University of Maryland, College Park, Md.) Personal communication.

Steiner, Rudolf. 1924. *Agriculture*, 1958 ed. London: Bio-Dynamic Agricultural Association.

Tompkins, Peter, and Christopher Bird. 1973. *The Secret Life of Plants.* New York: Harper & Row.

von Wistinghausen, Eckard. 1977. "The Quality of Carrots, Beets, and Wheat in Relation to Locale and Soil Conditions," *Bio-Dynamics* 123 (Summer), 10–22.

Walters, Charles, Jr. 1975. *The Case for Eco-Agriculture.* Raytown, Mo.: Acres, U.S.A.

Welch, L. F., F. A. Bazzar, R. H. Hageman, R. H. Harmeson, B. A. Jones, F. J. Stevenson, and R. L. Switzer. 1972. "Fertilizer Nitrogen Use by Crops and its Movement in Soil," in *Special Publication 26.* Proceedings of the Second Allerton Conference, Environmental Quality and Agriculture. Urbana, Ill.: College of Agriculture, University of Illinois, 36–39.

Wilkinson, S. R., and J. A. Stuedemann. 1974. "Fertilization with Poultry Litter," in *Yearbook of Science and Technology 1973.* New York: McGraw-Hill, 180–82.

Wilson, Charles. 1972. "Occupational Health and Safety Standards that Apply to Pesticide Exposure Situations Where Protective Clothing and Safety Equipment are Needed," in *Proceedings of the National Conference on Protective Clothing and Safety Equipment for Pesticide Workers.* Washington, D.C.: Federal Working Group on Pest Management, 63–64.

Chapter 8

Carter, Luther J. 1974. "Pollution and Public Health: Taconite Case Poses Major Test," *Science* 186 (4 October), 31–36.

CEA. 1976. *Economic Report of the President Together with the Annual Report of the Council of Economic Advisors.* Washington, D.C.: G.P.O.

Colamosca, Anne. 1974. "Health Foods Prosper Despite High Prices," *The New York Times* (November 17), Part III, 3.

Cornfield, Jerome. 1977. "Carcinogenic Risk Assessment," *Science* 198 (18 November), 693–99.

CP. 1972. "Eating What Comes Naturally," *Canner Packer* 41 (May).

Darling, Mary. 1973. *Natural, Organic and Health Foods.* Extension Folder 280. St. Paul, Minn.: Agricultural Extension Service, University of Minnesota.

ERS. 1976. *Fruit Situation.* TFS-199 (June). Washington, D.C.: Economic Research Service, U.S. Dept. of Agriculture.

Fryer, Lee, and Dick Simmons. 1972. *Earth Foods.* Chicago: Follett.

HFB. 1976. "Profile of a Retailer," *Health Foods Business* 22 (April), 33–46.

Krutilla, John V., Charles J. Cicchetti, A. Myrick Freeman III, and Clifford S. Russell. 1972. "Observations on the Economics of Irreplaceable Assets," in Allen V. Kneese and Blair T. Bower, eds., *Environmental Quality Analysis.* Baltimore, Md.: Johns Hopkins Press for Resources for the Future. C. 3, 69–112.

Lichtenstein, Grace. 1971. "Store Owner, Citing 98¢ Bread, Calls 'Health Food' Overpriced," *The New York Times* (9 December), 37.

NCFM. 1966a. *Organization and Competition in Food Retailing.* National Commission on Food Marketing, Technical Study No. 7. Washington, D.C.: G.P.O.

———. 1966b. *The Structure of Food Manufacturing.* National Commission on Food Marketing, Technical Study No. 8. Washington, D.C.: G.P.O.

Palasthy, A. 1977. (Service Migros Sano, 2 route d'Oron, 1010 Lausanne, Switzerland). Personal communication and pamphlets.

Parker, Russell C. 1971. *Discount Food Pricing in Washington, D.C.* Economic Report. Federal Trade Commission. Washington, D.C.: G.P.O.

PG. 1975a. "Product Performance '75," *Progressive Grocer* 54 (July), 32–122.

———. 1975b. "42nd Annual Report of the Grocery Industry," *Progressive Grocer* 54 (April), 87–166.

———. 1976. "Diet Foods Thrive, But Health Items Falter," *Progressive Grocer* 55 (January), 77–80.

Tennant, Richard B. 1971. "The Cigarette Industry," in Walter Adams, ed., *The Structure of American Industry*, 4th ed. New York: Macmillan. C. 7, 216–55.

USDA. 1972. *Food and Home Notes* (September 25). U.S. Dept. of Agriculture. Referenced in R. A. Seelig, "High Price of 'Organic Gullibility," *Supply Letter* (November 1972). Columbus, O.: Cooperative Extension Service, Ohio State University.

———. 1975a. *Agricultural Statistics.* Washington, D.C.: U.S. Dept. of Agriculture, G.P.O.

———. 1975b. *Handbook of Agricultural Charts.* Agriculture Handbood No. 491. Washington, D.C.: U.S. Dept. of Agriculture, G.P.O.

Wright, Robert A. 1972. "Health Foods—Only a Fad?" *The New York Times* (October 15), Section 3, 1.

Chapter 9

Bates, Angela. 1976. "L'Agriculture Biologique Commissariat Generale au Plan, Review," *The Soil Association (England) Quarterly Review* 2 (June), 1–3.

BR. 1974. "Agate Elevators Discontinue Selling Chemical Fertilizers," *Burlington Record*, Burlington, Col.(12 December), 5D.

Breimyer, Harold F., and Wallace Barr. 1972. "Issues in Concentration Versus Dispersion," in *Who Will Control U.S. Agriculture?* Special Publication 27. Urbana, Ill.: University of Illinois, Cooperative Extension Service. C. 2, 13–22.

Buck, Paul. 1975. (Formerly of the Dept. of Nutrition, Cornell University.) Speech to the Pennsylvania Organic Farmers-Consumers Organization Annual Meeting, November 28.

Dillon, John L., and J. R. Anderson. 1971. "Allocative Efficiency, Traditional Agriculture, and Risk," *American Journal of Agricultural Economics* 53 (February), 26–32.

Johnson, S. R. 1967. "A Re-examination of the Farm Diversification Problem," *Journal of Farm Economics* 49 (August), 610–21.

Lin, William, G. W. Dean, and C. V. Moore. 1974. "An Empirical Test of Utility vs. Profit Maximization in Agricultural Production," *American Journal of Agricultural Economics* 56 (August), 497–508.

NLR. 1975. "Results of Survey Show: Neb. Farmers Successfully Kick Chemical Habit," *New Land Review* 1 (Winter), 3–9.

Reinhardt, U. 1972. "A Production Function for Physician Services," *Review of Economics and Statistics* 54 (February), 55–66.

Simon, Herbert A. 1959. "Theories of Decision Making in Economics and Behavioral Science," *American Economic Review* 49 (June), 253–83.

USDA. 1975. *Handbook of Agricultural Charts.* Agriculture Handbook No. 491. Washington, D.C.: U.S. Dept. of Agriculture.

Wernick, Sarah, and William Lockeretz. 1977. "Motivations and Practices of Organic Farmers," *Compost Science* 18 (November–December).

Williamson, Oliver. 1963. "Managerial Discretion and Business Behavior," *American Economic Review* 53 (December), 1032–57.

Chapter 10

Abele, Ulf. 1973. *Vergleichende Untersuchungen zum konventionellen und biologisch-dynamischen Pflanzenbau unter besonderer Berucksichtigung von Saatzeit und Entitaten.* Ph.D. dissertation, Justus-Liebig-Universitat, Giessen, West Germany.

Auer, Ludwig, and Earl O. Heady. 1964. "The Contribution of Weather and Yield Technology to Changes in U.S. Corn Production 1939 to 1961," in *Weather and our Food Supply.* CEAD Report 20. Ames, Iowa: Center for Agricultural and Economic Development, Iowa State University of Science and Technology, 45–74.

Bremer, Michele. 1975. *An Examination of Some Aspects of Two American Diets.* Ph.D. dissertation, University of Massachusetts, Amherst.

Brokken, Ray F., and Earl O. Heady. 1968. *Interregional Adjustments in Crop and Livestock Production. A Linear Programming Analysis.* Technical Bull. No. 1396. Washington, D.C.: Economic Research Service, U.S. Dept. of Agriculture.

Buck, Paul. 1975. (Formerly of the Dept. of Nutrition, Cornell University.) Speech to the Pennsylvania Organic Farmers-Consumers Organization Annual Meeting, November 28.

Chapman, Duane. 1973. "An End to Chemical Farming?" *Environment* 15 (March), 12–17.

Conterio, W. A., Dale Bateman, and Louis Christen. 1971. *Pollution Solution Plots.* Tuscola, Ill.: Cooperative Extension Service, University of Illinois.

CRB. 1976. *Agricultural Prices. Annual Summary 1975.* Washington, D.C.: Crop Reporting Board, Statistical Reporting Service, U.S. Dept. of Agriculture.

Davidson, A., and R. B. Norgaard. 1973. "Economic Aspects of Pest Control." *OEPP/EPPO Bull. 3* (No. 3), 63–75.

Davidson, B. R., B. R. Martin, and R. G. Mauldon. 1967. "The Application of Experimental Research to Farm Production," *American Journal of Agricultural Economics* 49 (November), 900–907.

DeBach, Paul. 1974. *Biological Control by Natural Enemies.* Cambridge, England: Cambridge University Press.

Demmel, Dennis. 1976. "Nebraska Studies Methods to Use Wastes in Farming," *Compost Science* 17 (January–February), 31–32.

Dixon, Orani, Peter Dixon, and John Miranowski. 1973. "Insecticide Requirements in an Efficient Agricultural Sector," *Review of Economics and Statistics* 55 (November), 423–32.

Eggert, F. P. 1977. "The Effect of Several Soil Management Systems on Soil Parameters and on the Productivity of Vegetable Crops." *IFOAM Bull.* No. 22 (3rd Quarter) 3. Oberwil, Switzerland: International Federation of Organic Agriculture Movements.

EPP. 1965. *Restoring the Quality of Our Environment.* Environmental Pollution Panel, President's Science Advisory Committee. Washington, D.C.: G.P.O.

Farris, D. C., and J. M. Sprott. 1971. "Economic and Policy Implications of Pollution from Agricultural Chemicals," *American Journal of Agricultural Economics* 53 (November), 661–62.

————.1972. "Economic and Policy Implications of Pollution from Agricultural Chemicals: Reply," *American Journal of Agricultural Economics* 54 (August), 536.

Greenberg, Daniel S. 1975. "Cancer: Now, the Bad News," *Washington Post* (19 January), A1.

Griliches, Zvi. 1958. "The Demand for Fertilizer: An Economic Interpretation of a Technical Change," *Journal of Farm Economics* 40 (August), 591-606.

Hall, Darwin C., Richard B. Norgaard, and W. R. Z. Willey. 1975. *The Profitability of Integrated Pest Management Techniques Under the Advice of Independent Pest Management Consultants.* Unpublished paper.

Hawken, Paul. 1975. *The Magic of Findhorn.* New York: Harper & Row.

Headley, J. C. 1968. "Estimating the Productivity of Agricultural Pesticides," *American Journal of Agricultural Economics* 50 (February), 13-23.

Headley, J. C., and J. N. Lewis. 1967. *The Pesticide Problem.* Baltimore, Md.: Johns Hopkins University Press.

Heady, Earl O. 1952. *Economics of Agricultural Production and Resource Use.* Englewood Cliffs, N.J.: Prentice-Hall.

Heady, Earl O., and Ludwig Auer. 1966. "Imputation of Production to Technologies," *Journal of Farm Economics* 48 (May), 309-22.

Heady, Earl O., Howard C. Madsen, Kenneth J. Nicol, and Stanley H. Hargrove. 1972. *Agricultural and Water Policies and the Environment.* CARD Report 40T. Ames, Iowa: Center for Agricultural and Rural Development, Iowa State University.

Heady, Earl O., and John F. Timmons. 1975. "U.S. Land Needs for Meeting Food and Fiber Demands," *Journal of Soil and Water Conservation* 30 (January-February), 15-22.

Holcomb, G. D., S. D. Evans, W. W. Nelson, and C. J. Overdahl. 1976a. "Comparison of a Soil Conditioner and a Specialty Fertilizer with a Conventional Fertilizer, *Soils* No. 22, revised. Fact Sheet. St. Paul, Minn.: Agricultural Extension Service, University of Minnesota.

————. 1976b. "Comparison of Na-Churs Fertilizer with a Conventional Fertilizer," *Soils* No. 23, revised. Fact Sheet. St. Paul, Minn.: Agricultural Extension Service, University of Minnesota.

Ibach, D. B., and J. R. Adams. 1968. *Crop Yield Response to Fertilizer in the United States.* Statistical Bull. No. 431. Washington, D.C.: Economic Research Service and Statistical Reporting Service, U.S. Dept. of Agriculture, G.P.O.

ICES. 1972. "The $14 Pound of Broccoli." Urbana, Ill.: Cooperative Extension Service, University of Illinois.

Johnson, D. Gale, and Robert L. Gustafson. 1962. *Grain Yields and the American Food Supply.* Chicago: University of Chicago Press.

Kervran, Louis C. 1972. *Biological Transmutations.* Michel Abehsera, translator. Brooklyn, N.Y.: Swan House.

Langham, Max R., Joseph C. Headley, and W. Frank Edwards. 1972. "Agricultural Pesticides: Productivity and Externalities," in Allen V. Kneese and Blair T. Bower, eds., *Environmental Quality Analysis.* Baltimore, Md.: Johns Hopkins Press for Resources for the Future.

McCullough, M. L. 1975. "Biological Aids for Livestock Show Promise," *Hoard's Dairyman* (25 October), 1179.

Mayer, Leo V., and Stanley H. Hargrove. 1971. *Food Costs, Farm Incomes, and Crop Yields with Restrictions on Fertilizer Use.* CAED Report No. 38 (preliminary). Ames, Iowa: Center for Agricultural and Economic Development, Iowa State University.

NRC. 1972. *Genetic Vulnerability of Major Crops.* Washington, D.C.: National Academy of Sciences-National Research Council.

Perrin, Richard K., and Earl O. Heady. 1975. *Relative Contributions of Major Technological Factors and Moisture Stress to Increased Grain Yields in the Midwest, 1930–1971.* CARD Report 55. Ames, Iowa: Center for Agricultural and Rural Development, Iowa State University.

Pimentel, David. 1973. "Realities of a Pesticide Ban," *Environment* 15 (March), 18–30.

Polanyi, Michael. 1958. *Personal Knowledge. Towards a Post-critical Philosophy.* London: Routledge and Paul.

Senn, T. L., B. J. Skelton, J. A. Martin, and J. J. Jen. 1972. *Seaweed Research at Clemson University 1961–1971.* Research Series No. 141. Clemson, S.C.: South Carolina Agricultural Experiment Station, Clemson University.

Shaw, Lawrence H., and Donald D. Durost. 1965. *The Effect of Weather and Technology on Corn Yields in the Corn Belt, 1929–62.* Agricultural Economics Report No. 80. Washington, D.C.: U.S. Dept. of Agriculture.

Slife, F. W. 1973. "Costs and Benefits from Weed Control," in *Twenty-fifth Illinois Custom Spray Operators Training School.* Summaries of Presentations. Urbana, Ill.: Cooperative Extension Service, University of Illinois.

Sonka, Steven T., and Earl O. Heady. 1975a. "Agricultural Export Alternatives: Effects on Land Use, Crop Prices, and Land Values," *Journal of Soil and Water Conservation* 30 (May–June), 121–25.

———. 1975b. *Income and Structure of American Agriculture under Future Alternatives of Farm Size, Policies and Exports.* CARD Report 53. Ames, Iowa: Center for Agriculture and Rural Development, Iowa State University.

Squires, Arthur M. 1970. "Clean Power from Coal," *Science* 169 (28 August), 821–28.

Taylor, C. R., and E. R. Swanson. 1975. *The Economic Impact of Selected Nitrogen Restrictions on Agriculture in Illinois and 20 Other Regions of the United States.* AERR 133. Urbana, Ill.: Dept. of Agricultural Economics/Agricultural Experiment Station, University of Illinois.

Thompson, Louis M. 1969a. "Weather and Technology in the Production of Corn in the U.S. Cornbelt," *Agronomy Journal* 61, 453–56.

———. 1969b. "Weather and Technology in the Production of Wheat in the United States," *Journal of Soil and Water Conservation* 24 (November–December), 219–24.

Thompson, Richard L. 1975. "Farming without Herbicides," in *Organic Farming Yearbook of Agriculture.* Emmaus, Pa.: Rodale, 62–63.

Thorne, Charles Embree. 1930. *The Maintenance of Soil Fertility.* New York: Orange Judd.

Tompkins, Peter, and Christopher Bird. 1973. *The Secret Life of Plants.* New York: Harper & Row.

USDA. 1965. "Basic Documents Submitted by the Department of Agriculture Relating to the Use of Pesticides." *Interagency Coordination in Environmental Hazards (Pesticides).* Hearings before the Subcommittee on Reorganization and International Organizations of the Committee on Government Operations. U.S. Senate, 88th Cong., 2nd Sess., Appendix I to Part I. Washington, D.C.: G.P.O.

———. 1975. *Agricultural Statistics.* Washington, D.C.: U.S. Dept. of Agriculture, G.P.O.

von Wistinghausen, Eckard. 1977. "Bodenvergleiche nach 19 jahriger unterschiedlicher Dungung," *Lebendige Erde* (May–June) 91–100.

Wade, Nicholas. 1975. "Boost for Credit Rating of Organic Farmers," *Science* 189 (5 September), 777.

Chapter 11

Aubert, Claude. 1972. *Basic Techniques of Biological Agriculture and its Application in France.* AS/Agr (24) 7 Or. Fr. Strasbourg, France: Council of Europe.

Balfour, Eve. 1974. "Converting a Farm to an Organic Farm," in *Alternative Agriculture/Organic Farming.* Stowmarket, Suffolk, England: The Soil Association.

Cox, Jeff. Undated. "Organic Yields Challenge the Chemical Farm." Emmaus, Pa.: Rodale.

CRB. 1976a. *Agricultural Prices (May)*. Washington, D.C.: Crop Reporting Board, Statistical Reporting Service, U.S. Dept. of Agriculture.

———. 1976b. *Agricultural Prices. Annual Summary 1975*. Washington, D.C.: Crop Reporting Board, Statistical Reporting Service, U.S. Dept. of Agriculture.

DeBach, Paul. 1974. *Biological Control by Natural Enemies*. Cambridge, England: Cambridge University Press.

ERS. 1976a. *Fats and Oils Situation*. FOS-282 (July). Washington, D.C.: Economic Research Service, U.S. Dept. of Agriculture.

———. 1976b. *Feed Situation*. FdS-261 (May). Washington, D.C.: Economic Research Service, U.S. Dept. of Agriculture.

———. 1976c. *Wheat Situation*. WS-235 (July). Washington, D.C.: Economic Research Service, U. S. Dept. of Agriculture.

FFBDW. 1972. "Bio-ecological Approach to the Cultivation of Fruit, Vegetables and other Farm Produce—Present Position and Prospects in Germany," prepared by the Forschungsring fur Biologisch-Dynamische Wirtschaftsweise. AS/Agr (24) 5 Or. German. Strasbourg, France: Council of Europe.

FSMNS. 1976a. "Fresh Fruit and Vegetable Federal-State Market News." *Los Angeles Daily Wholesale Market Report* 62 (16 June, 23 June, 30 June, 7 July, 3 August, 11 August). Federal-State Market News Service, U.S. Dept. of Agriculture, Agricultural Marketing Service and Fruit and Vegetable Division; and California Dept. of Food and Agriculture, Bureau of Market News, Los Angeles, Ca.

———. 1976b. *Los Angeles Fresh Fruit and Vegetable Wholesale Market Prices 1975*. Federal-State Market News Service, U.S. Dept. of Agriculture, Agricultural Marketing Service and Fruit and Vegetable Division; and California Department of Food and Agriculture, Bureau of Market News, Los Angeles, Ca.

———. 1976c. *Rice Market News* 57 (July). Federal-State Market News Service, U.S. Dept. of Agriculture, Agricultural Marketing Service, Grain Division, and California Dept. of Food and Agriculture, Los Angeles, Ca.

Heinze, Hans. 1976. (Forschungsring fur Biologisch-Dynamische Wirtschaftsweise, Stuttgart, West Germany.) Letter to author.

Pfeiffer, E. E. 1945. "How to Convert a Farm to BioDynamics," in *Bio-Dynamic Farming*. Articles 1942-1962. Spring Valley, N.Y.: Bio-Dynamic Farming and Gardening Association.

Thompson, Louis M., and Frederick R. Troeh. 1973. *Soils and Soil Fertility*. New York: McGraw-Hill.

USDA. 1975. *Agricultural Statistics*. Washington, D.C.: U.S. Dept. of Agriculture, G.P.O.

Chapter 12

Aldrich, Samuel R. 1975. "Organic Farming Methods," *Science* 190 (10 October), 96.

Aubert, Claude. 1978. Advanced Biological Agriculture Seminar (May 7-13). Brattleboro, Vt.

Bates, Angela. 1976. "L'agriculture Biologique Commissariat Generale au Plan. Review," *The Soil Association (England) Quarterly Review* 2 (June), 1-3.

Berardi, Gigi. 1976. *Report on Conventional and Organic Wheat Farming in New York State and Pennsylvania*. M.A. thesis, Cornell University, Ithaca, N.Y.

Childers, Norman F. 1975. *Modern Fruit Science*, 6th ed. New Brunswick, N.J.: Horticultural Publications, Rutgers University.

CRB. 1975a. *Citrus Fruits*. RfNt 3-1 (October). Washington, D.C.: Crop Reporting Board, Statistical Reporting Service, U.S. Dept. of Agriculture.

————. 1975b. *Vegetables—Fresh Market. 1975 Annual Summary.* Vg 2-2 (December). Washington, D.C.: Crop Reporting Board, Statistical Reporting Service, U.S. Dept. of Agriculture.

EPA. 1974. *Farm's Pesticide Use Decisions and Attitudes on Alternate Crop Protection Methods.* U.S. Environmental Protection Agency and Council on Environmental Quality. Washington, D.C.: G.P.O.

EPAB. 1974. *Encyclopedie Permanente d'Agriculture Biologique.* Paris: Editions Debard.

ERS. 1977a. *Feed Situation.* FdS-267 (November). Washington, D.C.: Economic Research Service, U.S. Dept. of Agriculture.

————. 1977b. *Fertilizer Situation.* FS-8 (December). Washington, D.C.: Economic Research Service, U.S. Dept. of Agriculture.

————. 1977c. *Fruit Situation.* TFS-205 (November). Washington, D.C.: Economic Research Service, U.S. Dept. of Agriculture.

————. 1976. *Sugar and Sweetener Report 1 (May).* Washington, D.C.: Economic Research Service and Agricultural Marketing Service, U.S. Dept. of Agriculture.

Garrich, Carl. Undated. *A Very Brief Statement in Management and Method in Growing Rice Organically or Commercially.* Bel Air, Md: Laurelbrook Foods.

Hall, E. Raymond. 1972. "Down on the Farm," *Natural History* (March), 8–12.

Ibach, D. B., and J. R. Adams. 1968. *Crop Yield Response to Fertilizer in the United States.* Statistical Bull. No. 431. Washington, D.C.: Economic Research Service and Statistical Reporting Service, U.S. Dept. of Agriculture, G.P.O.

Klepper, Robert, William Lockeretz, Barry Commoner, Michael Gertler, Sarah Fast, Daniel O'Leary, and Roger Blobaum. 1977. "Economic Performance and Energy Intensiveness on Organic and Conventional Farms in the Corn Belt: A Preliminary Comparison," *American Journal of Agricultural Economics* 59 (February) 1–12.

Lockeretz, William, Robert Klepper, Barry Commoner, Michael Gertler, Sarah Fast, and Daniel O'Leary. 1976. *Organic and Conventional Crop Production in the Corn Belt: A Comparison of Economic Performance and Energy Use for Selected Farms.* CBNS-AE-7. NSF/RA-760084. St. Louis, Mo.: Center for the Biology of Natural Systems, Washington University.

NLR. 1975. "Results of Survey Show: Neb. Farmers Successfully Kick Chemical Habit," *New Land Review* 1 (Winter), 3–9.

NRC. 1975. *World Food and Nutrition Study. Enhancement of Food Production for the U.S.* Washington, D.C.: National Academy of Sciences–National Research Council.

OSU. 1976. *Ohio Crop Enterprise Budgets 1976. Horticulture Crops.* Columbus, O.: Area and State Extension Farm Management Faculty, Dept. of Agricultural Economics and Rural Sociology, Ohio State University.

Podany, Joseph, and Hilarius Fuchs. 1974. "Cost of Harvesting, Packing and Storing Apples for the Fresh Market with Regional and Seasonal Comparisons," *The Fruit Situation* 191 (July), ERS-562, 7–22. Washington, D.C.: Economic Research Service, U.S. Dept. of Agriculture.

Podany, Joseph C., Robert W. Bohall, and Joan Pearrow. 1973. *Harvesting, Storing and Packing Apples for the Fresh Market: Regional Practices and Costs.* Marketing Research Report No. 1009. Washington, D.C.: Economic Research Service, U.S. Dept. of Agriculture, G.P.O.

Rodale, J. I. 1961. "Preparing the Soil for Fruit Plantings," in J. I. Rodale, ed., *How to Grow Vegetables and Fruits by the Organic Method.* Emmaus, Pa.: Rodale. C. 23, 561–69.

Rose, Bruce. 1974. "Converting to Organic," *The California Certified Organic Farmer* (Summer), 21.

Snyder, Darwin P. 1975. "Fruit and Vegetable Crops Costs and Returns," from *Farm Cost Accounts, 37 Farms—1974.* A. E. Res. 75-27. Ithaca, N.Y.: Dept. of Agricultural Economics and Cornell University Agricultural Experiment Station, Cornell University.

———. 1976. *Cost of Production Update for 1975 on Sweet Corn for Processing, Red Kidney Dry Beans, Apples for Fresh and Processing.* A.E. Res. 76-9. Ithaca, N.Y.: Dept. of Agricultural Economics, Cornell University.

Stevens, George A. 1970. *Farm Data Manual.* Information Series No. 6. College Park, Md.: Cooperative Extension Service, University of Maryland.

Stoneberg, E. G., and R. Winterboer. 1973. *Cost of Crop Production in North Central Iowa.* FM 1565 (Rev.). Ames, Iowa: Cooperative Extension Service, Iowa State University.

Tukey, Loren D. 1969. "Cultural Practices of Apples as they Relate to Harvest Mechanization, Past, Present and Future," in B. F. Cargill and G. E. Rossmiller, eds., *Fruit and Vegetable Harvest Mechanization Technological Implications.* Rural Manpower Report No. 16. East Lansing, Mich.: Rural Manpower Center, Michigan State University, 653-71.

USDA. 1975. *Agricultural Statistics.* Washington, D.C.: U.S. Dept. of Agriculture, G.P.O.

Vogtmann, Hardy. 1977. (Director, Research Institute for Biological Husbandry, Oberwil, Switzerland.) "Organic Farming Research in Europe," Seventh Annual Composting and Waste Recycling Conference. University of Massachusetts, May 4-6, 1977.

Chapter 13

Acres. 1976. "A Humate Primer No. 1." *Acres U.S.A.* 6 (January), 13-14.

Aldrich, S. R. 1972. *Fact from Environment.* Atlanta, Ga.: American Potash Institute. Referenced in Singh 1975.

Beleau, M. H., N. D. Heidelbaugh, and D. van Dyke. 1974. "Open-Ocean Farming of Kelp for Conversion to Animal and Human Foods," *Food Technology* 29 (December), 27-45.

Bell, R. G. 1976. "Persistence of Fecal Coliform Indicator Bacteria on Alfalfa Irrigated with Municipal Sewage Lagoon Effluent," *Journal of Environmental Quality* 5 (No. 1), 39-42.

BLS. 1976. *Employment and Earnings* 23 (July). Washington, D.C.: Bureau of Labor Statistics, U.S. Dept. of Labor.

CEA. 1976. *Economic Report of the President Together with the Annual Report of the Council of Economic Advisors.* Washington, D.C.: G.P.O.

Chapman, V. J. 1970. *Seaweeds and Their Uses.* 2nd ed. London: Methuen and Co.

Cohea, Carol. 1975. "Humate Work in Soil Remains Puzzling," *Albuquerque Journal* (30 November), F-1.

DeBach, Paul. 1974. *Biological Control by Natural Enemies.* Cambridge, England: Cambridge University Press.

Ember, L. R. 1975. "Ocean Dumping: Philadelphia's Story," *Environmental Science and Technology* 9 (October), 916-17.

FWS. 1962. *Seaweeds Are Not Weeds.* Conservation Note 7. Washington, D.C.: Office of Information, Fish and Wildlife Service, U.S. Dept. of the Interior.

Hunter, Charles J. 1975. "Edible Seaweeds—A Survey of the Industry and Prospects for Farming the Pacific Northwest." MFR Paper 1123. *Marine Fisheries Review* 37 (February), 19-26.

King, F. H. 1911. *Farmers of Forty Centuries of Permanent Agriculture in China, Korea and Japan.* New York: Harcourt, Brace.

Kottlowski, Frank E. 1976. (Director, New Mexico Bureau of Mines and Mineral Resources.) Letter to author.

Kuchta, Francis W. 1975. "Baltimore Uses Sludge Instead of Dumping It," letter in *Compost Science* 16 (March–April), 26.

Larson, W. E., J. R. Gilley, and D. R. Linden. 1975. "Consequences of Waste Disposal on Land," *Journal of Soil and Water Conservation* 30 (March.April), 68–71.

MacEachern, Gordon A. 1975. "Animal Agriculture and Waste Recycling," in *Proceedings of the Conference on Waste Recycling and Canadian Agriculture*. Agricultural Economic Research Council of Canada.

Manson, R. J., and Clifford A. Merritt. 1975. "Farming and Municipal Sludge: They're Compatible." *Compost Science* 16 (July–August), 16–19.

Plimpton, Greg. 1976. (Atlantic and Pacific Research, Inc., North Palm Beach, Florida.) Personal communication.

Senn, T. L., and Alta R. Kingman. 1973. *A Review of Humus and Humic Acids*. Research Series No. 145. Clemson, S.C.: Horticulture Dept., South Carolina Experiment Station, Clemson University.

Shacklette, Hansford T., and R. C. Severson. 1975. *Sources and Use of Fertilizers and Other Soil Amendments for Food Production—An Outline*. Open File Report No. 75-23 (preliminary). Denver, Col.: U.S. Geological Survey.

Sheppard, Richard A. 1973. "Zeolites in Sedimentary Rocks," in Donald A. Brobst and Walden P. Pratt, eds., *U.S. Mineral Resources*. U.S. Geological Survey Professional Paper 820, 689-95.

Shipp, Raymond F., and Dale E. Baker. 1975. "Pennsylvania's Sewage Sludge Research and Extension Program," *Compost Science* 16 (March–April), 6–8.

Singh, Ambika. 1975. "Use of Organic Materials and Green Manures as Fertilizers in Developing Countries," in *Organic Material as Fertilizers, Soils Bull. 27*. Rome: FAO, United Nations, 19–30.

Stephenson, W. A. 1974. *Seaweed in Agriculture and Horticulture*. Pauma Valley, Ca.: Bargyla and Gylver Rateaver.

Taylor, Leland B. 1976. *How and Why Clod Buster Reduces Drouth Damage*. Albuquerque, N.M.: Farm Guard Products.

USDA. 1975. *Agricultural Statistics*. Washington, D.C.: U.S. Dept. of Agriculture, G.P.O.

Walker, John M. 1975. "Sewage Sludges—Management Aspects for Land Application," *Compost Science* 16 (March–April), 12–21.

———. 1977. "Wastewater Renovation and Sludge Utilization on Land Including Questions of Ownership," *Compost Science* 18 (September–October), 8–15.

Wilcox, Howard A. 1975. "The Ocean Food and Energy Farm Project." Paper presented at the 141st Annual Meeting of the American Association for the Advancement of Science, New York. Available from Code 0103, Naval Undersea Center, San Diego, Ca.

Wolf, Ray. 1975. "Sludge in the 'Mile-High' City," *Compost Science* 16 (January–February), 20–21.

Wolfbauer, C. A. 1976. (U.S. Geological Survey, Denver, Colorado) "Mineral Resources for Agricultural Uses." Paper presented to the Conference on Energy and Agriculture, St. Louis, Missouri, June 16–19, at the Center for the Biology of Natural Systems, Washington University.

Chapter 14

ERS. 1975. *Changes in Farm Production and Efficiency. A Summary Report*. Statistical Bulletin No. 548.

USDA. 1975. *Agricultural Statistics*. Washington, D.C.: U.S. Dept. of Agriculture. G.P.O.

Index

Grains and beans, 75, 158–62, 168–70, 184–86, 196–203, 229. *See also* individual grains
Green manure, 29, 49

Habit, 87, 163
Harvesting, mechanized. *See* Mechanization
Haughley, 44
Headley, J. C., 170–72
Heady, Earl O., 159–60, 168–70
Health Food Business, 130
Health food stores, 128, 137, 206
Health
  human, 9, 43, 60–62, 86, 147, 163, 232; livestock, 9, 147
Heart disease, 9, 62, 87
Heavy metals, 123, 219–20
Hedgerows, 82
Herbicides, 58–60, 122, 165–66
Herbs, 44, 118
Homeopathic medicine, 118, 163–64
Hormones, 21
Howard, Sir Albert, 113
Humates, 221–22. *See also* Soil amendments
Humility, 81
Humus, 120, 222, 24ff. *See also* Compost; Soil
Husbandman, farmer as, 108, 110, 126
Hybrid corn, 159
Hybrid varieties, 41, 162

IFOAM. *See* International Federation of Organic Agriculture Movements
Industrial farming. *See* Corporate farming
Inputs
  farm, 15, 150, 201; human, 106, 126
Insecticides, 55–58. *See also* Pesticides
Insect pest management, 65–66
Integrated control, 65–66
Intermediate technology. *See* Appropriate technology
International Federation of Organic Agriculture Movements, 123
International Rice Research Institute, 50
Ions, 25
Irrigation, 20, 190

Justus Liebig Institute, 164

Kepone, 58
Kervran, L. *See* Biological transmutations

Labor
  farm, 201, 204, 206–8, 216–17, 223, 230; productivity, 15; substitution of capital for, 13–14
Labor-intensive technical change, 13–14, 20
Ladybird beetles, 82
Land, relationship between man and, 126, 146–47, 147n
Large-scale production. *See* Economies of scale

Life force. *See* Living energy
Limits to Growth, 102
Livestock
  beef, 16, 21–22, 89–90, 191; chickens, 16, 43, 50
Livestock health. *See* Health, livestock
Living energy, 24, 164
Loans. *See* Financing
Local consumption, 124, 138
Lockeretz, William, 193, 195, 196–98, 200–1

Management techniques, 14
Manure fertilizer, 9, 40, 123–24, 165, 197, 218
Marginal benefit, marginal cost, 72–73, 73n, 120–22
Margins, retail and wholesale, 120–30
Market failure, 5, 75–92, 124–25, 150, 225
Market potential, 75, 78–79
Marketing, direct. *See* Direct marketing
Marketing orders, state, 83, 136–37
Marketing rights, 231
Markets, regional. *See* Regional specialization
Markups. 129–30. *See also* Margins
Mechanization, 9, 13–16, 161, 208, 211 harvesting, 211
Medicine, 24, 145–46, 163
Micronutrients. *See* Trace elements
Microorganisms, soil, 26, 63
Migration, labor, 15–16, 127
Milk production, 44–45
Minerals, 24–25. *See also* Trace elements; Fertilizer, chemical
Minimum tillage, 58–59
Mold, 17, 85, 185
Monoculture, 14, 27, 81, 145
Moon phases, 118, 164
Mortality, related to fertilizer, 44
Mushroom poisoning, 76
Mutations, 54, 60, 120
Mycorrhizal fungi, 27

National Academy of Sciences, 7, 221
National Institute of Health, 61
Natural Food Associates, 115
Natural foods, definition, 130
Natural food stores, 130–32
Natural toxins, 42, 122, 123
Net energy, 108–10
Nitrates, 24, 40–42
Nitrogen
  fertilizer, 29–31, 38, 62, 95, 169, 193, 217–21; fixation, 7–8, 27, 221; pest attacks related to, 54
No-till. *See* Minimum tillage
Nuclear power, 102–5
Nutrition
  human, 23–24, 37–46, 61; science of, 42–43; soil, 38–39. *See also* Fertilizer
Nutritional quality. *See* Food quality